Dedicated to the memory of George Galtress,
Frank 'Mickey' Lowe, Sidney Clouting, the late Reg Cox MM,
and especially to Benjamin Clouting, 1897 – 1990

OTHER BOOKS BY RICHARD VAN EMDEN:

Meeting the Enemy

The Quick and the Dead

Tommy's Ark

Sapper Martin

The Soldier's War

Famous 1914-1918

The Last Fighting Tommy (with Harry Patch)

Britain's Last Tommies

Boy Soldiers of the Great War

All Quiet on the Home Front

Last Man Standing

The Trench

Prisoners of the Kaiser

Veterans: The Last Survivors of the Great War

Tickled to Death to Go

Teenage Tommy

MEMOIRS OF A CAVALRYMAN IN THE FIRST WORLD WAR

EDITED BY
RICHARD VAN EMDEN

Pen & Sword
MILITARY

First published in Great Britain in 1996 by Spellmount Limited

Reprinted in this format in 2013 by
PEN & SWORD MILITARY
An imprint of
Pen & Sword Books Ltd
47 Church Street
Barnsley, South Yorkshire
S70 2AS

Copyright © Richard van Emden, 1996, 2013

ISBN 978 1 78303 287 7

Printed and bound in England
By CPI Group (UK) Ltd, Croydon, CR0 4YY

Pen & Sword Books Ltd incorporates the Imprints of Aviation, Atlas,
Family History, Fiction, Maritime, Military, Discovery, Politics, History,
Archaeology, Select, Wharncliffe Local History, Wharncliffe True Crime,
Military Classics, Wharncliffe Transport, Leo Cooper, The Praetorian Press,
Remember When, Seaforth Publishing and Frontline Publishing

For a complete list of Pen & Sword titles please contact
PEN & SWORD BOOKS LIMITED
47 Church Street, Barnsley, South Yorkshire, S70 2AS, England
E-mail: enquiries@pen-and-sword.co.uk
Website: www.pen-and-sword.co.uk

Contents

List of Maps

All maps © Derek Stone

The publisher would like to acknowledge the following for their permission to reproduce the photographs.

Captain Hornby's family	:	picture 5
The Imperial War Museum	:	pictures 10 and 25
The National Army Museum	:	pictures 13 and 15
The Royal Dragoon Guards	:	pictures 18 – 23
David Bilton	:	picture 34
Family of Louise Donnay de Casteau	:	picture 39

All other photographs © Richard van Emden

New Introduction

I am delighted that this, my first book, has been reprinted in time for the 100th anniversary of the Great War. It is 25 years since I met Benjamin Clouting and 23 years since his death. Yet the memory of a short but very close friendship remains with me. It hardly seems credible now that I knew someone who not only took part in the great heroic Retreat from Mons – Ben always said it appeared to him more of a shambles – but that this man, this sixteen-year-old boy as he was then, took part in the very first action of the British Expeditionary Force in France and, two days later, one of the last great cavalry charges in history.

I have been back to the locations of both the first action and the cavalry charge on a number of occasions, most recently to take photographs for the plate section of this book. The site of the first 'shot' has hardly changed since August 1914, and not much since I went there with Ben in May 1990. A small electrical sub-station has been built next to the château where the action occurred and on my most recent visit (on a Sunday, in the hope of finding the place free of traffic) I found to my frustration, a large articulated lorry parked outside the gatekeeper's house. Never mind. It might be argued that the British Army went to war in the first place so that Belgians might be free to park their lorries as and where they wanted.

There is no blue plaque to mark the spot where the first shot took place. I have wondered if anyone other than Ben knew that it was outside La Roquette Château. As for the location of the cavalry charge, that has hardly changed either, except for large wind pylons that now dominate the horizon. Sadly, Ben and I did not return to this place but I feel he would have easily recognised it too, as the ground near Mons was not shot-blasted like that of the Somme or Ypres Salient where Ben would later serve and where he was wounded.

Ben's story is republished with some new pictures but no added text. Questions that I failed to ask him back in 1990 can find no answers now. I hope Ben would have been pleased with this new edition. He did not live to see the book in print although he knew it was being written and he was delighted.

Richard van Emden, October 2013

Introduction

It was through one of those rare, spectacular coincidences that Ben Clouting and I came into contact. I had become fascinated with the British Expeditionary Force's 'first shot' of the continental conflict, and had long hoped to meet an old soldier who had actually been present. Research into the subject had, however, led me to the sad, if unsurprising, conclusion that the last witness, one Bumble Worrell, a Chelsea Pensioner, had died aged 91 in 1984. The action had seemingly passed into history.

In 1988 a Reading newspaper, *The Evening Post*, began a series of articles entitled 'Berkshire At War'. It was primarily concerned with memories of the Second World War, but nevertheless I wondered if any older soldier, from the First War, had been featured, and so I went to Reading County Library to request some back issues. Through a fortunate misunderstanding, an assistant brought a file of old press cuttings, among which appeared one from 1977 announcing the closure of the Reading Branch of the Old Contemptibles. It read: 'Early in 1914 a young private in the British Expeditionary Force saw the first shots fired in the First World War. Yesterday at his home in Hungerford Road, Reading, ex-Private Ben Clouting of the 4th Dragoon Guards recalled those shots...' A quick search of the register of electors, and the rest, as they say, is history.

A telephone call elicited the information that Ben was not only fit and well but still a working man, and any idea that I had had of interviewing him midweek was impossible. His work at a window-cleaning company ensured that he was out of the house by 6.30 each morning. 'Come and see me on Sunday,' he said. I did, and Sunday became a regular weekly date during which his memories were avidly recorded.

A friendship grew, culminating in a wonderful trip back to the battlefields in May 1990 on the final pilgrimage of the Old Contemptibles. This trip thrilled Ben as much as it did me, for although his health was rapidly declining – he died just three months later – any difficulties he had were put to one side and, armed with a walking stick for the first time in his life, he set about enjoying only his second return to the battlefields in seventy six years. The trip, which involved eleven other veterans, encompassed town functions, wreath layings, and a trip back to the battle sites including, for Ben, that of the first action at Casteau on August 22nd 1914. When the party of veterans left Ypres for England at the end of the tour, it seemed fitting that Ben was the last veteran to board the coach: the first one in and the last one out, I thought.

Unlike many veterans, Ben was glad he had gone to France. He was in fact tickled to death to go after the Regiment had tried to leave him behind, for he was still only a boy of sixteen. His experiences over the next five years remained close to him, but did not blight the rest of his life. He had excellent recall but, perhaps thankfully, he was not blessed with an over-imaginative mind, for it was often a fertile mind which was the root cause of so many soldiers' mental and physical collapse, either during or after the war.

Teenage Tommy is edited from tape recordings made between January 1989 and August 1990. On the whole, what Ben remembered proved correct or remarkably close to the known passage of events. There were time slips, when incidents were placed chronologically out of sequence, and these have been rectified, but, throughout, I have always sought to keep the flavour of Ben's spoken word in the written text. As the book was put together after Ben's death, there were many frustrations, when seemingly obvious questions cropped up, and I wondered why I did not think to ask Ben for the answers at the time. As I pondered on how to check or verify obscure facts, the outrageous fortune and coincidences that were a feature of Ben's service in France seemed to rub off on me, and I often found solutions in the nookiest of crannies! I would like to think he is co-ordinating my efforts.

During the writing of this biography, I have tried to be as accurate as possible in my narrative. However, while this is principally Ben's story, I have made a feature of two famous events in which Ben was involved, the BEF's first skirmish in Belgium on August 22nd 1914, and the famous charge at Audregnies two days later. In both cases, new and significant light has been thrown on proceedings as a result of follow-up research to what Ben told me.

This said, I am also aware that mistakes may have crept through, for which I apologise. Even so, I feel that this book is very readable, and gives a new and rare insight into the life of a cavalryman in the First World War. It is not a book of blood and guts. Other memoirs, mostly written by infantry or artillerymen, have far more of this sort of detail than appears here. Ben was a cavalryman, and for much of the war was an officer's horse orderly and therefore spared such great tests as going over the top, or participating in a trench raid. Ben did serve in the trenches; he shot and was shot at; he was wounded twice, and saw men die, yet the real strength of this book lies in Ben's deft insights into the daily life of a soldier in the First World War. These insights were often unwitting, but were nevertheless detailed, perceptive, and often very funny.

I have endeavoured to make this book attractive to read, for both seasoned researchers of the conflict and interested yet more casual readers. For this reason the notes, which could easily have become very expansive, have been sharply curtailed, and are limited to items of distinct historical importance, or to asides which will appeal to a mainstream readership. Within the text, the role of the editor has been to place stories in a broader context, or to narrate, in depth, stories of significant historical interest and appeal. I should mention at this point that in one instance a name has been changed, as Ben requested.

I would like to thank the following people and institutions for their help; firstly, the curators at the Royal Dragoon Guards Museum at York for their very kind help. The Imperial War Museum and the National Army Museum have both kindly consented to the reproduction of several photographs, which I greatly appreciate. I should also like to express my gratitude to the family of Louise Donnay de Casteau, and to the family of Captain Hornby. My appreciation also goes to the Clouting family, and Betty Williams, all of whom have been encouraging and supportive throughout. Thanks are also due to my parents, Joan, and my late father, Wolfgang van Emden, who proved invaluable sub-editors. I am grateful to Maurice Johnson, Tony and Teddy Noyes and David Bilton.

Finally, I should especially like to thank the superb staff at Pen and Sword Books for their work in bringing Benjamin Clouting's story to a wider audience. In particular, Jonathan Wright, who is not just someone I enjoy working with, but who has become a good friend too. I would also like to thank Dominic Allen for his excellent book plate design, David Hemingway, Matt Jones and, of course, Charles Hewitt.

Richard van Emden

CHAPTER ONE

A Sussex Childhood

Ben

Had luck not been kind to me, I might never have survived past the age of four. My earliest years were anxious times for my parents, who saved me from various dangerous exploits, exploits which lived on, as such things tend to do, as favourite family stories. I was born in the country, at Beddingham, a little village close to Brighton, in September 1897. My father was head groom on an estate called Little Dene, where he was in charge of a large number of hunting horses belonging to the local landowner and renowned huntsman, the Honourable Charles Brand. The stables were adjacent to my parents' tied house and it was inside these that I was found at the age of three trying to climb the hind leg of one of two horses in a valiant attempt to mount. By chance I had chosen a docile old mare which didn't react to the irritant clinging on to her back leg; the other horse, so my father later assured me, would have kicked my brains out. Fate saved me on this occasion, as did the fortunate intervention of my mother, one year later, when any number of fingers were saved as I endeavoured to show my two-year-old sister how the chaff-cutter worked.

My parents, William and Ellen, had moved to Beddingham soon after they married in the early 1890s. They had met at the Sussex home of the Sassoons, where my mother worked as a parlour maid and my father as a stable boy. I was the eldest of four children, being followed by Dorothy in 1899, Mabel in 1900 and William in 1902. We were brought up in a six-roomed house with three bedrooms. The children all slept in one bedroom in two double beds, my bed being an old wooden four-poster bed with the posts cut off and a seaweed mattress.

The estate was very much a model of its kind, with its farm and riding stables. The Brands entertained frequently, bringing their guests to the stables to walk round, my father always being on hand to give carrots to those who wished to feed the horses. There was also a walk round after church on Sundays when some of the local gentry paid a visit, so everything had to be spick and span, from the burnished harnesses right down to the painted blue wooden stable buckets, each sporting C.B. in white on the side.

1

The Brands had pots of money. The Honourable Charles had married a member of the Vanderbilt family and they had had four children, Betty, Ruth, Eve and Jack. They all lived a luxurious lifestyle, hence the two dozen employees needed to run what was a self-supporting estate which included a small herd of cows and a large number of sheep, all carefully selected and bred. There was the big house, then adjacent to it were tied cottages for the head gardener and his wife, who was the dairy maid. Then, the estate carpenter lived next door to the head carter, followed by another pair of cottages where the second gardener lived next door to Mr Weaver, the bailiff, who ran the farm.

My father had been taken on as head groom at the princely sum of five pounds a month. He had grown up with horses, trying his luck out in Canada as the driver of a Royal Mail coach. He had returned to work as a stable boy at the Sassoon family home and had worked his way up before getting the job with the Brands. No one could fail to notice my father's love of horses; he never hesitated to pass on his natural enthusiasm, talking to the horses as though they were his own children. As a boy, I watched admiringly the rapport he built with them, for they seemed intuitively to understand his chatter. I was barely two years old when my father put me on my first mount. From then on, I ran into the yard every time the horses came in from exercise and my father would place me on a horse's back as it walked into the stables. By the time I was five, he had begun teaching me all aspects of stable life, and by six I was riding my own polo pony. I was taught to ride military style, as my father himself had been, by an uncle who had ridden in the 11th Hussars.

I first rode without any reins, holding on with just my knees as the horse was led round the stables. From these humble beginnings, I was taught the basics so that by the age of seven I was able to ride independently, being taken out to go cub hunting with the hounds, a sport designed to break up fox families. A year later, I was riding every morning, taking the horses out for exercise with my father at 6am before returning for breakfast and dashing off to school. In the end I was excused religion, the first lesson at school, so I had more time to ride, although in return I attended Sunday School and sang in the Beddingham church choir.

Working on a country estate was a full-time job in every sense of the word. In those days, factory workers received a week's holiday a year but for farm or stable workers, such things didn't exist. Father worked at the stables every day of the year, with only the occasional break when he and I might go to Tattersall's to buy a couple of new hunters for the stables, or rarer still an occasional afternoon visit to the races at Brighton. Otherwise it was a daily routine from early morning when the horses went for exercise, to 5pm when the horses were watered, bedded down on soft straw and their day blankets exchanged for night. Night meant 6pm when the working day ended, though Dad, with paraffin lamp in hand, would walk round the stables before bed checking that everything was all right.

Large families were very much the norm, and mine was no different. I had some eleven aunts and uncles, and innumerable cousins. Throughout my childhood, an assortment of family members came to stay. There was Aunt Pat, a nanny to the wealthy, who came on many occasions but who would never take her hat off unless she was staying the night. Then there was Uncle Charlie, my father's brother. He was a great gambling man and former apprentice jockey who, it was said, rode the great Fred Archer to a close finish. However, his career was short-lived, as he was warned off the course for deliberately losing a race after making a deal with some bookmakers. As a result, he was always broke, so one season he came to work at my father's stables and lodged with us. Uncle Charlie had a fiery temper and could neither be told what to do nor criticised, and, as my father too was a bit sharp, it was an arrangement that could never work. On one occasion, my father gave Uncle Charlie half a sovereign, only to discover he had gambled it away. That was the last money he ever gave him. Uncle Charlie couldn't stop the gambling habit and died in a workhouse some years later. Then came my father's nephew, Sidney Clouting. He used to come down and spend his holidays with us, as well as occasionally helping out at the stables. He was the illegitimate child of my Aunt Nell, who was in domestic service when the butler got her pregnant. Money had apparently changed hands, and the scandal was hushed up, for, as an unmarried mother, she would never have got another job. Nell kept her job, and Sid was brought up by his grandparents, believing Nell was an aunt, and that his mother had abandoned him at birth. He was to die in the war, without Nell ever owning up to who she really was, although Sidney had his suspicions. Nell never got over the shock and died in 1929. Then there was Great Aunt Bessie, aged 103, on my father's side. I do not recall ever meeting her, but, it was said, she had planted her own potatoes in 1903 but didn't live long enough to dig them up. Lastly, there was Uncle Toby, a great character and a sergeant major in the Scots Guards. Even though he had been too young to fight in the Boer war and later somehow avoided the First World War, he nevertheless nurtured my interest in warfare.

3

From as far back as I can remember, I was crazy to be a soldier. As a child I brandished a wooden sword, with red ink spattered along the edges, and strutted around the estate like a regular recruit. I daydreamed about the heroic actions of former campaigns, and avidly read highly-charged tales of action in South Africa. At the annual village fair, known as The Club, rides on the roundabouts or shies at the coconuts always came second to the shooting range.

For a boy with army aspirations, five-shilling 'Blucher' boots were very important. Made on an army pattern, with hob nails and a broad toe cap, the boots were sold at the Crosskeys village shop, unstained and semi-watertight. Three days' work was needed to change them from brown to 'army' black, either by working in spitblacking (purchased in cakes and wetted with saliva or beer) or with the liquid blacking from an 'Everetts' stoneware bottle, conveniently sold with a brush attached to the bottle's cork so as to dab the paint onto the shoe before polishing. The hard work needed to properly prepare a pair of Bluchers was all part of military discipline, and the resulting glorious polish enough to make any sergeant major smile.

As soon as I was old enough, I bought an air rifle for the princely sum of three shillings and sixpence. This I had earned by becoming a company agent and hawking penny packets of flower and vegetable seeds door to door. Some ninety packets had to be sold to realise seven shillings and sixpence, which was then sent to the company in exchange for one of several gifts. There was never any question that I would choose the gun and I quickly became a dabster at shooting any number of sparrows tempted into our garden by bread for bait. Sparrows, as well as rooks and pigeons, were widely eaten and were caught in their dozens for home-made pies. In winter, when sparrows nested in haystacks, evenings were organised when the whole village turned out to catch them. Adults, armed with nets on poles, surrounded the stacks as boys flashed bicycle lamps into the hay, or beat tin cans. The clatter terrified the birds, flushing them out into the waiting nets, which were quickly brought round to trap them. My rifle made little further impression on their numbers but they were mine and they tasted better. I took them home, defeathered and held them by a toasting fork in the kitchen range, then ate them with some bread.

In 1908, I, like many of my friends, joined the rapidly expanding scout movement that had just been formed by Lord Baden Powell. Our local curate, the Reverend Finch, had formed the 1st South Down Troop with the help of Miss Betty Brand. No one knew anything about how a scout movement should work, the rules or the laws, so we all learnt together from the handbook written by Baden Powell. There were around twenty of us in the troop, mostly from Beddingham, Glynde and Firle schools, and being one of the oldest, I was made patrol leader straight away. The uniforms were provided free of charge and we met every Friday in a corrugated-iron hut at Glynde. Everything else had to be provided by us, so competitions were organised to make the things like stools that we needed.

Like all scouts, we had to learn to tie eight knots without looking, and then there were the badges for all the usual things such as cooking, gardening, cycling and riding. Quite often the Reverend Finch took us camping to Firle Park, just below Firle Beacon, or once or twice we went boating on the river Cuckmere near Alfriston. This was in a small boat which we pulled up the river until the tide turned, then we would float some three miles back down again.

The outdoor life always appealed to me, and I thoroughly enjoyed all my physical pursuits, riding, gardening, scouting. I disliked being stuck indoors and from four years old, when I attended Beddingham School, I found my education an uphill struggle. I did not stay long at the school, for soon after I arrived I was traumatised when a mad bull broke into the field where we were playing. It had broken out of a nearby farm and careered into our field, closely followed by several farmers running with pitch forks and shouting to us kids to 'run, run!' We scrambled through a fence, only for the bull to crash through the same fence farther up the field. Eventually the farmers cornered the bull between two carts and shot him, but the horror of the event stayed with me for years. Ironically, the field we had played in did not belong to the school, and normally the children played in the road instead. My mother disapproved of our having no playground and wrote to Mrs Weston, the headmistress, to inform her that she wished to move us to West Firle School in November 1905.

There were just three teachers at Firle Church School, one each for the three standards: Mr Price, headmaster and teacher of the senior class of some sixty children, Mrs Price, his wife, who took the twenty or so infants, while the twenty five or more children of the middle class were taught by a succession of supplementary teachers who were appointed only to resign a few months later.

Most of my school life was spent trying to avoid lessons as much as possible. I quickly got a reputation as a trouble maker, not in a bad way, for I was always considered the most polite child around, but because I simply would not pay attention. As a result I was always being kept behind after school to write lines for talking in class, and a week would never go by without my receiving the cane. Mr Price was a very nervous man who was always biting his finger nails (in reality he didn't have any nails left to bite). Owing to this, he was always quick to resort to the cane for all manner of minor infractions, though I think he enjoyed meting it out anyway.

On at least one occasion, Mr Price had cause to beat me all the way round the school playground. Both boys' and girls' toilets were earthen privies, simply a shed the back of which opened up when it was time to shovel away the waste. There were no toilets in the modern sense, simply a seat and a round circular hole. This meant anyone daring enough to climb over a protective fence would be in an ideal position to open the back of the shed and see one, or more, round and somewhat vulnerable bottoms sitting there.

Attacking these bottoms with a handful of brambles was a favourite trick. The suddenness of surprise, the shouts and shrieks, made for quite an amusing prank. Mr Price didn't agree. It was Mrs Price who happened to be sitting there on my next forage, and as I scrambled back over the fence, it was her husband who was waiting for me with the cane. He was in a flaming temper and grabbing me by the scruff of the neck, proceeded to thrash me all the way down the school playground. Later that day my sisters told my father what had happened. 'Oh, Mr Price didn't half thrash our Ben in the playground, he was hitting him on his legs, bottom and back,' to which my father remarked, 'Perhaps if I knew what he'd done, I'd give him another one'.

Most lessons during the year were badly and haphazardly taught. My favourites were maths and history, largely because all other subjects were made so boring. A typical geography lesson might entail drawing a map of England with all the seaports or major towns, or, alternatively, a map of Sussex with all the main landmarks. Geography was just about bearable but spelling, my worst subject, often necessitated a nose bleed which I brought about by pinching my nose tightly and blowing hard. This resulted in my being sent to the cloakroom where I bathed a cloth in cold water from an enamel bowl, and held it to the back of my neck.

Such inadequate teaching continued all year until two weeks before our exams, when life became not worth the living. For those fourteen days, Mr Price would cram us with exam information. He was well aware that Church School inspectors would come round to check on the results and it had to look like we had been taught properly. It all added up to a ridiculous situation. He was a very busy man but his fingers were in too many other pies and eventually he was sacked.

My education was markedly backward for my age. Because I was mischievous, Mr Price would always find a reason to send me out of the class and I was chosen for many shopping trips for the headmaster's wife. The village shop was a good half a mile away and I gratefully accepted the errand for the chance to get outside and into the open. Often I would return only for Mrs Price to say she had forgotten such and such, 'Do you mind going back?' Well, of course I didn't. I took other jobs too, from scrubbing, then swilling out, the boys' toilets on a Friday afternoon (after which I could go home early) to looking after his garden. Apart from the general foliage, Mr Price's garden also held seven or eight bee hives and in May, as the bees began to swarm, he would send myself and classmate Harold Clark to claim them for his hives. This was an important moment for the headmaster, for until the bees were 'claimed' they were anyone's property. With a key and a tin can at the ready, Harold and I would follow the swarm until it settled around the queen bee, then, as one of us tapped the can to signal our claim, the other would run and tell the headmaster. He would abruptly halt the class, collect his smoking outfit, skip and handbrush, and join us at the swarm. We would then watch as he smoked the bees into stupefaction before sweeping them into his skip and carrying them off to his hive.

Heartily tired of school, I jumped at the first legal chance to leave, when I asked dad if he would allow me to do just that on my fourteenth birthday. To my great annoyance my father refused, as I had no job to go to. However, my plight lasted just one month, for one of father's friends wrote and asked if I would like to be taken on at Colonel Campion's stables at Hassocks, near Brighton. Colonel William Campion was a local magistrate and brother-in-law of Charles Brand.[1] He was somewhat older, in his mid-seventies, an old soldier of several campaigns including the Crimean and the Indian Mutiny. As it turned out, his head groom required a stable boy, so without much ado my father gave me permission to accept the job and so leave school. That Monday I went to school for the last time to tell Mr Price I was leaving. 'Goodbye, Clouting, good luck and I'm damn glad to see the back of you.' I took it as a compliment, for no one was as glad to get away from that school as I was.

I left school on a Monday and, after packing and saying goodbye to my parents, left home that following Friday. The twenty-five-mile journey to Hassocks negotiated, I arrived at the Campion estate to be put to work under Costick, the head groom, and in times gone by an old stable mate of my father's. Costick had briefly been a trooper in the 5th Lancers, but had hated it so much that he bought himself out just as soon as he could. He was scathing about my obvious enthusiasm to join up, and wouldn't hesitate to tell me, often, that army life was no land of milk and honey. 'Well, boy, you think you're going into the army? You won't stick that for long,' he once said, on hearing me drum my fingers, military style, on a bucket.

At Hassocks I worked alongside another stable boy called Fred. Fred had a slightly mysterious background that I never did fathom. He was married, I believe, but was not meant to be; whatever the potential for scandal, everything about his personal life was kept quiet. In spite of a certain distance between us, Fred and I got on well and often we would ride out on exercise together to Danny Park near Thursbury Point, I on Colonel Campion's horse General, Fred on Speckles, a horse belonging to the Colonel's daughter. I worked a seven-day week, with Friday evening off to go to the scouts and Saturday evening off as of right, when I might go to the cinema at Hassocks or Hurstpierpoint. Work was hard but steady, and life by modern standards uneventful.

In the summer of 1912, I heard that Charlie Brand had died from the effects of a riding accident. I didn't go to the funeral but, in keeping with the close-knit community, the coffin bearers came from the estate employees, and included my father, Mr Weaver, and Mr Hayter, the butler. A month later, much of the estate was sold at auction, including some of the horses, and although my father remained at Beddingham, the writing was on the wall. The shock of Charlie Brand's early death at fifty seven was compounded at the reading of the will, for news quickly spread that he had left just £4,000. Clearly his wife's money, Vanderbilt money, had underpinned life at Little Dene for all those years.

In early July 1913, I finally resolved to join the army, so I gave notice at the stables, and returned home. At this time the Sussex Yeomanry were about to go to camp, but still needed someone to drive the officers' 'Maltese' mess wagon. News was that I intended to join up, so on the basis that this job would be good experience for me, I was asked if I would report to the Yeomanry's adjutant in Chichester, whereupon I would be given this wagon to drive. Our local butcher was lending a horse to the Yeomanry so I set out on the forty-five-mile journey, stopping off for a couple of hours at a pub so I could water and feed the horses. The job lasted two weeks, throughout which I watched the manoeuvres, following the territorials wherever they went, ready to supply the officers with food from the wagon. I was paid, though only a few shillings, for it was the experience that mattered. The manoeuvres were filmed and made into a short feature entitled something like 'A day out with the Sussex Yeomanry'. Shortly after, it was shown at the cinema in Lewes, where I made my cinematic debut, briefly appearing aloft on my wagon, much to my and my sisters' delight.

NOTES

1. Colonel William Henry Campion (1836–1923) married Gertrude Brand in 1869. She was the daughter of the 1st Viscount Brand, a former Speaker of the House of Commons, and sister of the Honourable Charles Brand (1855 – 1912).

CHAPTER TWO

Crazy to be a Soldier

Ben

I was still only fifteen years old when I came home from Colonel Campion's stables in July 1913, so it was necessary for me to get into the army any way that I could. The artillery was calling for boy trumpeters and, as I wished to work with horses, joining a battery appeared to be my best chance.

It was while I was weighing up my options that an officer, Captain Carton de Wiart of the 4th Royal Irish Dragoon Guards, visited the stables. Several officers from this Regiment regularly came over to the Brands' while they were stationed at Brighton, for Charles Brand was the Master of the Southdown Fox Hunt, and had a string of hunters these officers could borrow.

My father would drive down to meet the officers at Glynde train station, bringing them back to the house so that, as a youngster, I saw men such as de Wiart and Major Tom Bridges, another 4th Dragoon Guards officer, as I helped around the stables with the saddles and harnesses.

'I see your boy's home,' de Wiart observed. 'What does he want to do?'

'He's intending to join up,' my father replied, 'he's talking of the artillery.'

I was told that de Wiart exploded at this. 'He doesn't want to be a bloody gunner. Tell him he can join my Regiment, the 4th Dragoon Guards. I'll ensure he is looked after.'

That evening my father passed on the news. 'Well, it's up to you,' he cautioned, 'but don't expect me to buy you out if you don't like it. I haven't got the money even if I wanted to.' I did not need a second invitation. The following morning I went to enlist in Lewes, where a recruiting sergeant, dressed in khaki but sporting a broad red sash across his chest, made me welcome. After one or two informal questions, he began to put my details in his ledger. It was necessary to conceal my age so I could enlist as an eighteen-year-old, but in my excitement I told him I was born on September 15th 1895.

'Well, you're not eighteen, then, are you?' Lying did not come naturally and I sheepishly corrected myself.

10

He didn't care. The general rule was that if you were big enough, you were old enough, and if you were old enough, you were big enough; as far as he was concerned he'd got another recruit and that was all that mattered.

'What regiment do you wish to join?' he asked rhetorically. I put forward the 4th Dragoon Guards, whereupon the sergeant promptly put me down for the infantry. The standard height for the cavalry was five foot seven, he said, and, as I was nearly five foot nine, it would be better if I went into the foot guards.

'But the Dragoon Guards are already aware that I am to join them,' I said, stretching a point.

'Then I'll have to fill out a special application because you are too tall,' the sergeant said, irritated.

Whether he did or not, I don't know. More personal details were taken, after which I scribbled a short passage to prove my basic literacy. 'I fully understand that after my first double issue of kit I will have to pay for my own from the allowance that I will get.'

My papers had to be accepted, and I returned home to await formal confirmation. A travel warrant duly arrived with an order to attend a medical examination in Brighton, during which my measurements were taken along with the smallest physical characteristics, in case I should ever desert: a brown mark on the inner side of my left knee, and a 'scar small on back' where my mother had once used scissors to dig out a sheep tick. Lastly, the swearing-in ceremony before an officer and I was in the army; the date was August 28th 1913.

For the next three days, I stayed at Brighton Barracks before travelling by train to the Dragoons' depot at Seaforth, Liverpool, where the Recruits' Course of Training taught the rudiments of cavalry life. At Seaforth, I was allocated a barrack room and told to report to the Quartermaster Sergeant's stores to draw my equipment. There, I was handed a khaki uniform and told to change in a cubicle, parcelling up my civilian clothes with brown paper and string. These clothes were to be sent to my parents, but recruits were always ripped off and it didn't surprise me when they never reached home. No doubt they were pawned – a financial perk for someone in the stores.

Corporal Reagan, a full time drill instructor, was to show us the ropes during three months of foot drill and fitness training, that would mould each of us into the basic shape of a Dragoon. Much emphasis was laid on physical fitness. Gruelling hours were spent running across country, or round the barracks, leaping the water trough after each circuit, or in the gymnasium, working on the rings, vaulting, running, performing press-ups until we couldn't

11

press-up any more. To toughen us up, boxing gloves were dished out, and we were paired off for three-minute bouts. Heaven help anyone that did not fight like mad, for the instructor would step in and have a go at those who didn't give their all.

Almost as much time was spent on the parade ground, where barking NCOs fought to shape us up, with the usual verbal abuse to encourage obedience. One poor devil, a man from Somerset, became so nervous while marching that within a few paces his arms swung in tandem with, and not against, his stride. At first, the sergeants thought he was trying to be funny and aimed no end of shouts and shrieks in his direction. Soon they had him on his own, walking up and down, to and fro, and each time he would start all right and then revert, maddening his trainers and no doubt making the situation worse. In the end he bought himself out.

On Saturday mornings, drills gave way to fatigues, then to lectures, when we were told about the nature of Esprit de Corps, or about the importance of health and cleanliness. Many speakers simply passed the time of day, but one in particular had a marked effect. He was Sergeant Cole, a drill instructor from the Queen's Bays (2nd Dragoon Guards). I forget the theme but part-way through, he stopped. 'You young chaps take my advice. Learn your trade, learn everything you possibly can because, believe you me, in less than no time you'll be fighting for your bloody lives.' He was killed early on in the Retreat from Mons, but I never forgot his words.

During the final month of basic training, we were allowed out on to civilian streets for the first time. The wearing of khaki was forbidden until at least two years' service had been put in, so instead we appeared in newly-acquired full dress uniforms. Red tunics, dark blue collars and cuffs in velvet with a little yellow piping, were worn above blue 'strides', down the side of which ran a two-inch-wide yellow stripe, held tight underneath our Wellington boots by a buckle. We had to know how to carry ourselves, whip under the shoulder, so that at the very least we appeared a credit to our regiments. 'When you walk down the street, remember you are a cavalryman. You are not just walking down the street, you own the bloody street!' That was the message and I did feel very proud.

While we were at Seaforth, we saw one or two full-time officers who were sent from the various Dragoon Regiments to do stints as orderly officer at the recruits' depot. One such officer was a Lieutenant from the 4th Dragoons' barracks at Tidworth, Sir Arthur Hickman, a popular man but one who suffered from a pronounced stutter.

One of his jobs was to oversee guard duty. There were set procedures for this which had to be learnt, so that everything was done just right once the orderly officer had read the evening's orders and mounted the guard. If, for example, the guard was approached by the orderly officer and sergeant of the guard, they were challenged in the correct manner as follows: 'Halt! Who goes there?' The sergeant answered with 'Orderly officer doing his rounds,' before the officer asked the sentry to 'Hand over your orders'. The private then replied, 'Take charge of a post and all Government property in view. Report any unusual object to the Sergeant of the Guard.'

One evening, during a walk round the stables, Hickman met the sentry's customary challenge. 'Ha..ha..ha..hand over your orders,' said Hickman, whereupon the sentry began 'Take ch..ch..charge of a po..po..posts . . . ,' but got only so far before being cut short by Hickman who spluttered with rage, 'You bloody monkey! Don't you bloody well mo..mo..mock me or I'll punch your nose.' Unbeknown to Hickman, the sentry stuttered too. It would have been a calamity for an officer to strike a sentry but it took all the sergeant's persuasive powers to stop Hickman doing just that. The incident caused a sensation and was common knowledge all round the barracks within twenty four hours.

The night that I passed out to join my Regiment, I was also on guard duty. As a rule, seven men were on parade, six of whom would rotate the night's work, the seventh, the cleanest, being given what was known as 'the stick'. The inspecting duty officer would tap the winner on the shoulder, whereupon the rest of the guard dismissed and the orderly dumped his sword, collected his whip and reported to the sergeant. Being the Sergeant of the Guard's orderly was the cushiest job, for the orderly slept all night unless any messages needed delivering. That day I was immaculately clean, with everything in the highest state of spit and polish possible, for to be sent off the passing-out parade meant another month's training, and I had no intention of missing out. Two of us had been on the passing-out parade that morning, and the officer was having difficulty picking out the cleaner. Ordering us to step forward, he said 'Lift your foot'. Our strides were buckled underneath the boot to keep them straight, and I won the stick because my tiny buckle was polished and his wasn't.

Just before I left for Seaforth, I was woken in the early hours by a woman's voice screaming a torrent of abuse. The whole barrack block was up and about, peering out of the windows, trying to discover what on earth was going on, as regimental policemen were seen darting in and out of several barracks. Word quickly got around that a prostitute had been smuggled into the camp, but that the regimental police had got wind of what was going on, and a search was now underway to catch the troopers responsible. The culprits had dashed to evict the prostitute by dumping her unceremoniously over the camp's perimeter railings, but this was easier said than done, for the railings were spiked and, as the soldiers were finding, it was no easy matter to launch anyone over, let alone an ungrateful prostitute.

The screams signalled that they had been unsuccessful, and as the troopers beat a hasty retreat, the prostitute was left dangling from the railings, her skirt and various undergarments impaled on the spikes. The Military Policemen, more concerned with finding the offenders than helping the woman, were rushing about trying to catch anyone in bed with their clothes on. To most, the incident was hilarious, but privately I thought it was awful that she should be left hanging there.

I was just sixteen and had joined the army hardly knowing how babies were born, indeed I was utterly naive about anything sexual. While at Seaforth, a soldier considerably older than myself had become very talkative and friendly to me. His bed was in the corner of the room, and mine was next to his. One evening, another soldier took me aside. 'Boy, you want to sleep with your breeches on,' he said. I wanted to ask why, but instinct told me not to. Only later did it dawn on me that the man was homosexual, and that this was by way of a warning. Similarly, the Saturday lectures about private cleanliness had often left me wondering what on earth the instructor was talking about. 'If you must dip your wick, for heaven's sake make sure you wash when you come back.'

In December 1913, I left with a draft of twelve men for Tidworth camp. 'Is there a Private Clouting here?' asked a corporal, on my arrival. 'Right, C Squadron, report to Captain Hornby.' De Wiart had been seconded to another Regiment, but had ensured I would come under the able Hornby, another officer well known at the Brands' home, and therefore to my family.

The regiment was billeted in Assaye Barracks, in four of twenty eight camp accommodation blocks built in a large crescent. The regimental barracks were each named after an Indian town: 1.Aliwal 2.Assaye 3.Bhurpore 4.Candahar 5.Delhi 6.Jalalabad 7.Lucknow 8.Mooltan. Of these, Aliwal, Assaye, and Mooltan had stable blocks behind, so that, apart from the 4th Dragoons in Assaye Barracks, there were the 18th Hussars in Aliwal, and the 9th Lancers at the other end of the crescent in Mooltan. The other barracks held either battalions of infantry, such as the Rifle Brigade or men from the Army Ordnance and Service Corps.

The whole camp was more or less self-sufficient, for, even if we had had passes to leave Tidworth, Swindon, the nearest town, was twenty six miles away and we had precious little money to spend anyway. Outside the camp, there was The Ram Inn, the only civilian pub anywhere near the barracks, and half the time this was out of bounds because there'd been a row and a punch-up between soldiers and locals. We therefore relied on the camp. Symonds Brewery supplied beer at two pence a pint to our canteen, where the men would get drunk on a Friday night, while one or two shops in the middle of the camp supplied everything else. Entertainment was catered for by the camp's own theatre, our spiritual health by the camp's impressive church, and our physical well-being ensured by our own hospital in Candahar barracks. Finally, for those who had wives and children, there were married quarters, identical terraced houses which ran behind and parallel to the wide sweep of the barrack blocks.

Four barrack blocks were allocated to the 4th Dragoons. Every block contained eight rooms, each housing twelve men from the same troop. Six beds lined each side of a room, separated in the middle by two long wooden tables. The otherwise spartan room was heated at one end by a coal fire and lit by paraffin lamps, the glass chimneys of which were forever breaking. Outside each room there was a wide verandah, at both ends of which were the stairways, and between the stairways of each block were the wash rooms, the baths being in a separate building. Baths were held on Saturdays, and although there was nothing to stop one having a bath during the week, most waited until the weekend for there were so many duties to do.

As an unmarried private, I was allocated a bed upstairs in the block belonging to the 4th Troop of C Squadron, where I met my new comrades, among them my Corporal, Cushy Harrison, our Shoeing Smith, Sandy, troopers Spider Stevens, Cumber, Isted, Treacle Johnson, Shit Sharp and Ding Dong Bell.

Most soldiers picked up nicknames and mine was Cronkie, given after Cushy Harrison detailed me for a job under the impression that this was my name. 'Well, what is your bloody name?' he asked when I didn't respond. 'Clouting,' I replied. 'Uhh, well, Cronkie will bloody well do for me,' so Cronkie I remained. Of the others, Johnson, as I soon learnt, could never keep his fingers from the thick dark treacle given as a weekly treat to the horses; Sharp always managed to look scruffy – even when he was tidy – and Bell was inevitably Ding Dong.

I quickly slotted into the room's regime. Each person took turns as barrack room orderly, making sure that the fireplace was cleaned out, the paraffin lamps trimmed, the two barrack room tables scrubbed daily and the floor once a week. It was, of course, everyone's responsibility to ensure the room was tidy and that the beds were taken down, the three blankets, two sheets and pillow slip being folded and lined up properly with our towel on top. An inspection by the Orderly Sergeant ensured that any lapses were noted and punished with extra fatigues or 'jankers', such as weeding round the stables or extra latrine cleaning. As punishments were collectively given to the whole barrack room, plots were hatched to retaliate against anyone who let the side down. When Treacle Johnson spilt paraffin, staining the floor, he was grabbed and carted off struggling to the horse trough where he was dragged, fully clothed, up and down with a horse halter on his head. It was all in good humour, but it helped ensure that we strove not to let each other down!

Almost as soon as a new trooper was allocated to a bed, married soldiers came in and touted for his clothes washing. 'Have you made arrangements for your washing? No? Well my missus will look after you.' The charge was fourpence a week, for which his wife would wash a shirt, a pair of pants, socks and a towel, her husband picking up the washing, which he found rolled up at the end of the bed, on a Monday and returning it on a Friday or Saturday. Now and again we could get darning done, too; it was the married man's way of supplementing his income, for many were still privates and had children to support.

There were one or two others, ex-soldiers who remained at the camp and made a living doing odd jobs. One of the best known was Hoppy Martin, a fifty-year-old civilian allocated one of four small rooms attached to the barrack blocks and normally reserved for the Orderly Sergeants. Hoppy, so-called because of a wooden leg which he swung from the hip down, was the troops' official photographer and toured the regiments looking for commissions. His bread and butter work was group pictures at the stables, at the cookhouse, or on church parade, the troopers splitting the costs between them. Hoppy also took portraits, and carried with him a magnificent picture of a Dragoon in full dress uniform astride a beautiful horse. He would offer to take your picture, superimposing it on the photograph of the Dragoon with such expertise that it was impossible to see the join.

Many of his pictures were taken while we worked at the stables or as we undertook various fatigues. One of the principal fatigues was carting around the coal needed all over the camp; in the barracks, the cookhouse, the married quarters. Coal was drawn from the dump, enough for the barrack room for a week, although not sufficient to keep the fire going at night which, during winter, necessitated our sleeping in cotton shirts and long johns. In twos, we carried coal to the cookhouse or married quarters, using double-handed metal cauldrons, making two trips to the bunker at the back of each home.

Potato peeling was a daily routine, with twelve of us peeling potatoes for the whole Squadron. Everyone used his own knife, with those who'd never peeled before leaving as much spud on the skin as on the potato itself. To while away the time, we usually broke into a song, especially favourites such as 'Nellie Dean'.

For fatigues, we wore canvas trousers with turn-ups. Working in the muck of the stables, these turn-ups became filthy, and by the end of the week looked in a real state. It was our job, however, to keep them clean for the Monday morning inspection. As it was nigh impossible to wash them by hand, most rubbed soap into the sodden trousers, then scrubbed them vigorously with the bass broom from the stables, swilling them off with fresh water before pinning them up to dry. Even then, it was difficult to stop the turn-ups from becoming ragged at the edges, as Sergeant Major Steel coarsely pointed out one morning, while we were lined up for inspection. 'That canvas of yours! There is more bloody lace around the bottom of those than my old woman has round her drawers.' This man had been married for no more than three weeks, and was saying things like that, I thought. The language we heard from the NCOs did beggar belief sometimes, but this was different and my estimation of the man never went back up again.

Work was strenuous during the week, when sleep was all we wanted. Lights out was at 10pm and choice words followed from the Orderly Sergeant if we were slow to respond. At weekends, we sometimes played cards underneath the barrack room tables, pulling a blanket over the top before lighting a candle and beginning a few hands. These games included a spot of gambling, but with a wage of one shilling and threepence a day, it was only for pennies.

To catch up on lost sleep, it was possible to stay in bed an extra hour on Sunday mornings. Those due for stable fatigue rose at 6am while those on the Orderly Sergeant's list for Church Parade got up at 7am. Those on the list had to have volunteered, something I always did, as I loved singing so much. The extra hour was to ensure we were absolutely spick and span, but unofficially it was an extra forty winks. Each squadron provided a skeleton number of troopers for Church Parade, about thirty or forty, all in full dress uniform, brass helmets and swords. Two lines were formed for inspection, with the tallest men at each end so as to make both rows look about the same size. On 'eyes right' we turned to dress, shuffling forward or backward, ensuring we were in a straight line. There were two sittings at the camp's Church, which lay on a hill more or less behind Lucknow barracks, one for the Protestants and one for the Catholics. The band played the Protestants to church, hence the phrase 'Following the Drum', which was used to identify oneself as a Protestant, as often as saying 'C of E'. Once at Church, several minutes of assorted clatters and bangs followed as the infantry with their bayonets, and the cavalry with their swords sat, while the officers with their wives and children made their way more sedately to specially reserved seats. A regular selection of hymns was sung, led by the choir made up from the duty Regiment, while music was played by the duty band.

After the service, a parade was formed for the march back. All the regiments were represented, with their bands playing, the 18th Hussars going ahead of us, the Rifle Brigade behind. This caused all sorts of problems, for C Squadron was directly in front of the Rifle Brigade's band and therefore we could hear virtually nothing of our own band, making it almost impossible to keep in step, a problem compounded by the fact that the Rifle Brigade marched at a different speed from everyone else. The cavalry traditionally marched at 120 steps to a minute, the infantry 140, but the Rifle Brigade walked at 144. To stop us crashing into each other, our stride was thirty inches in length, the Rifle Brigade's twenty four, but all said and done, a farcical collision was only averted by careful concentration all round.

During the week we all got up at the same time. Reveille was a single trumpet call at 6am followed by a second once the trumpeter had had time to walk round to the other side of the barracks. We rose to the shouts of troop corporals to look lively, washing in tin bowls of cold water before dressing in fatigues and running downstairs (or shinning down the drain pipe) to answer the Orderly Sergeant's roll call at 6.15. At 7am, we left the barrack rooms to muck out the stables, cleaning out the wet peat and wheelbarrowing in new, dry, rough-cut peat distributed from huge loose bales. While straw looked nicer, peat made a better bed and could be evenly spread to a depth of six inches, to be topped up later to keep the horses comfortable. The horses were then taken for a drink and given their feed, hay throughout the week with a Saturday treat of bran mash mixed with hot water and a scoop of treacle. Only after the horses had eaten did we make our way to the cookhouse for breakfast, a couple of slices of bread, margarine and jam, or pozzy as jam was known, and a bowl of tea. During winter, bread changed to porridge, also known as burgue, for pozzy and burgue were Hindustani words, which we picked up from the older soldiers who used little phrases or counted up to ten, 'ikk, do, tin, char, panch, shey, saat,' etc, to impress us youngsters and to prove they'd been there.

The younger and older soldiers got on pretty well, although there were grizzly old soldiers that we learnt to watch out for. These men had certain ways of doing things, certain seats in the mess where they always sat, certain crockery they always used. One incident showed how petty some old soldiers could become. Tea basins were picked up as we entered the mess hall. Some were plain, others had red or blue bands around them, but all were basically the same in that they held over a pint of tea, poured out by one of the mess room orderlies. One morning trumpeter Patterson mistakenly picked up a 'favourite' bowl belonging to one of these old soldiers, who, grumbling loudly, embarked on his own crusade to find it, which he duly did. 'What are you doing with my bowl, boy?' he growled. 'Is this really your basin?' replied Patterson. 'Well, put a bloody chinstrap on it,' and standing up, plonked it firmly on the old soldier's head, showering the man with tea. Patterson was a favoured boy in the Regiment because he had joined as a boy trumpeter and was still only eighteen, despite having been in the Regiment for some five or six years. There would have been an uproar had this older man tried to hit Patterson, and he knew it. Soaked with tea, he stood his ground, furious, but at a loss to know what to do. In the end, he swallowed his pride and walked away, much to our amusement and the odd jeer.

After breakfast, at 9am, a trumpet call signalled the start of training exercises, followed at 11am by another call for stables, when the horses were groomed and taken out for inspection by the troop officer. This was a thorough inspection, the troop officer wiping a handkerchief over the horse to check it was clean, then examining the saddlery hung up behind. At evening stables, we'd water the horses, before night rugs, old and fairly dirty blankets, were put on to keep them warm. In the stalls, they were tied by a chain which ran from their head collar through a ring to a ball weight, giving the horse enough flexibility to lie down but not to leave the stalls.

There was no main gate guard at Tidworth, just a stable guard looking after all four troop blocks, ensuring that none of the horses became loose in the stalls or got a hoof stuck in the swing bar as it rolled in the peat. As others preferred to stay in bed, I could earn two extra bob by doing their stint, working two hours on, four hours off. Those on duty missed out on their normal night's sleep and this was difficult to make up, but I was young and felt I could manage, so to earn extra cash I often took two or three nights' duty in a row.

Next to the stable blocks stood a covered area under which was stacked the peat and a small amount of baled hay. One night, while on duty, I sat down on one of the bales for a few minutes and was soon asleep. I did not hear the orderly officer with Sergeant Dusty Miller as they came round on a routine check, calling 'Sentry, sentry.' As the two passed by, Miller spied me out of the corner of his eye and hit my legs with his stick, while continuing to call for the sentry. Waking with a start, I dashed round the other side of the block to meet them with a conscientious-sounding 'Who goes there?' It was very easy to miss one another when patrolling round four stable blocks, so the officer was none the wiser. Miller had saved me from a charge, for which I was more than grateful.

My first Christmas at the Regiment was a raucous affair, the whole Squadron in a mess hall eating and getting increasingly drunk together. Troopers stood on benches and gave their musical best to songs whose words were somewhat altered, before the Sergeant Major was persuaded to stand up and sing a parody of 'The Good Old Summer Time', to general cheers.

The festivities coincided with the old soldiers returning from their month's furlough, and this ensured that there was a great spirit of camaraderie between all the privates and NCOs, before the younger recruits took their yearly one week's leave in January. I returned to my parents' home and took the chance to show off my dress uniform on every opportunity, including walking down to my old school to pick up my brother, who was equally thrilled to see me coming. I was not able to show off to Mr Price, for he had finally been sacked in early December, a mistress and her sister taking over the teaching and, to my brother's disgust, handing out homework for the first time!

I returned to the Regiment, and soon after began formal instruction at the Regiment's riding school. That first morning, a corporal addressed us as we lined up for tuition. 'Any of you chaps used to horses?' he asked. I replied that I had been a groom, another that he formerly worked on a baker's van. But neither qualification seemed to impress the corporal much. 'Well, to start with you can forget everything you thought you knew about horses, you're in the cavalry now.'

For the first two days, we were only taught the names of the saddlery, and how to put on and take off a saddle. On the third day, we were given our mounts and within minutes the corporal rode up, inquiring who had taught me to ride military style, promptly moving me to a higher ride, from which I was promoted one notch further four days later.

The purpose of the riding school was to teach us how to be a fighting machine on horseback, and this demanded strict uniformity. Preparing to mount, we were called to attention standing on the left side of the horse's head, the reins in the right hand. At the command 'Prepare to mount!' we turned, taking the reins in our left hand, putting the left foot in the stirrup. At 'Mount!' we rose as one, but waiting for the man on the extreme right to nod his head before we swung in unison into the saddles, finding the right stirrup. When riding, all actions were controlled by the bugle, sounded by the trumpeter at any speed equal to, or faster than, the trot. To get the bugle steady enough to sound, it had to be blown downwards, the rider crouched in his saddle, not as Hollywood western films showed years later, bugles played at the charge, with the rider bolt upright.

On Salisbury Plain there was a 'manger', that is, a double ring of fences, five or six in each, the outer markedly higher than the inner ring. Both horses and riders were taught in the manger. Loose horses were driven round to teach them to jump naturally, while troopers rode round so that faults, such as leaning too far forward or back, could be pointed out. It was while on Salisbury Plain that I was moved to the highest ride. I had come to the attention of the Riding Master, a captain in charge of the riding school, who, after watching me ride, asked the corporal instructor who I was. I was told to ride round first the inner, then the outer jumps, before the officer asked, 'Will you take your saddle off and try it again?' At sixteen years old, I was as agile as you like, and, although I fell off, the horse stopped in between the fences and I finished the round. The Riding Master spoke to me again. 'I'm going to put you into the top ride, where you'll have to work hard, as they are more advanced than you. You'll also need to stop behind for a while to learn sword and rifle drill, but I think you can cope.' There were about six levels to reach the top ride and I still had much to learn, but this was one area where I could shine, and I passed out of the riding school in three months, when it normally took nine.

This was exceptional, for generally speaking few troopers had had any experience with horses, let alone the opportunity to ride one since childhood. Invariably, as new recruits learnt the ropes, accidents occurred. Bruises were par for the course, cracked ribs or broken arms an occasional hazard, but every now and again tragedy would strike, and one May morning a trooper from my Squadron was killed at the riding school. He was in a lower ride and had apparently slipped from his horse only to be kicked as he fell. Any death meant a full dress funeral when the Regiment's three Squadrons (in Church Parade numbers) turned out in respect. It was a blazing hot day for the trek to the Church and afterwards the cemetery, which lay a couple of miles away from Tidworth on the Collingbourne road. As the sun blazed down, everyone was sweating profusely under their tunics and brass helmets. If one man had fallen out, half the Regiment would have followed suit – but no one was willing to accept the inevitable consequences of being first, so we stayed in line.

It was a very sombre ceremony. We followed the cortège in which walked a jet-black horse with the soldier's boots placed eerily back to front in the stirrups. After the service we walked to the cemetery, arriving at the slow march, pointing the toe, standing to attention as he was buried and a volley of shots was fired over his grave. The Regiment came back across country, marching at ease with the regimental band striking up the popular tune 'Stop Thy Tickling Jock,' to shake the men out of any glumness.

Despite the dangers, troopers learnt trick riding. This was taught to give us self-confidence and mastery over our horses. At the gallop, we were taught to pick up objects from the ground, swinging over and hooking our spurs underneath our swords, our left hand holding the reins, the right scooping up a handkerchief, sometimes staying down to pick up a second one fifteen yards farther on. We were also taught to come into action at the gallop, whereby a horse holder at the gallop took the reins of another trooper's horse, while he, the trooper, jumped down holding on to his saddle while getting into step with the horse. Gripping on to his rifle with the left hand, the trooper ran on, throwing himself to the ground, and coming into action as the horse holder rode away. Similarly, to remount at the canter, the same trooper would leap into the saddle as the horse holder spurred his mount on.

Basic rules for musketry were taught in the same way as horsemanship. Our first lessons had been at Seaforth where we stood around a rifle mounted on a tripod, a sergeant taking us through the rifle's mechanics, before showing us how a target should sit on the blade of the foresight and on the shoulders of the backsight. Our first shots were on an indoor rifle range, shooting over thirty yards. As an economy measure, we used Lee Enfields converted to take .22 ammunition, firing at targets balanced on old railway sleepers buttressed by sandbags. By shooting indoors, we could be trained intensively in all weathers, for it was not until we joined our regiments that we shot outdoors on proper ranges.

Except for initial foot drill when we were issued with Marks One and Two Lee Enfields, the cavalry had changed over to the Mark Three. This was a rifle with several important modifications, principally a shorter barrel and longer stock, which strengthened the muzzle, and a reduced sight, the Mark Three being sighted to 1,800 yards, 1,000 fewer than her predecessor. Each trooper became attuned to a particular rifle, learning to compensate for any slight anomalies it had, so improving his own accuracy. This was the rifle that would be taken to war and so he was naturally loath to change it, let alone to allow anyone else to shoot with it. To avoid confusion, each rifle was identified by a number on the butt plate and on a small disc on the stock, mine being 231.

Musket training was on the sixteen-target Sidbury range, built into the side of the hill. If there was a strong cross wind, we used what was called a sighting bullet. As a strong wind affected the path a bullet took over a long distance, we were allowed to fire one bullet using our windgages to counteract its effect, moving the wind gauge one, two, or three clicks left or right, depending on the wind's direction. The shooting at number sixteen target was always notoriously bad, for just off the bank to the side of the target was a pathway on which rabbits were often seen and the boys could never resist having a pot at them.

Not everyone eligible to shoot would fire each day, for a fatigue party was needed to work the ranges. On many occasions I took a turn sitting in a long, ten-foot-deep trench, working the iron-framed apparatus below the targets. Two men worked each pair of targets, sitting on little chairs as the bullets cracked overhead. One mended the 'down' target, pasting, then slapping black or white square patches over the holes, while the other signalled shots on the 'up' target with a long 'lollipop'-like pole. The disc on top of the pole was painted black on one side, white on the other, so that either side could be used to highlight the bullet hole, depending on which of the target's concentric black and white circles had been hit. A bull was shown by displaying the edge of the disc against the target, and a complete miss was signalled by the waving of a flag. The fatigue party remained underground for about two hours, having a chat and a laugh before a whistle blew to signal the all-clear.

During musket training we practised shooting at a life-size cut-out of four horsemen. It was built on a four-wheeled platform and pulled over the brow of a hill by a team of horses appearing for a few seconds at 400–500 yards range. It was a lesson in just how difficult it was to hit a target travelling at speed, especially one coming across our front and at the gallop, and I don't believe it was hit more than half a dozen times throughout the summer months of 1914.

To pass out as a fully-trained soldier, a trooper had to fire fifteen aimed rounds a minute at 400 yards, starting with five rounds in the magazine and nothing in the breech. This took a lot of practice, and not just on the ranges. In the evenings, as we lay on our beds, we sought to speed up the time taken to work the rifle's bolt action so that by the time we were due to pass out, most of us could get off seventeen aimed rounds a minute, starting with one in the breech.

Finally, after two years' service, a trooper was automatically tested for an extra sixpence a day Proficiency Pay, awarded for putting five bullets in a four-inch circle at a hundred yards, slow firing. No practice shots were allowed to gauge wind strength and, although one miss was allowed, it had to be very close. Further tests included firing fifteen rounds rapidly into a six-foot target at 400 and 600 yards.

Those were exciting days. I was up to my neck in army life, and loving every minute of it. None of it was really hard because I was so keen to be a soldier. Conversely, many chaps let it drop that they would rather be in civvy life, but, as they had nothing else to do, often nowhere else to go, they enlisted to get something to eat. They were not literally starving but, in my experience, 50% of recruits joined up because they had no work or money. One shilling and three pence was the basic daily wage in the cavalry, and expenses came out of that, such as cleaning materials or deductions for breakages. Joining the army meant the security of daily food and accommodation, and that was worth more to many than the weekly four or five shillings in our pockets.

A good proportion came from orphanages, joining for the comradeship and the sense of belonging more than for anything else. One man in my barracks at Seaforth had come from a Dr Barnardo's home; he had no family and to him, as to all these men, the army was their new family, most, not suprisingly, never receiving any mail from the outside world at all.

The Regiment was a hotchpotch of men, from many backgrounds. The 4th Dragoon Guards was an Irish regiment, but the number recruited from Ireland had reached an all-time low. More came, as I recall, from the Birmingham area than from Ireland, while among the officers only Lieutenant Gallaher stands out in my memory as an Irish officer with an accent to match. In the army were several men who were a source of speculation and intrigue. One man I first met at the depot at Seaforth was very well spoken, clearly well educated and, as it turned out, of some financial means. No one knew the circumstances behind his wealth, or why this man wasn't an officer. Despite signing on as a private, he had taken on the services of an older ex-trooper, one of several who lived at the depot working as storemen, who turned this private out immaculately each day, acting in effect as his batman.

Another man at Seaforth told me that he had deserted twice from infantry regiments before joining the cavalry. It was obvious, even to new recruits, that he had been in the army before, for he picked up the drill too easily. The drill sergeants knew it too, but no one could find out where he had been before and no further investigations were made. He was happy, he said, to stick with the cavalry, and eventually joined the 3rd Dragoons.

Given the varying reasons for joining up in the first place, it was hardly surprising when a trooper nipped out of Seaforth or Tidworth not intending to return. On average, a trooper disappeared every three months at Tidworth and, although a search was made, if he wasn't found after twenty one days his property was auctioned, the money going to regimental funds. One deserter, trained in the same squad of recruits as myself the previous summer at Seaforth, had failed to return from leave in January, and so an auction was announced for the next pay day. This was an organised event with items being put on display for pre-sale viewing, before a sergeant offered the pieces lot by lot. I was in need of a new tunic. The one I owned had a tar mark in the middle of the back, after I had inadvertently leaned against a fence. It was no longer than an inch, but although I used chalk, the mark stubbornly refused to go away. I had been on parade several times with this tunic on, and while nothing had been noticed, I knew it was just a matter of time. A new tunic cost about three pounds, but they were only ever sold for a fraction of that price at auction, so when I immediately bid a princely three shillings, I warded off any rival bids and got it.

March 17th – St Patrick's Day – was the Regiment's special day of the year when the massed trumpeters, all twenty four of them, sounded reveille, before the band struck up and marched round the barracks playing old regimental tunes. Apart from looking after the horses and mounting the guard, all duties were suspended for the day. All disciplinary sanctions regarding the excessive consumption of alcohol were also lifted, allowing the men to celebrate St Patrick's Day by getting blind drunk. Just as long as things were back to normal the next morning, nothing was said, even to those who literally had to be carried to their beds by our military police.

In the evening there was a concert and a raucous sing-song. Beer was free, and I vividly remember trumpeter Patterson lying on a table, trumpet in mouth, drinking the beer that was poured through the top. He did not attempt to play lights out that night!

For many men, these evenings provided brief breaks from the control the army exerted over our lives from morning to night. This went much further than the bugle calls which woke us in the morning and put out the lights at night, or the ever-present NCOs who ordered our working day. The Regiment itself was omnipresent, and could sanction everything from whom a trooper married to whether he grew a beard. Even our top lips belonged to the King, and to shave off what fluff might have accumulated there was, at least in theory, a court martial offence. This law continued until mid-way through the war when, through the mud and the shell holes, an order arrived to say that 'moustaches were optional'.

There was an enormous gulf between ourselves and the officers, so that other than soldiering, a troop officer, ex-Harrow and Sandhurst, could have had nothing in common with an orphan from a Barnardo's home. It was a gulf that was the accepted norm, particularly within a cavalry regiment, when almost without exception every officer had to come from a wealthy background to afford the lifestyle. They were all ex-public school boys,[1] a few of whom had perhaps been to university but all of whom had certainly attended Sandhurst. Poor officers were only relatively poor, those who might have to borrow a polo horse from the Regiment. Not that we were supposed to know. Yet it was an open secret among the ranks who had money and who was struggling to get by. Later on, during the war, money did not matter a damn, but pre-war it was very important to keep up appearances, and many officers might have been surprised to know what rumours, unfounded or not, had seeped their way down to the men as barrack gossip. For an officer rarely spoke directly to a trooper, and we could not speak to an officer except through the intermediary of a senior NCO, and then as we stood to attention.

While our lives were tightly controlled, the officers lived in relative freedom, pursuing mainly sporting or hunting interests, the one unstated rule being that they maintained the reputation of the Regiment in all its forms. Great emphasis was placed on sporting prowess among the officer élite, and when we were off-duty, some of us would walk up to Tidworth Park where the officers played polo. Polo was always a great thing in a cavalry regiment; all the wealthier officers owned their own horses with civilian servants looking after them, while we had one officer, Major Hunter, who actually played for England.

By contrast, the use of our spare time appeared mundane. A round of cards was a common pursuit, as was Crown and Anchor, a gambling game on which there were always players willing to chance their arm, even though it was frowned upon by the army. Crown and Anchor was the simplest of games: a canvas sheet squared off into six areas, each of which had one of six symbols, a spade, club, diamond, heart, a crown and an anchor. Money was placed on any of the squares and three dice each carrying the same six symbols were thrown. If three hearts were thrown, for example, the banker paid out three times the money on the heart, scooping up the rest. Not surprisingly, the bankers were rarely out of pocket and were always the sort who could look after themselves, so there was hardly any trouble. The only permitted game was Housey Housey, or bingo as it is now known. Organised amongst the men, it didn't take much for the caller to form a league with a friend and only by keeping a close eye on exactly which numbers were pulled from a bag could a fair game be enforced.

Every summer, it was traditional to mark the King's birthday, when the Brigade's three Regiments joined up on Perham Downs for a ceremonial review. The King wasn't there, rather, a senior general would take the salute, watching the Dragoons, Hussars and Lancers performing various trot-pasts. On parade we sat tight, gripping firmly and rising with the horse, rather than posting in the saddle. The full Regiment turned out, including officers' servants who, because of their other duties, usually escaped parades and were therefore more lax when it came to spit and polish. Just before one of these parades, a servant came into the barracks in a panic. His helmet wasn't clean and he needed to borrow one from a younger recruit not far enough advanced to take part in the parade. The Regiment had just finished a trot-past when this servant began complaining that the helmet was too big and was chopping down on his ears, so at the next opportunity, when the Regiment was dismounted, he tore up handfuls of grass to cushion the inside of the helmet.

Unfortunately for him, it was traditional to finish the parade with all three Regiments performing a charge over 200 yards. We were gradually brought into line as senior regimental trumpeters sounded the canter, then the gallop and finally the charge, the three Regiments riding as one, all immaculately dressed, with polished jackboots, glinting brass helmets, and, with arms locked, swords pointing forward between the horse's ears. The speed is that of the slowest horse, about 25 mph, making sure that no one broke the line as we passed before the assembled military dignitary. To the onlookers, it was a perfect exhibition of collective horsemanship. No one had noticed the grass which, during the canter, gallop and charge, had silently slipped beneath the helmet of the officer's servant and now covered his face. But he did not escape the attention of his troop officer and a subsequent charge, nor all manner of jokes as the Regiment made its way back to barracks.

Whenever we rode back to Tidworth, we were allowed to relax and permission would be given to smoke. The officers could smoke cigars, but while on horseback, troopers were restricted to smoking pipes, not cigarettes. This suited me. I had never liked cigarettes, and instead smoked a twopenny cherrywood pipe, partly to look and feel older in front of the others, often lighting up my pipe while cleaning the saddlery, or, as others smoked, to help me fit in.

In the summer months of July and August, the Regiment went on manoeuvres. Built up from Troop and Squadron training during early July to Regimental and full Brigade manoeuvres by August 1914, we were, as it happened, in a heightened state of readiness when the war broke out. Training took place on Salisbury Plain and was for those classified first class soldiers. I had just qualified, having finished all my drills by July. Each day the Troop went out practising various left wheels, right wheels, and troop actions.

With so many horses on manoeuvres, it wasn't uncommon for one to get loose and charge off. These horses either turned up at the barracks by themselves or were picked up along the way. Whoever had lost his horse did not receive a lift home but was expected to walk back. This was fair enough, had it not become an unwritten rule that if an NCO lost his horse, he would take the first trooper's horse he came across, leaving the poor private to walk back. That summer, Bridges, the squadron leader, decided to put a stop to this practice.

Troop manoeuvres had progressed to Squadron manoeuvres, when one fine morning we got the order 'Action front, dismount, three rounds rapid fire.' As usual, the horse holders took the reins of three other mounts, wheeling round to get under cover, as those who were to come into action ran forward, knelt down and opened up with blanks, at 200 yards. To orchestrate this action, our troop officer, Swallow, dismounted just as Shoeing Smith Sandy passed his horse. 'I couldn't resist it,' he told us later. The horse had raised its tail and Sandy, needing no further invitation, put his rifle up behind the horse's backside and pulled the trigger. Others were already in action, muffling his shot, and Swallow's horse ran haywire – down a slope and on to the road beyond. 'Whose horse is that?' inquired Hornby. Swallow had to admit that it was his. 'Well, you know the orders,' said Hornby.

Crestfallen, Swallow was forced to trudge back to Tidworth that evening, while in the barracks the men took turns to buy Sandy a drink. No one had a high opinion of Swallow, but I don't suppose for one minute that Sandy realised that he would have to walk back. Poor horse, apart from the shock, it would have hurt to get a blank fired at so sensitive an area, and it must have itched for days.

Final manoeuvres, when the whole Brigade came together, took place just as war broke out. On this occasion, 'H' Battery came over from the Artillery Camp at Bulford Barracks, a short distance from Tidworth, and commenced live firing. It was during these final manoeuvres that we were ordered over to Sidbury Hill to charge some men of the infantry. The idea was to give them a feel of what it was like to be attacked by cavalry, to demonstrate that when infantrymen kept their nerve and lay flat, it was a devil of a job for those on horseback to run them through. If they stood up and ran, they were far more vulnerable to being run down by the horses. The infantry lay six yards apart as the Regiment galloped through their lines. As we passed, I looked to my right to see a face peering up with an expression of considerable discomfort; he patently didn't like the experience one little bit.

Editor

Ever since 1911, when General Sir Henry Beauvoir de Lisle had been appointed to command the 2nd Cavalry Brigade at Tidworth, the Dragoons had been preparing for the expected outbreak of hostilities. As de Lisle in his memoir, *'Reminiscences of Sport and War'*, wrote, 'Knowing that war was inevitable and imminent the two years at Tidworth were spent in training for war. Major-General Allenby, who was Inspector of Cavalry, was equally confident that war must come, and we had many conferences at my home as to the best way to train the cavalry to meet it.'

Ben

With the news that war had broken out, Tidworth went crackers. Everyone was very excited at the prospect of a fight, troopers firing off blank cartridges in a show of delight. We were going to war; we were going to do something. No one stopped to think about what that actually meant. We were about to wipe the floor with the Germans and anything else was inconceivable.

Our first instructions were to let everything go rusty. Nothing was to be polished – buttons, cap badges, buckles, stirrup irons – anything that could reflect sunlight and so give notice of our presence in France. Items blancoed in peace time such as horses' ropes,

```
      The Officer Commanding,

           " B " Squadron.
      ----------------------------


           The following message received from Headquarters is
      forwarded for your information. Please take action.
      " Mobilize .

      "Brigade parade for tomorrow holds good ".


      Tidworth,                                        Captain,
                          Adjutant 4th.Dragoon Guards.
      4/8/14.


      ORDERLY ROOM
     4th DRAGOON GUARDS
        4 - AUG.1914

      Register No.................
```

The order to mobilise for War

gun slings, the lanyards that fitted in our top pockets, were washed down or stripped. New, darker horse halters were distributed, while our sword belts, in peace time whitened by pipe clay, were handed in to stores. Even our white handkerchiefs were discarded to be replaced by red and white spotted alternatives.

All belongings had to be sorted out. Personal items had to be parcelled up to be forwarded by the army to nearest and dearest. Anxious not to lose treasured possessions, I sent a separate parcel from the local post office, a shrewd move as it turned out, for the army parcel never arrived.

Orders were issued that each man must take his 'full kit' to France, to which was added an extra shirt, one pair of socks and underwear. Like our private possessions, everything that was spare had to be put into kit bags, labelled and taken to stores. This meant we lost – as it turned out, forever – our distinguished full dress uniform, but other than that, in footwear alone we bagged up our stable clogs, one spare pair of standard 'Hilton' army boots, one pair of Jack boots and a pair of Wellingtons worn underneath our strides. All these stores were later raided by the Quartermaster Sergeant to help fit out the Kitchener men.

Tidworth was a hive of activity heightened by the arrival of a steady stream of reservists from August 6th onwards. These reservists were allotted to different troops, and more beds were drawn from the stores to fit them into our barrack rooms. There were umpteen strange faces, and not knowing any of them I was intrigued to watch these old soldiers, some with seventeen or eighteen years' service, settle in and renew old friendships. They knew the ropes and slotted back into army routine quickly, going off to be inoculated, and wasting no time in getting all their hair whipped-off with clippers. The younger recruits, such as myself, waited for the order to visit the barber's, and were a little more circumspect about how much we lost – given how short the war would be! With everyone busily preparing to leave, most of these old-timers were not spoken to until we got to France, and with old nicknames being banded around, it was a while before we found out who they actually were.

During peace time, many of the military's horses were put on the reserve, but when the army was mobilised these horses were recalled. Two days after the outbreak of war, I was detailed to travel with six other troopers and two veterinary officers to Birmingham's R. Whites' mineral water factory, commandeering heavy draught horses, not for us, but for the artillery and Army Service Corps. Our job was simply to wait around until the veterinary officers had passed each horse fit and healthy, and, once each horse was numbered, ride one and lead another to the local train station. These mammoth horses had never had anyone on their backs before, and didn't understand our spurs' commands. Each time we dug them in, they stepped backwards as if to get away. We soon tumbled to the fact that if we wanted them to move we would have to give verbal commands.

At the station a train was waiting, and once loaded, off it went. The job done, I and a couple of other troopers had time to look round the R. Whites' factory, where our presence aroused much interest, and some over-excitement among some of the ladies working there. We were soldiers about to go to war and in August '14 this impressed everyone.

Flushed with pride, and giddy at the prospect of going to France, I returned to Tidworth. During my absence, the Squadron and Troop lists had been pinned up on the notice boards, so I went to have a look. My eyes scanned the notice: Lieutenant Swallow; Johnstone, my troop sergeant; Patterson; Tilney; Cumber; Thomas; Bell; Jury. I was dumbfounded, my name had been omitted from C Squadron's 4th Troop list. Stubbornness quickly over-rode bitter disappointment. 'I cannot be left behind and I will not be left behind!' I thought, so returning later I carefully rubbed out the bottom name and added my own. The next day Sergeant Johnstone spotted the alteration and, unmoved by my determination and enthusiasm to go, changed it back. Once more my name appeared on the list, at which point Johnstone marched me to the Squadron Office to see Captain Hornby. 'Why are you doing this?' said Hornby. 'You know your age, you are not entitled to come out with the Regiment.' 'According to my enlistment papers, sir, my age is officially nineteen and with all due respect I am coming out.'

Hornby knew I was a fully trained soldier but he also knew I was still sixteen years old. Desperate to go, I even threatened to abscond with the 9th Lancers, although this cut no ice with Hornby. 'One way or another I will be there when the Regiment reaches France,' I insisted. Finally he said, 'Fair enough, it's against my wishes but you shall come.' I don't know who dropped out but I can't imagine all the reservists were itching to fight. Several were veterans of the South Africa campaign and from experience may not have been so keen to go to war again.

Editor
Hornby's change of heart proved no error of judgement. In a letter he wrote in February 1915 to Adrian Carton de Wiart, he included the following:

'. . . that boy Clouting, son of the groom, did most awfully well, a real tiger with an exceptional cool head on him, so good that Bridges took him away to the 4th Hussars with him. Clouting was in C Squadron so I saw quite a lot of him, in fact I tried to leave him behind when we left as he was so young but he flatly refused to be left.'

Ben
Before leaving Tidworth, each trooper drew a hundred rounds of ammunition. Our rifles were to remain empty until otherwise ordered, so ninety rounds were stashed in the bandolier each trooper wore around the shoulders, and ten rounds in a pocket. About this time we were allocated the horses we were to take to France. Apart from the horses which carried the Regiment in peace time, others had been called up from various riding schools and hunting stables. Inevitably, I was not given the one I had trained on, but, rather disappointingly, an old riding school 'hack', distinguished by its doctored tail. This meant that instead of having a horse with a long flowing tail, I had one with a bob that couldn't grow back. Yet any annoyance that I had not been given a real troop horse was tempered by the knowledge that I was only too glad to be going at all. If not the youngest man in the Regiment,

I was certainly the youngest to go to France, no argument about that.[2]

Editor

The Regiment left for France on the night of Friday August 14th with 27 officers, 524 men and 608 horses, as part of the BEF's Cavalry Division, under Major-General Allenby. Five brigades of cavalry went with the BEF to France, the 4th Dragoon Guards belonging to the 2nd Cavalry Brigade, under Brig-General H de B de Lisle. This Brigade also included the 9th Lancers, 18th Hussars and H and K Batteries of the Royal Horse Artillery.

On that Friday night, the 4th Dragoons paraded outside Assaye barracks, before leaving around dawn for the train station a short distance away. A Squadron left first, followed by B and C Squadrons in successive trains. Their destination was to be Southampton, the first troops arriving at the docks in drizzling rain around 4.30am, the last about six hours later.

Ben

With everything ready, the Regiment left for France. First stop, Tidworth station, where a train was already waiting, so we handed over our horses to be loaded on cattle trucks and boarded the carriages. There were a few interested civilians to see us off, and as we got under way, troopers hung out of windows shouting at passers by. I recall in particular Patterson, our Squadron trumpeter, shouting 'Get those turkeys fattened up, because we'll want them when we get back for Christmas.' Ironically, less than ten days later he was taken prisoner of war, returning home some five years and as many Christmases later.

Detraining at Southampton, we immediately started boarding a little old cattle boat, HMT *Winifredian*, each trooper carrying his horse's saddle as well as his own equipment up one of two parallel gangways and on to the ship. Meanwhile, the horses were stripped down to their bridles, and were led, each following the one in front, down into the hold of the ship for stabling. One horse, too big to go the conventional route, had to be hoisted aboard by means of a pully and a canvas sling.

Editor

The *Winifredian* sailed around 12 noon, arriving some eighteen hours later in Boulogne. It had been a quiet, if long, crossing, for the fear of submarine attack had held up the ship shortly after leaving harbour. Indeed, many troopers were fooled when a first glimpse of Continental Europe turned out to be no more than the town lights of Hastings.

Ben

On leaving the quayside, I was promptly detailed for lifebelt duty at the stern of the ship. Here I stood until midnight with two lifebelts, ready to throw one overboard to any trooper who might be unfortunate enough to fall in. I was left on duty until, after six hours, I asked a sergeant strolling by if I might be relieved as I hadn't had a meal, a break, or anything at all, for that matter. My request granted, I made my way below deck to get a meal in a part of the galley rigged out as a mess room.

It was dark below deck, for with the threat of submarine attack, all lights had been dimmed, and portholes closed and firmly screwed shut. Up on deck there was a strict order banning all smoking, but the crossing was calm, and the night warm enough so that many troopers seemed content to just sleep the night away where they liked up on deck.

It was light when we pulled into Boulogne, and we excitedly crowded along the ship's railing to get some early impressions. Walking along the quay we spotted French soldiers wearing their blue jackets, red trousers, and peak caps. 'Blimey,' said one man, 'even the postmen have got bayonets.'

Editor

It was Sunday morning and the bells were ringing for early morning mass. Though few people were to be seen near the quayside at first, enterprising shopkeepers were soon up and around, and though few soldiers had any knowledge of French, hand gestures and verbal approximations, including *'du pain'* for bread, ensured that some quick trading was done.

Ben

We disembarked around 6.30am, though my impressions are that we sailed up the river some distance before getting off. We came down the narrow gangway and waited to take any horse which came down the adjacent ramp with just its bridle on. They were then taken, lined up and sorted out into their respective squadrons and troops. There weren't too many people around, a few sight-seers, though by the time we'd sorted out the horses and saddled up, more people had stirred and we were cheered with *'Vivent les Anglais!'* as we made our way into camp. Shortly afterwards, we went down to the beach and rode the horses bareback into the sea, sliding off their backs to swim alongside, or, as horses can't kick under water, to grip onto their tails to be pulled along. A pleasant introduction to France was not marred when, on leaving the sea, we were surprised by a French battery of 75s which had

34

hastily arrived on the beach, unsure of who we were. We eyed the crews and their small-looking guns, which to our minds didn't look as well built as the British 13-pounders.

The Regiment went into camp for two days before we rode to a goods yard to board trains to begin our move east. Once again the horses were stripped of their saddles. Eight horses were loaded to a truck, the first four being turned around to face the following four, with the saddles heaped in the middle, gravel being put down to help the horses grip. Two men were detailed to look after the horses while the rest of us scrambled aboard, six to a third-class carriage. We were advised to get as much sleep as we could, so we tossed up for who had the luggage racks, who the seats and who the floor. I lost, so got the floor.

It was a bruising trip. The drivers appeared to be amateurs, for every time the train stopped, carriages banged together with such force the men in the luggage racks fell onto the men lying on the wooden seats. Towards the front of the train, horses became loose as restraining ropes were broken by the constant shunting, and horse handlers were trampled underfoot trying to put new ropes across.

The trains were painfully slow and there were several stops oen route, not least to feed and water the horses. Where possible, troopers dashed along the side of the train to the engine. Here a queue would form as the driver tapped off boiling water from a pipe into our mess tins enabling us to make quite drinkable tea.

Editor
Records show that the Regiment left Boulogne at around 12.30am on Tuesday August 18th, travelling by train via Amiens to the small town of Hautmont. From here it moved forward on horseback, to Damousies on August 19th, then to Harmignies and finally to the Bois La Haut on August 21st.

Ben
When we finally left the train, the order was given 'Right, you are in suspected enemy country, load.' Two clips of five rounds filled the magazine, with the tenth in the breach. Safety catches remained on and, as was the rule, the tenth round was taken out and put into a pocket. We had met nothing but friendly greetings, but were now warned about speaking to civilians. 'Some may be sympathetic to the Germans,' we were told, 'others might even be informers, so be wary of what you say.'

As the Regiment rode through the Belgian countryside, a Connecting File was adopted. The purpose of the File was to give the

Squadron early warning of danger ahead by sending out scouts in advance of the main body of troops. These scouts rode on both sides of the road, followed some 200 yards behind by two troopers who would pass on signals between the scouts and the Squadron. Signals were given with a rifle. A vertical movement up and down meant trot, a rifle held vertically still meant halt. If the enemy were spotted, the rifle was pushed up and down three times in a horizontal position, and so on. The rifle sling was always turned towards those you were signalling to, for despite being khaki, it showed up better than the dark brown wood of the rifle. On Connecting File, on one early occasion, the order was given to dismount. We had just entered a small village and as we stopped I was approached by several people including a lady who handed me a small piece of cooking chocolate. Translating for the rest, one, an English groom working in Belgium, asked me, 'When are you expecting to fight? What are you hoping to do? Is your equipment better than the Germans?' I knew little more than he did, and, mindful of our orders, said there was not much I could tell him.

By August 20th, the Regiment had reached the small village of Damousies. The village was strung out along two sides of a large common, with an estaminet the most notable feature. As we were billeting here for the night, the men were to sleep at one end of the village, the officers at the other. As the afternoon wore on, some of the troopers were allowed to visit the pub for a beer. However, French beer seemed to go through soldiers like potato water, and it wasn't long before the toilet was in demand. This was simply a five-foot screen erected in front of the pub, behind which a funnel had been attached to a wall. The funnel ran down to the floor, across, underneath the screen and simply stopped dead a few inches above the ground. As each trooper relieved himself, the urine simply spilled out on to the street before meandering away towards a gutter.

As we settled down for the evening, we saw at the far end of the common a round, and, to our amazement, high-backed hip bath. This bath had been conjured up from somewhere, and was now being filled by water from the village pump. Some of the officers were going to have a bath before their evening meal, and in due course we watched as an orderly tipped water over them as and when they required it. The sight alone made me realise just how innocent we all were to what this war was to be all about.

Later, at about 9pm, we witnessed one of the earliest air-to-air combats of the war. Two aircraft, one British, the other German, had met in the skies above us and, as we listened to the drone of their engines, we saw the flash of rifles or revolvers being fired in the evening light. Very slowly the two planes circled each other before breaking off the fight without a result. No doubt neither could afford to stay and fight with only a limited amount of fuel.

NOTES

1. For example, Captain Fitzgerald was ex-Eton, Captain Oldrey, the adjutant, ex-Uppingham. Lieutenant Railston ex-Radley, 2nd Lieutenant Gordon-Munro and Lieutenant Aylmer both ex-Wellington College, Captains Sewell and Hornby both ex-Harrow.
2. A check on the regimental numbers of all those who went to France on HMT *Winifredian* shows that Ben's number, 8292, is exceeded only by one soldier, Private C F Lees 8300 (denoting that he joined the Regiment after Ben). Given the measures Ben had to take to be allowed to leave with the Regiment for France, it is highly unlikely Lees would have been younger than Ben.

CHAPTER THREE

The First Shot

Editor

August 21st dawned misty and dull, making aerial reconnaissance impossible until the afternoon. Cavalry patrols continued to be pushed onwards towards Mons, crossing the Mons-Condé canal during the day and spreading out along the banks between Maurage and Obourg. During the day, reports indicated that German forces were massing to the north, and in particular that there were 2,500 hostile cavalry at Soignies. These were substantiated that evening, when patrols from both the 4th Dragoon Guards and the 9th Lancers made visual contact with their German counterparts to the east of Mons, Lieutenant Jones reporting that he had also seen Germans under bivouac.

By this time on August 21st, the Regiment of 4th Dragoons was positioned east of Mons. Apart from these tantalising sightings, no reliable information had been collected as to the whereabouts or definite strength of German forces, so C Squadron was detailed to move forward in an attempt to make contact with the enemy. Travelling light, the Squadron moved off towards the village of Maisières, where a halt was made for the night. But Bridges, the 43-year-old Squadron leader, felt uneasy. Local civilians had been seen cycling out of the village to the north, so, unwilling to take risks, he moved his force across the main Mons to Brussels road to a nearby hill he had earlier noted. From here, a precautionary screen of pickets was put out, while Lieutenants Jones, Harrison and Aylmer, and Corporal Savory went out on patrol to gather further information. There was still no contact with the enemy, although the news gleaned from local residents earlier in the day was unmistakeable. Large numbers of enemy troops were pouring south on every road from Brussels. Figures could only be estimated at some 400,000.

Ben

All four Troops of C Squadron were on outpost that night with two troops on standby, saddled up, ready to move at a moment's notice. Our Troop was in a cornfield, along the back of which ran a wood. A screen of sentries was sent out, allowing those not on standby to eat something or catch up on some sleep. Everything was still and quiet; everyone was tense. We tied the horses' reins round our wrists, while those too nervous to rest talked to each other in whispers. We were warned that for all we knew we might already be surrounded and that we mustn't speak to anyone. A few of us slackened our horses' girths to let them breathe freely. But silence was the order and, as horses were prone to play with their loose bit bars, we held or tied handkerchiefs around the bars to muffle any sound.

Editor

Another trooper on standby that night was Private Tilney,[1] a reservist and orderly to Captain Hornby. 'We crossed the Mons-Condé canal, and reached some woods and a village on the main Soignies road. I was in the 4th Troop, which was for duty, so we found the picquet. Corpl Thomas was in charge, with Carb Facey, Jury and myself, and we had orders to fire on anyone coming down the road. It was agreed that Corpl Thomas should shout "Halt! who goes there?" and we were to fire.

Nothing happened until about 2am ... [when] suddenly we heard a horse coming down the road and it seemed to us, waiting for him, hours before he was within hailing distance. At last we could see a red glow: whoever it was, was smoking a cigar. Just as we were taking aim, the horse stumbled and the rider's pet name for it being the same as ours, we recognised the voice of Trooper Goodchilds.'

Despite everyone being in a high state of expectation, the rest of the night passed peacefully enough. At around 6am on an already bright, sunny morning, the Squadron moved off towards the village of Casteau, on the outskirts of which we made a brief stop, although there was time enough for several soldiers to enjoy some bread, butter and coffee, courtesy of a man from Windsor living nearby.[2]

Ben

At about 6.30am, we arrived at a farm on the corner of a staggered crossroads and began watering our horses in a trough. There were already a few people about and as we waited, a farm worker came in saying he'd seen four Uhlans coming down the road.[3]

Once this was confirmed, there was a flurry of action, and a plan was hatched to capture the patrol as it passed. Four men from 4th Troop were dismounted and ordered to fire a volley of shots into the patrol at close quarters. This would be followed by 2nd Troop charging forward and bagging the remainder. I, along with the rest of 4th Troop, was placed out of sight, mounted, waiting with drawn sword. I believe a man was sent out behind a hedge to signal when the Germans were about to arrive, but in his excitement he ran to grab his horse and gave the position away.[4]

Editor

It is not certain if this sudden movement made the Germans turn and retreat back up the steep, tramlined road, towards Casteau, but it now put Bridges in a difficult position. It was one thing to capture an advance guard of Germans, quite another to go hurtling after them not knowing how many more might appear over the brow of the hill. But Hornby was in no doubt that chase they should, so, with Bridges' assent, on to and up the main road the 1st Troop charged.

The Squadron leader was to follow on with the 2nd and 3rd Troops and what was left of the 4th, for some were still on patrol, and Tilney had gone careering down the road with Hornby. In 1932 Tilney wrote, 'I followed the Captain as he went down the right-hand side of the road. He took a German on the point of his sword, just as I saw the lads do at Shorncliffe with the dummies. I couldn't have a hand in the fun, so I crossed over to the other side of the road and took on a chap with a lance, whom I captured.'

Ben

The 1st Troop of C with Hornby at their head went after them, and the rest of the Squadron followed on in support, with drawn swords. Our troop officer, Lieutenant Swallow, led the Troop at a fast canter, everyone was highly excited and I recall looking round to find our saddler sergeant major, not with a sword, but with a cocked '45 in his hand.

As the Germans retired into the village they met up with a larger group of Uhlans, and, owing to the congestion, were soon caught by the 1st Troop. A fight immediately broke out. However, we arrived after the Germans had scattered, with the main body splitting off and carrying on up the main road. We continued to give chase, our horses slipping all over the place as we clattered along the square-set stones.

Editor

The German lance proved ineffective at close range against the English sword and a number of lances were thrown away though to no advantage. Several Germans were killed in this engagement, possibly as many as eight, with Captain Hornby being credited with drawing first blood.[5]

Ben

Our chase continued for perhaps a mile or more, until we found ourselves flying up a wide, rising road, tree-lined on both sides. The Germans, reaching the road's crest, turned and, though they were still mounted, began firing back down the hill. 'Action front, dismount,' rapped Hornby, 'Get the horses under cover!' In one

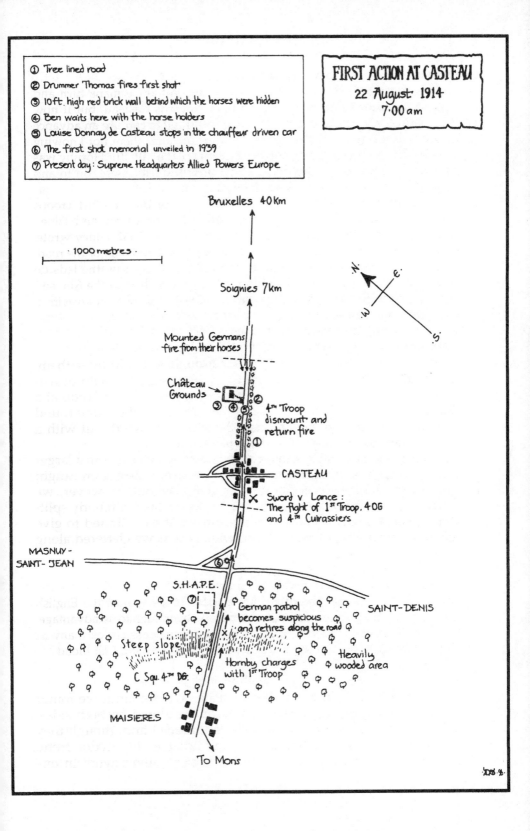

① Tree lined road
② Drummer Thomas fires first shot
③ 10ft. high red brick wall behind which the horses were hidden
④ Ben waits here with the horse holders
⑤ Louise Donnay de Casteau stops in the chauffeur driven car
⑥ The first shot memorial unveiled in 1939
⑦ Present day: Supreme Headquarters Allied Powers Europe

FIRST ACTION AT CASTEAU
22 August 1914
7.00 am

Bruxelles 40 Km

· 1000 metres ·

Soignies 7km

N. E. W. S.

Mounted Germans fire from their horses

Château Grounds

4ᵀᴴ Troop dismount and return fire

CASTEAU

Sword v Lance: The fight of 1ˢᵀ Troop, 4 DG and 4ᵀᴴ Cuirassiers

MASNUY - SAINT- JEAN

S.H.A.P.E.

SAINT-DENIS

German patrol becomes suspicious and retires along the road

Steep slope

Heavily wooded area

C Squ. 4ᵀᴴ DG.

Hornby charges with 1ˢᵀ Troop

MAISIERES

To Mons

movement the Troop returned their swords, reached for their rifles and dismounted, dashing for cover, lying flat on their stomachs behind the trees. Glancing up the hill, I saw several Germans filling the road. They made a perfect target, and Thomas, the first into action,[6] shot one from his horse.

The Troop's rapid fire sent bullets swarming up the road, but as a designated horse holder, I did not come into action. Before dismounting, the Troop had been riding in fours, and being number three, it was my job to take the reins of the two horses on my left and those of the one on my right. Spurred on by Hornby's command, I made for a high redbrick garden wall that surrounded the grounds of a château and which, because it stood at right angles to the road, offered us suitable protection. A gate was rushed open into the neighbouring field and I, along with the other horse holders, rode through to comparative safety. It is not an easy job to bring four horses through a narrow opening; even in battle, each of us had to ensure our horses didn't catch their hips on the gate. However, we almost accomplished our minor feat without problems when the very last horse through got a bullet in her stomach.

Editor
From now until the ceasefire, Ben and the other horse holders could see little or nothing of the mêlée taking place just yards away. It was a question of waiting and, as Ben recalled, steadying the horses with quiet words of encouragement. In the temporary absence of Bridges, who had still to arrive on the scene, Hornby was giving the orders. He had left the skirmish in the village to join the 4th Troop farther up the road, although he was not the only officer present. 4th Troop still had its troop officer, Lieutenant Swallow, but in action his nerve had given way.

Ben
Under fire, Lieutenant Swallow simply went to pieces. He was sitting on his horse shaking like a jelly, totally unable to pull himself together. Hornby was absolutely furious and seeing that Swallow was of no further use, turned on our troop officer shouting, 'Get back with the led horses, you cowardly bastard!' Hornby was barely able to control his disgust at Swallow's behaviour; the first action of the war, and Swallow had been left looking completely hopeless in front of the men he was supposed to lead. Swallow joined us, disgraced in front of the whole Troop.[7]

The whole action can't have lasted much more than three minutes and as the fighting abated, the order was given to cease fire and withdraw. As the troopers ran back to collect their horses,

I noticed a dark green chauffeur-driven limousine pull up outside the gateway to the field and, though the fighting had scarcely stopped, out stepped a young, fair-haired woman who proceeded to walk over and speak to the dismounted Captain Hornby. It transpired that she was a nurse and she asked, in the light of what was already taking place, if she might be allowed to go on duty at Mons.

Editor

In later years Hornby professed that he had no recollection of this occurrence. Perhaps too elated at the Dragoons' obvious success to register this strange incident, he was aware that the 4th Dragoons had more than fulfilled their brief by capturing some prisoners as well as giving the Germans a sharp rebuff. Bar minor flesh wounds, the Dragoons had had no casualties and later they were to ride back victorious with a cart full of lances and at least three prisoners.

Ben

We never knew the extent of German casualties, although as we rode back to Casteau, a civilian ambulance passed us to render the Germans any assistance it could. As far as I am aware, we came out of the action with three prisoners, all suffering from sword wounds. We suffered no casualties except among the horses, which included the one with a bullet in her stomach. She managed to bring her man out, but she was finished, being poleaxed in a village nearby and handed over to a Belgian butcher.

Editor

The delighted Dragoons had captured the first German prisoners of the war, though they were not Uhlans as Ben (and many others) have mistakenly described them, but troopers from the 4th Cuirassiers, 9th Cavalry Division. They were not all tough, regular soldiers like the British Expeditionary Force, rather, many were no more than 'Young Bavarian Ploughboys in German uniforms,' according to Arthur Osburn, the chief medical officer attached to the 4th Dragoon Guards. Later, he wrote about the incident. In his book, *Unwilling Passenger*, he confirms Ben's estimate of the number of German prisoners, for he met them. 'I could speak a few words of German and as I dressed their wounds I asked them what they thought of the War. They said they did not know what to make of it, nor what it was all about. They had, they said, been called up for military training only a few weeks before the War broke out. . . Apparently they had all shown very little fight.' One admitted that 'he himself was very pleased he had been taken prisoner and would not have to take any further part in the war'.

Ben

Naturally the whole Squadron was alive with talk about the fight. According to one tale being bandied about, the Squadron's fencing champion, 1st Troop's SSM Sharpe, had faced one Uhlan, parried the German's lance thrust before swinging his sword, and chopped all the Uhlan's fingers off.

Other stories no doubt changed with the telling. One concerns Thomas' first shot. To my mind, he set his sights at 350 yards and saw his first shot ricochet off the road. Only then did he up his sights, shouting 'Four hundred yards, give the bastards hell'. I can't say I saw his first shot but he was in my Troop and that was the talk at that time.

Editor

There has been a certain amount of confusion as to the exact sequence and timing of events. There is disagreement over the time, 6.30 or 7am, disagreement over when Thomas actually fired the first shot, and even disagreement as to who fired down the road at the 4th Troop: retreating German cavalry, or a group of German cyclists.[8]

After such a lengthy passage of time, the truth is difficult to ascertain. The official history states that as the German patrol turned and retreated, so 'the first shot by the British Army in the war was fired by Corporal Thomas'. But this is not supported by Thomas' own words. In 1939 Thomas gave this version of events. 'My Troop was ordered to follow on in support and we galloped through the village of Casteau. We could see the first Troop using their swords and scattering the Uhlans left and right. We caught them up. Captain Hornby gave the order, "4th Troop dismounted action". We found cover behind a château wall and possibly because I was rather noted for my quick movements and athletic ability, I was first in action.'

C Squadron withdrew across the Mons-Condé canal to a point south east of Mons, where they linked up with the rest of the Regiment. The men were rightfully jubilant as they paraded past the rest of the cavalry division, A Squadron's Lieutenant Chance noting in his diary that he saw the prisoners that afternoon as Bridges rode his Squadron 'among the chestnut trees at the foot of the Bois La Haut ... [where] a few townsfolk joined us to stare at the Germans'.

The prisoners had been put under the guard of Corporal Regan, who with Private Tilney rode back to the canal which they found guarded by a Troop of the Queen's Bays. It was there that Tilney 'recognised a chum, and he asked me where we had been. I pulled his leg, said we had been out to fetch a sample, and if they saw any chaps like these they were to shoot them, as they were Germans. When we reached the Regimental H.Q. Colonel Mullens asked "Who caught this one?" I stuck out my chest and said "I did, sir." He told me I was a damned fool, and then the second-in-command, Major Solly Flood, told me a few more things. (The order was that prisoners should be searched, stripped and turned away to avoid dealing with them and so hampering the advance guard.) The C.O. said "Take them down to Brigade H.Q.", which we did. Brigadier General de Lisle asked the same question as the Colonel, and we stood there whilst an interpreter asked a few questions.'

Editor
After the Dragoons' action, the following Operational Order was issued by Brigadier General de Lisle:
'The Brigadier desires to congratulate the 4th Dragoon Guards on the spirited action of two Troops of the Squadron on reconnaissance, which resulted in establishing the moral superiority of our cavalry, from the first, over the German cavalry.'
Extended note: The chauffeur-driven car.
The scene could almost be described as surreal: out of a sharp, if short, engagement suddenly appears this lady of obviously wealthy means, putting herself in immediate danger of being killed or wounded by any resumption of fire from German soldiers still just up the road. The car had came from the château, for Ben noted that it pointed down the road, away from the Germans. No other memoir, published article or book refers to this incident, though at the time other troopers must have watched it with some interest. For this reason one might doubt the story's veracity, but for the fact that Ben was to meet this lady twenty-five years later. The occasion was the unveiling of a plinth commemorating the Dragoons' action that day.[9] Some thirty-five veterans attended the unveiling, including Captain Hornby, while among the onlookers from the village, Ben recognised the lady and when he went to speak to her, she recounted her version of events.
She was Louise Donnay de Casteau, the youngest of seven children and sister of Lieutenant-General Gaston Donnay de Casteau, commander of the Belgian cavalry during the First World War. In August 1914, Louise was about thirty-five years old and was indeed a trained nurse, in which capacity she served throughout the war before returning to the family's château.
Apart from the disruption of war, in which she lost a brother, Emmanuel, life later became tranquil, even boring for Louise. She helped bring up the many children of the large Donnay family, remaining at the château for the next thirty years. She never married and in 1950 moved to Paris, where she lived until her death in the early 1960s.
The château was built in the 1790s and was one of two in Casteau owned by the family. As the British retreated from Mons, it was briefly occupied by the Germans, a minor inconvenience as it turned out com-

pared with the four years of German occupation during the Second World War. In later years the château (known as La Roquette) fell into disrepair and with spiralling maintenance costs was finally demolished in the late 1970s. While the family still owns the land, little remains except for the keeper's lodge by the main gate, the stables, and the red brick wall behind which Ben helped hide the horses.

NOTES

1. Private, later Corporal, Tilney became one of the most popular and best known faces in the Regiment. Transferring to the 4th from the 2nd Dragoon Guards in 1904, he went to the reserve in 1908, before rejoining at the outbreak of war in 1914. He was made a Sergeant in September and was wounded at Neuve Chapelle in October. In 1915, after becoming separated from his Regiment, he led a mixed bag of French troopers in a charge, routing the enemy, for which he later received the Croix de Guerre with Palms. In 1916 he was awarded the DCM for repeated gallantry. He survived the war, joining the army of occupation in Cologne, before being demobilised in April 1919.
2. In 1964 The Dragoons revisited the village of Casteau, where they met Ben Gunn, an Englishman who had lived in Casteau almost all his life. He wore in his lapel a cap badge belonging to the 4th Dragoon Guards, and said he was given it during the war by troopers of the Regiment. The soldiers, he said, were picking fruit from the trees in his garden when he engaged them in conversation, giving them whisky-laced coffee.
3. According to Tilney, it was a look-out who first gave notice of the Germans' imminent arrival. 'Vincent (3rd Troop) came round the corner. He was awfully excited, and said to Major Bridges: "They're coming! they're coming!'"
4. An anonymous account of the first action written in the Regimental Magazine cites SSM Rowlatt's horse as showing itself on the road 'giving the game away'.
5. Hornby was awarded the DSO for his action, and received the medal at a formal investiture at St James's Palace on February 16th, 1915.
6. Drummer Thomas undoubtedly fired the first shot of the BEF, but only on Continental Europe. The British soldier to fire the 'first shot' in the First World War was RSM Alaji Grunshi, DCM MM of the Gold Coast Regiment, at the capture of Togoland on August 6th, 1914.
7. Swallow remained with the Regiment until November 30th when the 4th Dragoons' War Diary merely states, 'Weather mild with occasional heavy showers of rain. Lieut Swallow left for England'.
8. According to Tom Bridges, in his book, *Alarms And Excursions*, published in 1938, it was a battalion of cyclists in position on the crest of the road that had halted Hornby's men.
9. It had been the Mayor of Casteau, not the Regiment, who had originally suggested that a memorial stone should be placed in the village. His idea was to order a stone not dissimilar to the metre-high demarcation stones which were laid after the First War to show the farthest extent of the German advance into France and Belgium. The Regiment was asked if it wished to help, which it did with aplomb, so that on August 20th 1939 a far more prominent plinth was unveiled, resplendent with a bronze plaque recording the events of twenty-five years before. The ceremony was a grand affair with the Belgians laying on military bands, and sumptuous hospitality in Mons for the thirty-five

veterans and many other serving soldiers from the Regiment who were present that day. The Commandant of the local Belgian garrison was also present at the ceremony, as were many of Casteau's villagers. Major-General Mullens, who had led the Regiment to France, unveiled the memorial by removing a large Union Jack draped across the plinth. Wreaths were laid and the two national anthems played.

Of the other veterans, Captain Hornby was present as were well-known 'personalities' including ex-sergeant Tilney and ex-trumpeter Patterson. The two notable figures missing from the occasion were Corporal Thomas and Major Bridges. Thomas, who for many years after the war had been a well-known commissionaire at a cinema in Brighton, had died in February of that year, his widow and daughter attending the ceremony. Bridges was seriously ill with chronic anaemia in Brighton and died shortly afterwards. With the Second World War breaking out just two weeks later, nothing was seen of the plinth until after that war; however, despite heavy bombing by the Allies in the area of Mons, the monument remained undamaged, save for one bullet fired at the plaque on the plinth by a disgruntled German officer in September 1941.

CHAPTER FOUR

Audregnies and the Retreat from Mons

Editor

On the night of August 22nd, the Dragoons made their way through a countryside of small mining villages, before they reached the outskirts of Thulin at 11pm, where they halted for the night. The next day, August 23rd, during a hot and sultry day, the battle of Mons began in earnest. The 4th Dragoon Guards had moved forward to the outskirts of the town. Less than 1,000 yards ahead of the Regiment, the clear, unmistakeable crackle of rifle fire began, growing in intensity and sounding, as Osburn wrote, like an 'October bonfire into which a cartload of dry holly boughs has been suddenly thrown'. One Squadron was despatched to help escort some artillery into action. However, in the main the Dragoons were held back to await the outcome of the infantry's fire fight, waiting and watching, as a trickle and then a stream of walking wounded retreated from the front line, along the Mons-Condé canal. As the bursts of shrapnel were heard overhead, the Dragoons moved to a field a few hundred yards to the left and dismounted. As they waited, the road bordering the field gradually began to fill with Belgian families pouring out of Mons with whatever belongings they could carry.

The British infantry of II Corps fought heroically against overwhelming odds, as German troops tried to force a crossing of the canal, only to be rebuffed with heavy casualties. Eventually by weight of numbers they crossed east of Mons at Obourg and, by late afternoon, had slowly begun to push the British infantry out of Mons. The day's fighting had cost the Germans dear, and by evening they were able only to hold the positions they had won, making no real effort to renew the attack until the following morning. Meanwhile the heat of the 23rd gave way to the cool of the evening and to rain which came down with increasing intensity, soaking everyone including the Dragoons, waiting, exposed in their cornfield. The Regiment was to stand to all night, listening, as Lieutenant Chance wrote in his diary, to the slow tap of the German Maxim machine guns, and watching the red glow of the flames rising from Thulin.

If the 22nd had belonged to the cavalry and the 23rd to the infantry, August 24th belonged to both. It was the first day of the retreat from Mons, and it dawned bright and sunny, promising another warm, clear day. The order to retire had been given at about 1am, and later that morning the 4th Dragoons were sent to cover the retirement of General

Sir John Fergusson's 5th Division from around the villages of Thulin and Audregnies.

At around 6am, and as a prelude to the day's fighting, the 9th Lancers and 18th Hussars contested the northern approaches to the smouldering town of Thulin with units from the enemy's 7th Division, retiring south as the full weight of the German advance was felt.

Later, at around 10am, L Battery of the RHA shelled relatively small numbers of German troops seen advancing southwards from the same village. These troops had quickly retreated, and as 'L' was itself coming under sporadic fire from German artillery, the battery began to retire with the rest of the 2nd Cavalry Brigade, until 'L' was ordered to a new position on high ground, 600 yards south of the Audregnies-Elouges road.

The order to fall-back had been given by Allenby in view of the overwhelming forces ahead of him. It was to be a staged retirement, the main body of Fergusson's 5th Division moving south along three roads east of Elouges, with the 2nd Cavalry Brigade acting as the Division's rearguard. By mid-morning everything seemed to be going according to plan; the Independent 19th Brigade had already pulled back towards the village of Angre at 10am, and now the 5th Division's 13th and 14th Brigades were following suit, covering each other's retreat with little difficulty.

Only at around 11am did Fergusson begin to realise the ominous threat to his left flank. A considerable gap of around 4,000 yards existed between Elouges and Audregnies, and reports from the Royal Flying Corps clearly showed that huge columns of German troops were heading southwards in an unstoppable tide, and that, more immediately around Quiévrain and behind the Valenciennes-Mons road, an entire army corps, the IVth, was preparing to advance, supported by artillery. In response, Fergusson sent forward his only reserves, consisting of 15th Brigade's 1st Cheshires, the 1st Norfolks, and the 119th Battery Royal Field Artillery; their job was to hold back an enveloping attack to be launched with the full weight of the German 7th and 8th Divisions, some twenty four battalions and nine batteries of artillery. Realising the weakness of his position, Fergusson called on Allenby for assistance, in response to which he received the support of the Second and Third Cavalry Brigades, themselves retiring on Angre.

The 4th Dragoons arrived in the vicinity of Audregnies, halting in a stubble field near the railway station. As they awaited further orders, they would have surveyed their surroundings: a maze of slagheaps, light railways, sunken roads, and villages interspersed with a few cornfields and cornstooks. It was a dry, dusty day, grey cleg flies buzzed around the horses, while troopers, waiting under a bright midday sun, sipped from their water bottles, or smoked cigarettes.

The 4th Dragoons were just behind Audregnies, the 9th Lancers a little in advance, but to the left and right respectively of the Chaussée Brunehaut, an old Roman road which drove through Audregnies and then northwards towards, and directly in line with, the anticipated advance of the German 8th Division. To the Lancers' right, spread out along the low ridge which ran towards Elouges, were Fergusson's reserves, the Cheshires and Norfolks. To their rear, perhaps a mile apart, stood L Battery and the 119th Battery RFA, while half a mile north west of Elouges and under cover of a railway cutting, two squadrons of the 18th Hussars waited for further instructions.

At around 12.30pm, as Lieutenant Chance of A Squadron recalled,

'Bull Allenby turns up, nods at Oldrey and rides off. "Get girthed up," says Oldrey, "Stand by your horses, prepare to mount, mount!" The commands are rapped from troop to troop and "walk-march" follows. There is a whee-thump of shells and a crash of house tiles from the village ahead.'

If each squadron had a designated purpose in the attack, it became hopelessly lost in the excitement of the now famous charge. At the very least, contemporary accounts do not always square with official accounts which have attempted to add a semblance of order to the events that followed. It was almost the entire Regiment of 9th Lancers which went into action first, with the help of a few men of the 18th Hussars. They attacked to the right of the Roman road, closely supported by the 1st and 2nd Troops of B Squadron, 4th Dragoon Guards, led by Lieutenant Sir Arthur Hickman. These two Troops charged along the road in an attempt to seize a house variously referred to as either a cottage or a farm, which lay on the outskirts of the village of Baisieux. Coming under almost immediate shell, rifle and machine gun fire, both were forced to take cover, though not before a dozen or more casualties were sustained including Lieutenant Hickman, who was thrown from his mount, his knees shattered by shell splinters.

The direction of B Squadron's attack was now followed by at least two Troops of C Squadron under Major Bridges, which, in charging to support B Squadron, managed to reach the house, before being swept off to the right by the intense German fire. Moments later A Squadron attacked, making for the north-east edge of the village, where the 4th Dragoons' Machine Gun Section gave covering fire. Led by Major Hunter, A Squadron, with the remaining Troops of C Squadron galloped out and across the open fields in front of Audregnies, and were cut down.

During this attack several men were seen to plummet head first into a narrow, fifteen-foot deep cutting which ran across the line of charge, while those that got past were quickly forced to arc eastwards by a torrent of fire coming from the direction of Quiévrain. Such was the confusion that men from all three Squadrons were seen among the survivors who rallied some twenty five minutes later near Elouges, to the east.

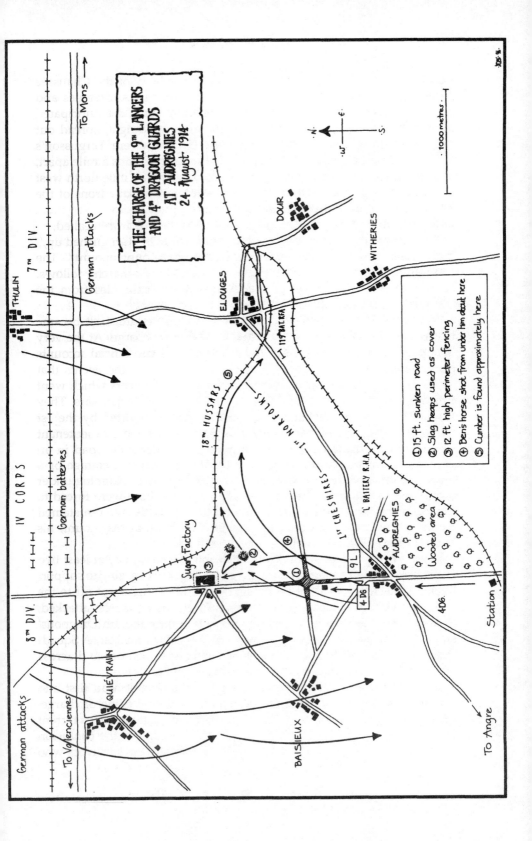

Ben

After the order to mount, we led off at a canter up a narrow lane, swords drawn, the blade resting on the shoulder. As we passed a corner in the road, I believe I saw de Lisle looking on, then we began to gallop, fanning out into the open fields beyond the village.

It was a proper mêlée, with shell, machine gun and rifle fire forming a terrific barrage of noise. Each Troop was closely packed together and dense volumes of dust were kicked up, choking us and making it impossible to see beyond the man in front. We were galloping into carnage, for nobody knew what we were supposed to be doing and there was utter confusion from the start. All around me, horses and men were brought hurtling to the ground amidst fountains of earth, or plummeting forwards as a machine gunner caught them with a burst of fire. Ahead, the leading troops were brought up by agricultural barbed wire strung across the line of advance, so that horses were beginning to be pulled up when I heard for the one and only time in the war a bugle sounding 'troops right wheel.' I pulled my horse round then, with a crash, down she went.

Editor

Major C H Levinson of B Squadron, 18th Hussars had watched the charge with a grandstand view. His Squadron was taking shelter in a railway cutting, when 'Suddenly there was a tremendous increase in the hostile gun and machine gun fire on our left. I looked in that direction straight down the railway line (we were at the left end of the cutting) and I saw our cavalry moving forward at the gallop . . . The first three squadrons carried lances (and were in open column of squadrons – the remainder had no lances) and appeared to be in column of troops as near as possible but in both cases the formation, if even made, was being rapidly lost as they were being exposed to a terrific shell and machine gun fire – a dozen shells bursting over them at a time – and I could distinctly see the men falling off their horses – others evidently wounded just clinging on.'

Arthur Osburn, who watched the confused scene, wrote later that 'Nearly every German gun within range had at once been put on to the small area on which our cavalry were moving. Presumably to counter this, our Field and Horse Artillery had also been compelled to open fire. . . A first-class "battle" had in fact developed with the rapidity of a whirlwind. . . Every rifle and machine gun on their side was now also blazing away at our rather desperate and rather objectiveless cavalrymen.'

Ben
I hit the ground at full tilt and with my sword still firmly attached by a lanyard to my hand, was lucky not to impale myself. Dazed, I struggled to my feet and can now recall only an odd assortment of fleeting thoughts and sights – a single image of chaos. A riderless horse came careering in my direction and, collecting myself, I raised my hand in the air and shouted 'halt' at the top of my voice. It was a 9th Lancers' horse, a Shoeing Smith's mount and wonderfully trained, for despite the pandemonium, it stopped on a sixpence.

Running through the field to my right was a single track railway, and mounting, I rode off in that direction. The racket was engulfing, but as I was about to cross the line, I caught a voice crying out, 'Cronkie, don't leave me'. I turned and saw Thomas Cumber, one of my own Troop. He'd been brought down on the railway line, and there he lay, prostrate, with one side of his face smashed in and bleeding profusely. I pulled up, jumped down and struggled to get him on his feet.

Editor
Ben was just part of the general flight from the inferno of fire. Little could be achieved except to buy a momentary respite for the 5th Division; otherwise it was nothing short of a chicken shoot, as several men later testified. One recalled how 'we rode across the enemy's firing line absolutely galloping to death, the noise of the firing was deafening, being mingled with the screams and the death shouts of men'. Another remembered comrades falling on all sides with horses 'sprawled all across the road breathing their last . . .'; another, Lieutenant Chance, watched as a trooper, crouched in his saddle, was blasted to smithereens by a direct hit.

Among the Dragoons' ranks, Corporal Murphy of B Squadron was shot through the chest, while Private Burgess, also of B Squadron, dropped from his horse, his mount racing away, the sword hilt covered in blood. Trumpeter Patterson of C Squadron had become pinned down in No Man's Land after his horse had fallen, as had Lance Corporal Cornall of 'B' who found himself spreadeagled on the ground, plumb between 'our infantry fire and that of the Germans'. Among those of A Squadron, Sergeant Talbot was brought down in a crashing somersault while Lieutenant Wright's horse slithered over the top of three other horses brought down by fire. Just yards away, Lieutenant Gallaher lay, one leg trapped under his dead horse, while Sergeant Hynes had begun painfully to drag himself towards a cottage, having broken at least two ribs in his fall.

Those who were mounted rode to whatever cover they could find. One trooper wrote later that, 'A party of us who seemed to have kept together – God only knows how – saw a small cottage in front and made for the scanty shelter it offered, several of us coming to grief in trying to jump the wire fence which surrounded the little garden... It was here that we found Major Bridges standing against the wall with blood streaming down his face and smothered in dust.'

Brought to earth early on in the charge, Bridges had been kicked in the head by another horse as he lay stricken on the ground. Only semi-conscious, he had nevertheless collected himself enough to order others to get out of the action as fast as possible. 'They won't hurt me, I'm an officer,' he is reputed to have said before fainting. The cottage, already heavily pitted by shell and Maxim machine gun fire, was proving too hot for those who were still there, so they left, dashing for a sugar factory half way between Audregnies and Quiévrain.

Surrounded by a twelve-foot high wire fence, the factory was a large imposing building with high brick walls. Two days before, it had offered the 1st Field Squadron, Royal Engineers, overnight billets. Now it appeared to offer shelter of a different, more urgent kind as several dozen troopers crowded in behind. But it was an illusion of safety, quickly dispelled as first the German artillery and then machine gunners readjusted their range, plastering and splattering the walls with shrapnel and bullets, flushing the hapless troopers out. There was certainly no way forward, and really no way back; the only chance appeared to be eastwards to two large conical slag heaps, 600 yards east of the sugar refinery.

Already at the slag heaps was Lieutenant Chance, the junior subaltern, keeping remarkably cool despite having his haversack shot away and his right collar badge broken. He had found himself among those halted by the wire and had veered right, with men of the 9th Lancers arriving at a slag heap 'like a flock of sheep'. Sergeant Talbot, remounted after his dramatic tumble, was there with a mixed bag of men from all three squadrons, as was Major Hunter and Captains Wright and Sewell, Sewell's chestnut horse coughing foam and blood at Chance. Those with Talbot were ordered to dismount and get into action on top of the slag heap, but like the sugar refinery it proved too dangerous, for the German gunners quickly reset their sights and began to take the top off the mound with several well-aimed rounds.

The order was retracted, and a mad dash was made, under fire, in the direction of Elouges. Levinson records that five or ten minutes after he witnessed the charge '... a mob of men and horses, many wounded, poured into our cutting. I recognised Capt Sewell of the 4th DGs and Capt Grenfell of the 9th Lancers, and I believe I saw Colonel David Campbell of the 9th Lancers. They galloped on down the cutting taking some of my led horses with them.'

It was on the same railway line, probably a little to the east, that Ben had come across the prostrate Cumber.

Ben

Cumber had apparently broken several ribs in the fall, and was in severe pain. I managed to pull up another loose horse and with difficulty helped him to mount before we followed the railway line back out of the action, Cumber more or less bent over the horse, half conscious and in a very sorry state. A dressing station had been rigged up near Elouges over which flew a makeshift Red Cross. There were already around forty men there as we arrived, but a doctor came out to help Cumber off his horse, quickly diagnosing that my friend had no choice but to stay put. Cumber was very distressed and said he wanted to carry on, but the doctor made it clear this was not possible, and I had no choice but to leave him behind. It was heartbreaking to go, for Cumber, like the rest who were in no fit state to ride, was now left to become a prisoner. Saying goodbye, I took his horse and rode on, joining a mixed bag of Lancers and Dragoons, straggling down a road, all looking for their units. I was fortunate in finding the remnants of my Squadron almost straight away, but it was days before the Regiment was anything like together again.

Editor

Hundreds of men and horses now lay strewn across several fields, some dead, most wounded, some suffering from horrific injuries. Troopers like Private Cumber and Corporal Murphy could count themselves lucky, for although wounded they had found help, while the luckiest of all, those who had come through unscathed, were out of sight at Elouges and Audregnies, congratulating each other and shaking hands as adrenalin and jubilation mixed freely.

To those who took part, the ill-fated charge became known as 'Shrapnel Monday' or the 'Joy Ride'. Yet despite the ferocity of the Germans' rifle, machine gun and artillery fire that day, much of it was poorly directed against the on-coming cavalry. The Germans, as Osburn noted, 'seeing a comparatively large mass of cavalry suddenly let loose and galloping towards them, got a bad attack of nerves'. Their lack of resolve may also be attributed to the accurate fire of both the RHA and RFA Batteries which, while unable to locate their German counterparts, caused havoc among the closely formed ranks of infantry advancing from Quiévrain. They had advanced in the open and at a distance of little more than 2,000 yards. Twice they broke, retreating beneath a veritable hail of low bursting shrapnel, before finally pushing round the west of Audregnies at 2.30pm, forcing the batteries to retire. Captain Francis Grenfell of the

9th Lancers, who had been badly wounded, and Major Ernest Alexander of 119th Battery, were later awarded Victoria Crosses for helping to extricate the guns of 119th Battery under fire.

The batteries had been admirably helped by the Norfolks and Cheshires on the ridge, and by the machine guns of the 3rd Cavalry Brigade west of Angre which, for a time, checked the Germans' enveloping movement by firing down a valley towards Baisieux. Only when it was clear the Germans could not be held did the Norfolks' Commanding Officer Colonel Ballard (temporarily in charge of the Cheshires, Norfolks and 119th Battery combined) order the withdrawal. This order was sent three times but failed to reach the Cheshires, so that by 4.30pm they were left to fight on alone. They were finally overwhelmed and forced to surrender at around 8pm, at which point they had lost some 800 men, killed, wounded or taken prisoner, leaving 200 of the Battalion's original complement to fight another day.

And what of the charge? In little more than ten minutes, the Brigade had lost 234 men, killed, wounded and missing, although it could and perhaps should have been much worse. The 4th Dragoons' two-and-a-half squadrons lost eighty one men (two Troops under Major Hutchison and Captain Magillicuddy were elsewhere) of whom just nine were killed, including their principal French liaison officer, the Vicomte de Vauvineur, shot straight through the forehead. Of the remainder, most were wounded and subsequently taken prisoner, Hickman, Murphy, Cumber, Patterson, Cornall and Burgess among them. The 9th Lancers lost fourteen killed, including one officer, and seventy three wounded or missing. The 18th Hussars, though not principally involved in the charge, lost nine killed, including one officer, and fifty seven wounded.

In the hours that followed, the Germans gradually rounded up the wounded from the fields in front of Audregnies, and from the many small farm holdings in the area. The majority were taken to one of two convents in Audregnies, and included among their number Lieutenant Gallaher of the 4th Dragoons. He recalled that a mixed bag of some 190 British POWs (including many officers and men of the 1st Cheshires) remained there under guard for at least a week until well enough to be moved. Shortly before they were due to go, Gallaher and Sergeant Hymes made a bid for freedom and on August 31st undertook a dramatic escape northwards, on foot to Tournai and by train to Bruges, before travelling onwards to Ostend and eventually all the way back to Britain. They achieved this remarkable escape despite both suffering from injuries, Gallaher in particular being handicapped by a head wound and, incredibly, a broken leg.

After the charge at Audregnies a Special Order was issued by Brigadier-General de Lisle:

'I wish to express to the 2nd Cavalry Brigade my extreme pride and satisfaction with their conduct at Audregnies on Monday August 24. The fight was necessary to save the 'V' Division from an organised counterattack during their retirement and the object was achieved by the gallant and steady conduct of the Brigade. Major-General Sir Charles Fergusson, commanding 'V' Division, thanked me personally for saving his Division, adding that, but for the Cavalry Brigade, his Division would have been destroyed to the last man. I specially wish to commend the 9th Lancers in daring to charge unbroken infantry, in order to save neighbouring troops, and the 4th Dragoon Guards in the effective support given, without hesitation or thought of danger. I intend to bring to the notice of high authority, how greatly I value the devotion of my Brigade.'

While de Lisle was rightly proud of his Brigade, and Mullens of the 4th Dragoons, both now had to make the best of the few men left at their disposal. Trooper Dyer of B Squadron noted that immediately after the charge he saw Mullens with only fourteen men, and that, at a roll call taken later that day, some 400 Dragoons were missing, some seventy per cent of strength. To all intents and purposes the Regiment was momentarily broken, although large numbers were able to rejoin over the following few days. Lieutenant Wright, for example, joined up with remnants of the 9th Lancers riding to Bavai, Landrecies, and Le Cateau before finding the Regiment three days later at St Quentin.

The Regiment had also lost around 300 thoroughbred horses, many of which had come from the Rothschild stables on mobilisation. Despite being badly wounded, some of these horses attempted to follow the Regiment as it moved south, a heartbreaking sight for anyone, but particularly for those in the cavalry. In the end those horses which could not be saved were shot.

Note on the absence of wire:

It has been thought that barbed wire fences of one form or another halted the headlong attack by the Dragoons and Lancers that day. But a 'Statement about the non-existence of wire during the Charge of 9th Lancers, 24 August 1914', to be found at the Public Records Office, appears to contradict the evidence of the time. It reads:

'Accompanied by a friend, I visited the area Quiévrain – Audregnies – Elouges, on August 25th 1921. There was no sign of any wire fence near the Sucrerie de Carochette, or anywhere else in that neighbourhood. Four men were ploughing on the spot. They each informed me separately that they had lived there continuously before, during and since the war, and never had there been any wire fence in the neighbourhood. A sportsman with a gun who was standing near also made the same assertion; he also had lived all the time in that place. All five appeared absolutely positive in their belief and statement.'

A.H.Burne Maj. R.A, Sept 28th 1921.

This may be where the apparent contradiction lies, for once the cavalry were driven to the right of the Chaussée Brunehaut by both frontal and enfilade fire, then the large sugar factory complex in effect steered what was left of the attack away to the east, barring any further advance. The assertion might be made that other than a quickset hedge which bordered the single track railway from Quiévrain to Elouges, there were few impediments at all other than the fence which surrounded the sugar factory. Most troopers were unable to see anything owing to the liberal amounts of dust kicked up in the air, and by the time they could see most had been driven off eastwards. It is possible that the principal wire fencing was that which surrounded the sugar factory, but which has been dismantled by discussion and oft repeated stories into a network of field partitions. Certainly there is no indication that the advancing German infantry were hindered in any way other than by the accurate fire of the British infantry and artillery.

The charge at Audregnies briefly stemmed the German advance and closed the door on the Battle of Mons. As men rejoined their troops, so the Regiment was divided by Mullens into two squadrons, to act in conjunction with the 1st Cavalry Brigade on the right flank of General Smith-Dorrien's Army.

During the night of August 24th, the Dragoons withdrew with survivors of the 5th Division in the direction of St Waast and Bavai, before continuing along the old Roman road, past the Forest of Mormal, in the direction of Le Cateau. By the morning of the 25th, while the infantry retreated, the Regiment zig-zagged across the BEF's line of retirement, to Le Cateau on the 26th, to Rancourt and St Quentin on the 27th and on to Noyon and Compiègne on August 30th.

Ben
August 25th – September 6th 1914

There was complete confusion in the retreat from Mons, for no sooner had the BEF been forced to pull back than the roads became clogged with entire families on the move, abandoning their homes in a futile flight from the advancing Germans. Horses, trucks, handcarts, and carriages poured onto every highway, accompanied by the old and the young, all carrying anything they could manage, and all moving at walking pace. It was a terrible sight, a morass of jumbled, doubtless treasured belongings piled high onto people, who, almost without exception, looked utterly forlorn. What happened when they were overtaken by the Germans, heaven only knows, for these people who had cheered and shouted *'Vivent les Anglais!'* on our march up to the front, were now left to fend for themselves. We felt sorry for them, we had let them down, but there was nothing we could do. It was simply a question of self-preservation.

Our job was to protect our own men by acting as a fast-moving cover across the line of retreat, holding out to the last possible moment to let the infantry get away. The Squadron became involved in a series of brief actions, firing on distant German infantry, or, just as likely, shooting in a given direction:

'Dismount! Three rounds rapid! Cease fire, remount!'

On other occasions, we would line up behind a hedgerow and wait for ten, twenty perhaps thirty minutes, before pushing on. I'm not sure if our officers had a clue where we were, I don't even know if they had any maps, but we implicitly trusted that our officers' judgements were sound. I well remember spending most of one day in a wood, only to ride over a crossroads we had passed some five hours earlier. We had ridden in one enormous circle.

After Audregnies, we retreated south through village after village, mostly small grubby affairs, surrounded by coal mines and slag heaps, a feature of the region. It was hot, dry and dusty, and very quickly the horses began to look exhausted and dishevelled. Where we could, we rode along the road's soft, unmetalled edges, for the paving stones were very hard on their legs, but our horses soon began to drop their heads and wouldn't shake themselves like they normally did. Many were so tired, they fell asleep standing up, their legs buckling. As they stumbled forward, striving to stay upright, they lost their balance completely, falling forward and taking the skin off their knees.

To ease the horses' burden, excess kit was dumped. Shirts, spare socks and other laundry were all thrown away along with our greatcoats. It helped, but the horses really needed a good rest and this was an impossibility. The best we could do for them was to halt, dismount and lead on, a short-lived order to walk that usually lasted for no more than a mile or so. As a result, the horses' shoe nails wore down at a terrific rate, each lasting little more than a week or ten days, before the chink, chink sound of a loose shoe meant falling back to find the farrier. It was sad to see our horses, so coveted and closeted at Tidworth, go unkempt. Saddles, once removed after every ride, now remained on for several days and nights with only the girths being slackened. The horses became very sore, their backs raw from over-riding, although they tended to suffer less than the French horses, which were simply ridden into the ground. The French cavalry never walked anywhere, and when they finally halted to give their horses a breather, it was not unknown for part of the horse's back to come away with the saddle. One horse went mad, banging its head against a wall, before it was finally put out of its misery. It was appalling to see. For our part, we did the best we could, bandaging our horses' grazed

59

knees with rags or bits of puttee, but the majority could consider themselves lucky if they got a rub down with a bit of straw, or a pat on the back to bring back the circulation.

By far the greatest strain for cavalrymen, worse than any physical discomfort or even hunger, was the gut-wrenching fatigue. Pain could be endured, food scrounged, but the desire for rest was never-ending. The motion of riding was enough to send a man to sleep. I fell off my horse more than once, and watched others do the same, slowly slumping forward, grabbing for their horse's neck, in a dazed, barely conscious way. At any halt, men fell asleep instantaneously, and required a good shake, or the 'gentle' prod of a sergeant's boot, to wake again. They struggled to their feet, hollow-eyed and giddy with fatigue, hauling themselves back on their horses. History judged the Retreat heroic, but from where I was sitting, it was a shambles.

I never thought we would lose, but I did wonder just how we were ever going to get out of the mess we were in. The reservists in particular found the going unbearable. Many had been called up after five years on the reserve and had not marched in all that time. Their feet simply weren't up to the stone-set roads, in stiff, unbroken boots. Blood oozed through shoe soles, or from bits of rag tied round blistered feet. Boots, jackets, caps, everything was dumped, except rifles and ammunition. The roadsides became strewn with bits and bobs of every description as stragglers sought desperately to stay in touch with their regiments. In grim determination, they hobbled along in ones or twos, often hanging on to our stirrup leathers to keep going. Some began to hallucinate. It was heart-rending. To help, an officer would carry another rank's kit, a stronger man, two rifles or another's pack, while we commonly transported an infantryman's rifle a couple of miles up the road, leaning it against a tree for him to collect.

The retreat continued to Le Cateau, through the Mormal Forest to St Quentin, Guiscard, Noyon, and then onwards still. At the time, of course, these places meant nothing to me; one or two men did keep diaries, but it is only since the war that I learnt where we were. To me, there were only villages on fire, or not on fire, towns that were filled with panicky civilians, or abandoned to the Germans. The forests, too, were remembered only for the relief they gave from the sapping sun, cocooning us briefly from the war.

During this time, concealment from the enemy was as important as engagement. The wire that in peacetime made our caps flat and rigid was dispensed with, making the caps' edges soft. Without the wire the caps lost their mass uniformity which could otherwise draw the attention of spotterplanes. It was not long either before our cap badges which reflected the sun were removed too, replaced much later by a blue cloth alternative.

For the first few days, the Regiment remained scattered, and only gradually got back together. What was left of the Regiment continued to respond to emergencies, frequently breaking up advance guards of German cavalry, too close on our heels for comfort. As a consequence, we were in a constant state of readiness, although we rarely went into action. As far as my Squadron was concerned, I do not recall any casualties during the Retreat. As a result, morale remained high, while rumours and counter-rumours ran through the ranks about where we were headed and when we might make a stand.

Food came from Army Service Corps ration dumps, which were just boxes of biscuits, tins of bully beef, and corn for the horses, stacked at the side of the road. Very occasionally, a chalk notice marked the food up for a particular Regiment, but more often than not we just helped ourselves, stuffing what we could into every pocket, and filling up a couple of nosebags of corn. If we were fortunate, and the drivers of the Squadron and Regimental General Service wagons were with us, then they picked up what they could.

Hunger and thirst sapped everyone's energy and, as there was no water at the dumps, the Regiment was left to fend for itself. Clean water was of great importance to a Regiment on the move, and whenever possible, water bottles were kept topped up. On one occasion, the Squadron turned into a stream and the horses, tired and thirsty, went to drink but we were told to 'Ride on', so on we went. I've no idea where we were, but things were quiet. The water was less than a foot deep, clear and inviting, and it seemed such a waste. Why we couldn't have halted for a few minutes, even for the horses' sake, I will never know. Several troopers did try to get water into their enamelled bottles, quickly removing the cork and slinging them over into the stream. But most bottles were already too light, and despite tipping and dipping them in the water, most failed to collect much before reaching the other side.

The compensations of summer were the grapevines, plundered for our horses' buckets, and the apples and pears scrumped from the trees which lined the roads or filled private gardens and orchards. We were warned early on that anyone caught stealing from private property could be shot and all Regiments had taken their own 'Red Caps', or Military Police, to France, a Provo Sergeant and a couple of Provo Corporals who enforced military law. Whether fruit was technically considered 'loot', I never knew, but there was no sense in leaving anything to feed the Germans.

More questionable was our scrounging round empty houses, many abandoned at such speed that a *'Marie Celeste'* scene of normality remained, with cutlery on the table and, on one memorable occasion, food still in the oven. On many farms we found a mess, with abandoned animals roaming around, some in a bad state. On one farm, we came across sheds containing several dozen cows all blowing their heads off, desperate to be milked. In their anxiety to clear out, the owners had loaded up their carts and left the animals locked up and unmilked. We were told to go and unchain them and let them out into a field, otherwise they would starve. They were in obvious pain as they came into the yard, their swinging bags so full that milk was actually squirting out.

To scratch a living off the land, we butchered smaller animals, often chasing prey around a farmyard, to general humour. 'Look at that blinkin' goose,' I said, at one farm where we had briefly halted. 'Drive him round the back of the barn, quick.' Nipping round the corner, I drew my sword and as the bird came shooting round, gave it such an enthusiastic swipe that I chopped its head off in one movement, blood spraying everywhere. I found some string, tied its wings and feet together and hooked it over my sword. Later that day, General de Lisle himself passed the Regiment and with a wry smile said to me, 'I see you have got your supper with you, lad'.

Scrumping apples, eating turnips, stealing chickens; baking odd potatoes in the embers of a fire; chewing a smoked hock of bacon whilst on the move, eating a crust of bread found by the roadside: every opportunity was taken to get food.

Relieving myself inside the edge of a small copse one day, I looked round just in time to see a rabbit shoot down a hole. Most animals which live underground dig a bolt hole as well as an entrance, and a rabbit, particularly a rabbit, won't wait around; if someone is at the front door, it's out the back and gone. Fortunately, the man detailed with me had stood near the bolt hole. 'There's a rabbit in there, shove the butt of your rifle at the front of the bolt hole,' I said. I passed him a stick, which he thrust down the hole while I at the other end stuck my arm down and grabbed the rabbit's hind legs. Dragging it out, I broke its neck, took my Jack-knife and gutted it. I tied it to my saddle, then rode on to catch the Squadron up, farther down the road.

If the Regiment was on the move, permission from a sergeant or corporal had to be sought to fall out in answer to any call of nature. We were riding from dawn to dusk, and the risk of being caught by the Germans quite literally with our trousers down was enough to warrant another man being detailed to act as look-out. While he held the horse, you tried to make yourself a little less conspicuous behind a tree or a hedge. Where there was none, it was down with your breeches and that was that.

To help share the workload, the Regiment ran a system of rotating duties with A, B or C Squadron being assigned as 'Duty Squadron' for up to four days at a time, each Troop taking a full 24 hours as 'Duty Troop'. This Duty Troop would be first to react in an emergency, the Duty Squadron supporting the Troop should a bigger threat materialise. On the move, day or night, the 'Duty Troop' rode at the front of the Regiment where most problems were likely to occur, providing the advance guard of scouts up to a mile ahead of the Regiment. At night, if the Regiment was resting, the Troop would be expected to provide outposts. Fighting died down at night. The Germans could ill afford to out-run their supplies and halted while they were brought up, but still there was no chance to relax. The stress was immense. On those occasions when the Regiment camped, there were hours of work for those on outpost duty. Standing on guard, two on, four off, no one could be sure they would not fall asleep as they took watch from the edge of a wood, or at a crossroads, leaning against a wall, or the side of a ditch. Being caught asleep on duty was a shooting crime, so the battle to stay awake was all-consuming, numbing one's faculties.

One night, while I was on duty, an officer tried to take my rifle from me, a trick to test whether a trooper was asleep or not; I passed not because I was awake, for I was darn near asleep, but because I had learnt from other old sweats to tie the rifle strap to my wrist. As I felt the first tug, I shuddered awake as the officer – my assailant – stood right beside me. I was relieved by our sergeant that time, but there were others during the war who were court martialled under similar circumstances, caught asleep without their rifles attached to their wrists.

It was very easy, when on Duty Troop, to become temporarily separated from the Regiment. Dawn came early and brought new alarms to which we had to respond, breaking camp at 3, 4 or 5am, to return to the roads. The 4th Troop was on outpost when such a thick fog set in that by daybreak, when we moved off, it was impossible to see even across the road, so Swallow ordered the Troop to ride one behind the other, keeping close to the roadside hedges. Suddenly, 'Qui va là?' ('who goes there?'), erupted out of the fog, then bang, bang, bang. Three shots fizzed down the centre of the road, then there were more anxious shouts. Barely fifty yards ahead was a twitchy French outpost and, taking no chances, they had opened fire. Swallow immediately shouted out, and as we rode forward there appeared a detachment of French Dragoons, complete with plume helmets and brass breastplates. They too were of the 4th, and as lost as we were, so linking up, we rode with these men for the rest of the day until we rejoined our Regiment.

Editor

As an indication of the pressure the Dragoons were under, it is interesting to note the following daily reports, taken from the regimental diary for the first week in September 1914:

1.9.14 Received orders to be ready to march at 4.30am.

2.9.14 Orders received at 2am to turn out as quickly as possible.

3.9.14 Marched at 4.20am

5.9.14 Ditto

6.9.14 Marched 5am

This is not exceptional. Similar requirements were made of many cavalry regiments during the Retreat. It is worth noting, however, that after August 24th until the Germans' abrupt about-turn on the Marne on September 6th, the 4th Dragoons suffered only two casualties, both wounded. This gives some indication of the style of hit-and-run skirmishing undertaken by the Regiment during that time.

Ben

In the event of the Regiment being called into action, the theory was that the most recent 'Duty Troop' would be the last to go. We were having a short midday break when news came through that three German cavalrymen, probably scouts, had been seen outside a village we had only just passed through. As 4th Troop was on duty we were ordered to round them up. We split up into two groups to push round both sides of the village. However, our group, finding no sign of the enemies' presence, headed back by way of a track that ran up the side of a small wood ... a blue flash followed by a tremendous, almost simultaneous bang, bang, bang, bang and the road a hundred yards ahead spattered into a cloud of dust. Not only had the three Germans broken through, but apparently half a battery of light artillery had followed suit. We'd ridden right across their line of vision and they'd opened up with shrapnel. We were ordered to gallop past the point where the shells had exploded and got out of sight on the far side of the wood, and no further rounds were sent over. The German gunners had narrowly over-set their fuses so that the shells burst in the air directly above us, shooting forward a curtain of metal. Had those shells burst behind us, they would have wiped out the entire Troop.

On another occasion, the Squadron was riding in open country. It was a beautiful day and we were in open order, each man riding ten yards from the next man. We'd been ordered through scrubland with drawn swords to ensure that the area was clear of Germans, but as none were there, the Squadron halted, closed in, and formed up in troop order while we awaited instructions. As was normal in these circumstances, two men were sent out on point to guard against any possible attacks, and, as I was one of the two, I took up a position on the left of the Squadron while another man was sent out right. A position at the edge of the neighbouring field was pointed out to me, so returning my sword I reached for my rifle and jogged lazily out towards a haystack I'd seen.

On reaching the haystack I sat back, relaxing, when fzzz, a bullet whipped past. The Mauser rifle used by the Germans was as good as ours over short distances, so this sniper was either a poor shot or, just as likely, a good half a mile away. I was a stationary target and didn't care to find out for sure, so I gave my horse a quick kick and got close in behind the haystack. It was to be the only occasion in the war when I could say that I had felt personally targeted, at least as far as Jerry's participation was concerned.

Before the Retreat was over, the Germans had forced their way practically into Paris. In the end, we went east of the city, then farther south to the Marne, but in those first few days of September I clearly remember seeing a 9km signpost for the city. 'Here's one who's not going into Paris,' said the man next to me. I asked why, and he told me of the siege of Paris in 1870 and how the inhabitants were forced to eat rats to survive. It was around this time that we saw twenty to thirty French taxi cabs commandeered to race urgently-needed reinforcements to the front, although, as we passed, they were merely sitting in the road waiting to move off, each taxi containing three or four soldiers.

Editor

These were troops of the 7th Division of the French Third Army, rushed forward to the front near Gagny, in the taxis of the Marne. They then pushed onwards to Le Plessis where they came to a halt, around 4,000 men travelling thirty miles. They were put into the line at a critical stage of the Marne Battle, as the newly-formed French Sixth Army's flank attack on von Kluck's First Army had faltered and was now fighting off intense counter-attacks. Ben had seen some of the men who on September 6th would finally end the retreat and help to begin the re-advance to the Chemin des Dames.

CHAPTER FIVE
Behind Enemy Lines

Editor

In the first few days of September, Ben was attached to an intelligence officer, Lieutenant Archibald Harrison. This officer had joined C Squadron at the outbreak of war, and had already made a name for himself as Bridges' translator, becoming well-respected for his obvious intelligence and daring. While the BEF continued its retreat south, Harrison would go off to collect information about the enemy, criss-crossing the countryside, in the hope of finding out anything that might be of use. It was while he undertook these escapades that Ben was ordered to accompany him.

Ben

Harrison was a larger than life figure. Out-going and entertaining, he was also a highly astute, flexible and gifted man who spoke about five different languages including French, German and, I believe, Russian too. He was an intriguing officer, and a man not immune from scandal, for the story ran that shortly before the war, he had been discharged for 'Disorderly Conduct' from the 4th Hussars for doing what was known as the Pursuing Practice with the officers' mess door.[1]

Possibly owing to the war emergency, Lieutenant Harrison was back in the army, and early in September I was detailed to accompany him as he went behind the German lines to collect intelligence about the strength and whereabouts of the enemy. It is now known that the Germans were making a last effort to break the BEF and French armies in order to win a quick war, but in the first few days of September, it appeared that the Teutonic wave would simply roll on and on.

Each morning, as dawn broke, I would scramble a quick breakfast before saddling up and joining Harrison as he chose the direction we would take. Most of the time I rode behind him, but now and again when he wanted to talk, he'd call me up to ride alongside. He liked to chat, and after the second day asked me my Christian name. This was very unconventional and would have been considered highly improper had anyone known, but while I naturally remained 'Clouting' within the confines of the Regiment, I was 'Ben' while we were on our own.

Once we had left the Regiment, Harrison got his bearings and we switched from the roads, moving from hedgerow to hedgerow, wood to wood, always keeping cover and trying not to appear out in the open, the roads being left to the Germans. We frequently stopped so that Harrison could use his field glasses to survey the land ahead, although much time was spent collecting information from the French people. German patrols were popping up everywhere and many civilians were understandably jumpy, having heard about the German 'atrocities', the gory details of which spread fast and furiously among scared country folk. Most appeared willing to offer advice, but were anxious not to be caught red-handed helping a couple of British scouts. Days later when Jerry began to retire, most were less reticent; then a flurry of questions often had them pointing in various directions, fanning their hands over the horizon. Sometimes they pointed furiously, which I took to mean our arrival had only narrowly followed the Germans' departure.

Harrison never shied away from using farmhouses to water the horses or procure a quick meal or sandwich, and it was on one of these detours that we had a very narrow squeak.

'We can get a meal here, Ben,' Harrison said after talking with one farmer. 'Water the horses, then take them to the stables and off saddle them. Be sure to give their backs a good rub, feed them and as soon as you are done, come into the farmhouse.' An elderly farm hand joined me in the stable, bringing with him some corn for our horses' nose bags, and I patted their backs to bring the blood pressure back up, a form of horse massage. In the farmhouse, I found Harrison, as usual, in animated discussion with the farmer, before we both tucked into an excellent omelette beefed up with bread and butter. We were just finishing, indeed the farmer's wife had just put some coffee on the table, when one of the farm labourers, sent out to keep watch, bounded in to say that Uhlans were headed towards the farm.

There was no time to get away, and as our horses were in the stables there was little point in hiding. So we waited, standing stock still behind the kitchen table, watching through the kitchen's thick lace curtains, Harrison drawing his revolver. Presently a dozen lancers rode into the courtyard to use the water trough. As we watched intently, I thought how strange it was: we could see them, barely an arm's length away, yet they were blissfully unaware of our presence. My mind turned to the two horses in the stables, then I looked at Harrison who appeared composed. I had brought my rifle indoors as normal, and steeled myself, for I knew that Harrison, being Harrison, would shoot if we were discovered. As it was, the Germans seemed content to remain on their horses, talking to one another as they milled around waiting their turn at the trough. They showed no interest in either coming into the house or taking a look round the stables, and after what felt like an inordinate amount of time, they pulled their horses round and rode off.

'For Christ's sake get those bloody saddles on!' Harrison was very excited, and did not want to hang around. I ran to saddle and girth the two horses quicker than I ever had before, and off we rode smartly in the other direction. Seeing the enemy at such close quarters was genuinely exhilarating. I was still not seventeen years old and was too curious to be frightened.

The area was positively crawling with German cavalry and the fun was far from finished, for we hadn't left the farm ten minutes when we were spotted by another patrol. Turning in his saddle, Harrison saw them first, and spurring his horse on, led the way down a cart track. We were more or less in open countryside with little cover, and Harrison's horse, somewhat stronger than mine, quickly got ahead while I struggled to keep in touch. After perhaps a mile, we came to a steep grassy bank, and after a moment's hesitation, Harrison plunged over the side with a sharp 'Come on!' It was a display of sheer horsemanship, for the bank was all of forty feet high which meant we had to sit right back on the horses to keep them straight as they slid down almost on their behinds. The Germans, on reaching the bank, decided not to follow and resorted to firing at us, the report of their carbines cracking in our ears. I didn't care to look back, but they were a fair way behind and we were by now a fast receding target. That evening, Harrison somehow found the Regiment and complained about the horse I had been riding, ensuring that I was issued with an altogether stronger mare the following morning.

Editor

September 6th proved to be the turning point of the Retreat. The Germans, finding themselves over-extended, were forced to fall back, first to the river Marne and then the Aisne. Over the following six days a total of five rivers, the Morin, Marne, Ourcq, Vesle and Aisne, were crossed by the British, the 4th Dragoons being engaged most notably at the Petit Morin where Lieutenant Jones led a valiant charge to seize one of the two bridges over the river, and again on the Aisne where the 4th Dragoons lost its first officer killed.

Ben

The Germans were now retreating to the Marne, and while they were in some disorder it was Harrison's job to get in behind their lines to discover the strength and location of units and where they might attempt to dig in. The Germans were retreating in some haste, and were leaving all manner of bits and pieces as they went. It seemed promising that personal kit had been dumped in the fields, for it was reminiscent of the way we had been forced to cast away ours only two weeks before. More significant than the items of kit were some wagons loaded with abandoned military supplies, and not a small number of items plundered from French homes.

By the 8th, Allied troops had re-crossed the Marne, pushing on towards the Aisne, into countryside that was in complete contrast to the low-lying, featureless land we had retreated from, near Mons. Steep hills surrounded shallow valleys while rivers wound their way through the countryside.

There was no telling where the Germans were, except for the debris of war they left behind, the dead horses which littered the roadways and the occasional body, too. On more than one occasion, Harrison veered away down a track on instinct, only to find we had narrowly missed bumping into German cavalry. On other occasions, it was quite possible to be within shouting distance of British troops and then to meet two or three German stragglers making their way back. These soldiers were usually dead beat and, strange though it seems, there was no animosity between us. On the contrary, Harrison talked to each one and I shouldn't wonder if he didn't tell them to keep going and rejoin their regiments. It wouldn't have been out of character! The land was full of surprises.

On cresting one hill, we came across a Troop of Hussars about to charge a Troop of German Lancers in the valley below, some half a mile or more from our position. Around twenty five troopers had formed up on both sides. There was a momentary pause before the Hussars attacked, swords pointed forward between their horses' ears, the Germans responding with lances outstretched. Both sides were in fairly close formation until, at about sixty yards distant, they suddenly broke and fanned out. There was no collision of horses, not one fell, indeed each side passed through the other without an apparent casualty. 'That is a sight you'll never see again,' said Harrison, and with that we moved off without waiting to see the conclusion of this little war.

One evening as it was getting dusk we came across a house on the very edge of the wood. The house had been taken over by several Germans who were busily settling in, lighting fires as they prepared dinner. We watched them for a minute or two, and then Harrison said, 'Cover me, Ben, I'm going to find out who they are.' German and British officers dressed similarly at the beginning of the war, down to the Sam Browne style belts, and, as it was now dark, khaki was indistinguishable from grey. He pulled his hat right down to imitate the German peak cap and rode forward, right up to a German sentry, stopped for a moment, turned round and calmly came back. 'Come on, I think we can get out of this,' he said with a big smile on his face. 'What happened, sir?' I asked, intrigued. 'I had a go at him for neither challenging me properly nor standing to attention when he spoke to an officer,' Harrison said, laughing. 'Then, once I'd ruffled his feathers a little, I asked him which regiment he belonged to and rough directions.'

The weather had well and truly broken by this time, with sweeping showers soaking us to the skin, and rumbling thunder that crashed around the valleys to great effect. German resistance was stiffening. Until this time, Harrison had contented himself with relying on the daily British advance to overtake and, in effect, release us from behind German lines. Normally, we waited in a wood until it was safe to move, but it became apparent this strategy was beginning to fail. The first time we were forced to stay out overnight, we stayed at a large farmhouse, Le Château Vert near the small hamlet of Mont Notre Dame, a few miles south of the Aisne. On entering the house, we discovered that five French Dragoons were drifting through, and had decided to stop for the night. As usual, Harrison was quick to strike up a conversation, but as it was late I was excused to make a last check on the horses before turning in. Harrison slept the night in another part of the house, while I bedded down in the straw-filled loft which the owner had made available. Presently the other Dragoons climbed into the loft, and it crossed my mind that I should try and say something. But there was little we could communicate, so I quickly got my head down and slept like a log.

When I woke it was still early, but the Frenchmen had gone, so I went downstairs and had a quick breakfast before feeding and saddling the horses. As we were about to leave, the farmer's wife produced a wicker basket with two dozen eggs and offered them to us. 'Can you carry those without breaking them?' Harrison asked. 'I can try, sir,' and I thanked the lady in my pidgin French. The *entente cordiale* was very much alive, or so I thought, until I discovered that my wallet was missing. It was possible that I had lost it in the hay, but I retained the sneaking suspicion that one of the French Dragoons had relieved me of it during the night.

Editor
Harrison and Ben re-found the Regiment as it passed through the town of Cerseuil to the west. The Germans by this time were digging in on the Aisne, but there was still enough confusion for Harrison and Ben to effect a crossing of the river unseen on September 11th, two days before the British launched their attacks to seize the bridges over the Aisne.

Ben
Harrison was nothing if not courageous, for despite the dangers he decided to continue probing the German defences. To do so, he chose to cross the Aisne early one morning in torrential rain, pushing onwards to a village I later discovered was Moulins, some two to three miles north of the river. Like most of the villages in the area, Moulins consisted of a few sleepy houses strung out along half a dozen rough track roads, more a hamlet than a village. It was dusk when we arrived, and Harrison halted to discover whether any Germans were around. None were in sight, so we carried on down one of its narrow streets. We had just turned a corner when Harrison suddenly said 'Get in there quick!' To our right stood a barn with its doors wide open, and we rode in, scrambling off our horses to shut the doors. 'Germans,' he said, 'right at the end of the street.' Harrison had reacted so quickly that I had not seen anyone, and we had apparently got under cover without being seen either. Working fast, we piled up straw in front of the door to give the barn the appearance to all but the most inquisitive that it was full, after which Harrison nipped out of a back door to make contact with the owner of the neighbouring estaminet. The village had been anything but empty when we had first arrived, for within half an hour we were able to watch, through the eaves of the barn, German soldiers sauntering up and down the road right under our noses, so close that we could clearly hear their chit-chat. There was no chance of getting away, so Harrison told me to improve our new billet, making sure the horses were as comfortable as possible.

While I remained in the barn, Harrison nipped back to the estaminet. Everything would be all right, he told me, but in the meantime we were to give the estaminet owner our emergency rations to help supplement whatever we ate. Except when he came back to sleep, Harrison spent most of the time in the back of the house while I remained in the stables looking after the horses, although, fortunately, a horse rarely whinnies when there is another one with it. In the end it all became almost boring, as I kicked my heels around for hour after hour, or popped up into the loft to watch out for any Germans who might pass by.

On the second day, the gunfire near the river increased considerably, and shells began to land in the near distance, which I took to be a promising sign, though I could see nothing. September 13th remained cold and showery but, as I was to find out later, the Dragoons had, on this dull, inauspicious day, taken part in an attack to capture a bridge that crossed the Aisne at the village of Bourg. This bridge had been hurriedly destroyed by the Germans. However, the Dragoons were able to cross by the use of an aqueduct, which I was to cross myself a few days later.

Editor
September 13th was very wet, the rain on occasions coming down in torrents, and soaking everyone and everything. B Squadron under Captain Sewell had been given orders to occupy the village of Bourg on the other side of the Aisne. This village had been reported clear of the enemy, but on reaching the canal bridge the 4th Dragoons were suddenly fired upon.

Ben
In an attempt to stall the British advance, the Germans tried to blow up a canal that crossed the river. This they failed to do, and only managed to put a hole in the adjoining footpath that crossed the river as part of an iron aqueduct. The aqueduct still had water in it, and three planks of wood, each about two and a half feet wide, were laid across the hole. The footpath was not that wide, so we had to get off our horses and lead them across in single file.

The Regiment had been supported by a battery of artillery in their attack, taking the bridge at 7.30am and a number of prisoners, after which the whole Brigade pushed on and seized the high ground a mile north of Bourg. The Germans had put up some resistance, with strategically-placed machine guns around the various bridges but B Squadron had carried all before them, although at the moment of victory our machine gun officer Captain Fitzgerald, was shot in the forehead and killed instantly.[2]

In my barn I was quite ignorant of all this and other attacks unfolding for the various river crossings. Because I had to stay with the horses all the time, my food was brought to me either by the owner, or by Harrison. Finally on the third morning, I saw British troops coming up the street. Before we left, we were invited for a meal in the kitchen, where I noticed a picture standing on the mantelpiece of the lady outside her estaminet. Keen to have a souvenir, I motioned to her if I might have the picture as a keepsake and she nodded.[3] We said goodbye and rejoined the war.

72

The Germans had just begun to shell the village and we were thankful to go, finding, by sheer chance, that the Regiment had just passed the village. The Germans finally stopped retreating to dig in on the Chemin des Dames some few miles to the north, and as a consequence Harrison and I parted company.

Shortly after the Regiment crossed the Aisne, I was involved in a curious incident, which caused consternation at the time and achieved some notoriety in later years. In brief, it concerned two Lieutenant-Colonels, Elkington and Mainwaring, who were respectively in charge of the 1st Warwickshires and 2nd Dublin Fusiliers. During the confusion of the Mons retreat, a few of the 4th Dragoon Guards, most notably Major Tom Bridges and Lieutenant Harrison, arrived in a town called St Quentin to find several hundred exhausted men from both battalions slumped in the town square.

Their two commanding officers were at first nowhere to be seen. At the end of their tethers from days of fighting with little sleep or food, these officers had surrendered their commands, and a note to that effect was on its way to the Germans, a few miles to the north. Trying to restore some hope and discipline, Bridges tried to get the men to move but to little effect, so he resorted to the unique action for which he is remembered. Seizing his trumpeter, he went to a toy shop in the square where he purchased a toy drum and whistle, and with as much strength as both could muster, they marched around the square playing for all they were worth. The troops responded to the spectacle, and some minutes later began to fall in, to be led out of the town under the noses of the German cavalry. The two colonels were subsequently court martialled.[4]

Where I was while these famous events unfolded, I do not now recall. However, my own path was to become briefly entangled with the fall-out from the events at St Quentin. Some time later, the Regiment was on the outskirts of a town when I was one of eleven troopers and a corporal called to fall in with our rifles by one of our sergeants. We were given no explanation, and although we asked the sergeant, we were none the wiser. Told to wait on a street corner until further orders, we hung around for a couple of hours before abruptly being stood down. Nothing was said. I was curious, and waited for the first opportunity to ask the sergeant what it was all about. He told me that we were to shoot two Lieutenant-Colonels had a court martial passed death sentences on them. Instead, the court martial adjudged both to have had a mental breakdown owing to severe stress, and cashiered them from the army.

Editor

The Courts Martial of Elkington and Mainwaring are recorded as taking place on September 11th and 12th 1914, or in other words at exactly the same time that Ben and Lieutenant Harrison were being hidden in the stable in Moulins. This contradiction currently remains unexplained.

Ben

In the days after my exploits at Moulins, I rejoined my Squadron. The weather continued to be dismal; everyone was soaked through and covered in mud. Severe fighting was in progress as the infantry engaged the Germans time and time again, and the enemy continued to dig in on the heights of the Chemin des Dames. The Regiment criss-crossed the battle front, while shells continually passed over our heads. On a number of occasions the full Regiment, or one or more squadrons, was called into dismounted action, when we would dismount and run forward to dig in. We had no way of knowing that static warfare was about to overtake us on this front, nor that it would start a race to the sea. That race, when opposing armies tried to out-flank each other, succeeded only in creating the long lines of trenches. Our scoops in the ground, in which we lay, were, in a sense, the forerunners of the trenches. They were hastily dug by loosening the earth with small picks, which were then turned around to become shovels, the shovels being used to heap the earth in front, giving us a little more protection from bullets.

We were to fight a sharp action from scoops when, a couple of days later, two squadrons were sent into action to support some hard-pressed infantry. Our orders, as I recall, were to ride to a ridge and open fire on the Germans reportedly advancing in mass formation on the far side. As we rode forward, I saw on our left a battery of Royal Horse Artillery come into action at a gallop, absolutely to drill. We'd seen them fire before, but this was the first, and indeed the only, time that I saw the lead gunners drop from their horses, unhook the guns and limbers, while the lead riders swung the horses round to take them under cover. It was picturesque.

The six-gun battery came into action in support, opening up shortly before we arrived on the brow of the ridge. As a horse holder, I ought to have stayed behind, but older troopers were quite happy to let the likes of me go instead. Leaving our horses at the bottom of a ridge, we ran up the slope, where we dropped into small scoops made by some recently-departed infantry. It was such a beautiful clear day as the Germans came on, packed together, hundreds of them, marching four deep and at a distance of some eleven hundred yards. They were coming down the far slope of a valley, marching through agricultural fields, as we opened up with our fifteen-rounds-a-minute fire. The vision was perfect. I could see Germans toppling over as the rest came relentlessly on, but, with our artillery pounding away, the Germans could only take so much. All of a sudden they turned and bolted back up the valley, and the ceasefire was ordered; the action hadn't lasted much more than five minutes. We waited in those scoops until the evening, during which time a message was passed along from man to man. It came in an empty Bully Beef can and was tossed from scoop to scoop. It said, 'Brave A and C Squadrons 4th Dragoon Guards. You are a credit to both infantry and cavalry.' I am not sure who signed it, though I have a feeling it was General Lomax. When we were finally withdrawn, I went to draw fresh ammunition from the limber. It was then that I found I had just fourteen rounds left of the ninety I had gone into action with.

The Regiment pulled back across the Aisne and went into billets at Longueval, an undistinguished village some four miles south of Moulins and Paissy. The Regiment had briefly halted there the day before the attack on Bourg, and now returned to be billeted there for a couple of weeks while the fighting around the Chemin des Dames continued. Although well within the range of German heavy artillery, Longueval had been relatively undisturbed, offering us a chance to clean up and get some sleep, as almost to a man we were exhausted and filthy.

While we were not required for duty, the Regiment could properly settle in, in which case the horse lines were put down. Around every horse's neck there was a picket rope with a toggle at one end, while at the other end the rope was doubled back to make a loop. This loop was passed through the toggle of the next horse and so on until all were linked together in one long line, the line being fixed by the two tent pegs which all horses carried and which were knocked into the ground. These tent pegs had a further loop through which the picket rope was run. To stop the horses turning round at night, a further peg was placed behind the horse's hind leg, held by means of a leg hobble.

The horses were so hungry, they were barely able to wait for their food, and impulsively strained forward in the horse lines at meal times, mouths open, hoping to get a mouthful of corn. As soon as a nose bag was on, they bolted the food, throwing their heads up into the air to get as much corn as possible into their mouths. The problem was that whole oats passed through the horses' digestive systems and straight out again in the manure, doing no good at all. To slow down the rate at which they ate, pebbles were put in the nose bags with the corn, although, strictly speaking, we were not supposed to do this. As the horses bit down hard, they received a salutary shock, ensuring that they chewed their food more gingerly thereafter. There was only one other reason why a horse might pass whole oats and that was if its teeth were not grinding properly. This happened if the molars had become a bit ragged, in which case it was up to us to file down the offending tooth or teeth. One man steadied the horse by using a twitch on its nose, or by pinching the nose between two fingers; either way the horse stood mute. The other man then opened the horse's mouth and caught hold of its tongue with one hand, while the other hand ran across the teeth, filing down the problem tooth until the horse could properly grind its food again.

One incident stands out in my memory at Longueval at this time. The Regiment had just come back to the village and I was detailed to help feed the Troop's horses, so I went to pick up a couple of feed bags and walked over to the horse lines. The horses had become noticeably agitated, but one, over-excited at the prospect of food, shot forward and in one movement bit my stomach, dragging me slightly across him before letting go. I had just a shirt on and the pain was excruciating, and I grabbed the nearest thing to hand, an entrenching tool, and gave the horse an almighty thwack across the nose. I had hit the horse so hard that it fell down just as our veterinary officer, Lieutenant Welch, happened to be strolling by. The horse regained its feet straight away but the officer had witnessed my attack and put me under immediate arrest, without even inquiring as to the whys and wherefores. Within half an hour, I had been brought up before Bridges, and Welch gave his evidence. Bridges asked me if I had anything to say, but believing that actions would probably speak louder than words, I pulled up my shirt to reveal my stomach, still oozing a little blood from the wound. 'The horse bit me, sir, so I hit it,' I said. He appeared unconcerned but stood up and had a look. 'Get your stomach dressed straight away. Two days Number One Field Punishment for hitting it in the wrong place.'

Field Punishment was a serious reprimand, and meant being tied to a gun or limber wheel, but on this occasion no one was interested in carrying it out to the letter of the law. A sergeant was detailed to take me to a limber, but as we arrived he pointed to the wheel hub and said, 'That looks a little dirty, let's get a horse's nose bag on there so your trousers won't get greasy.' He wrapped some ropes loosely round my wrists, whispering as he did so, 'Wait until I'm out of the way and then you can slip your hands out of the loop when no one is around'. Field Punishment normally lasted two hours a day, so I made myself comfortable, sitting on the hub. I hadn't been there half an hour when the order came to saddle up, as the Regiment was moving out. Bridges may have known this while passing sentence; either way I never had to complete my punishment, nor was the sentence entered into my paybook as it should have been.

Editor

On September 3rd, Bridges was given command of the 4th Hussars, after the previous Commanding Officer, Lieutenant-Colonel Ian Hogg DSO, had died of wounds after a short fight with the Germans near Roye-St-Nicolas. Bridges was promoted to Lieutenant-Colonel, and joined his new Regiment on September 27th, with Ben as his horse orderly. However, Bridges' time with the 4th Hussars was short-lived. On October 2nd, Bridges received orders to proceed at once to the Belgian GHQ, and in the morning duly motored on his way, leaving Ben behind. Ben stayed with the Hussars, as an orderly to Bridges' successor, Temporary Lieutenant-Colonel Philip Howell, formerly second in command to Hogg.

Ben

Bridges was a regular soldier of the old type, a disciplinarian but without being silly about it. He was a fine specimen of a man, all of six feet and fourteen stone in weight.

When with Bridges I always rode to the rear, automatically dropping to a position about a horse's length behind him, only riding forward when he called to give me instructions. When I had been with Harrison, he would call me up to ride alongside because he wanted to have a chat, something Bridges would never have done. Bridges had an aura about him, and it was a great disappointment when no sooner had we arrived at the Hussars than he left for the Belgian Army. Howell, the new Colonel of the Regiment, took over Bridges' horses, and I was asked if I would continue to look after them. I was to stay with Howell and the 4th Hussars for the best part of the next six months.

Towards the end of the first week in October, the 4th Hussars left the stalemate of the Aisne for the new battle front opening up to the north, around Ypres, and the Messines Ridge. We arrived at Ypres by about the middle of the month after a hard march, passing through the soon-to-be-famous town before virtually any damage had been done.

This was a fairly inactive period as far as I was concerned. I did not see much of Howell, as he was kept busy ensuring the smooth running of the Regiment and often drove over to Bailleul to the Brigade's HQ. Inevitably, when he was away, I spent much of my time with the transport, or at the canteen, where I palled up with a former groom in civvy life, Fred Meakin, an awfully nice man with whom I whiled away many hours in conversation. It was there that I met a friend from home, Alf Goldsmith. He came from Glynde and was a driver in D Battery, Royal Horse Artillery, one of two batteries attached to the 3rd Cavalry Brigade. By this time the weather was rotten, cold and raining most days, and he grumbled to me that the battery was having severe difficulties getting the guns around on roads and dirt tracks which disintegrated beneath the guns' wheels. I saw him on several occasions, once by the side of the road when his battery had halted for a snack, and again when we overtook the gun teams on the way to some village or other. It was always nice to see a face from home, and we always looked out for each other, trading remarks as we passed or swapping a wave.

I would also hear snippets about how the Dragoons were getting on, although they were not always happy ones. It was around this time that I heard that my Troop Sergeant, Johnstone, had been killed in an attack on Neuve-Chapelle, when the Regiment had suffered a lot of casualties. I was saddened by the news, for he was a good soldier, but more than that, he was a darn nice man. He had made an impression on me, not least because he was almost unique among NCOs in that he never swore.

During the first cold snap, we received our first rum issue. Early in the war, the quartermaster dished it out in a glass, which we were to drink straight down. The old soldiers showed no hesitation, tipping their heads straight back, so following suit I downed my share. My goodness, my eyes nearly popped out of their sockets! I'd never tasted rum before in my life, and this was neat navy rum; I thought my throat was on fire. Its effects were nevertheless miraculous, banishing the cold in seconds, as a sense of warmth extended all the way down to a soldier's toes. During October and November we got an issue pretty well every night, and though it was supposed to be good for us, medicinal you might say, I never got used to it. Early on, there was no possibility of passing the rum on, it was either a question of taking it or missing out. Later, when the rum was watered down, it was served out into our mess tins and then it was possible to pass it to others, which I did frequently.

Unlike the cavalry, the infantry were fortunate in having a travelling field kitchen which could serve up food more or less as a battalion arrived back from the firing line. This was different in the cavalry where, by the very nature of mounted work, we might be ordered to travel considerable distances across country. Indeed each trooper was himself semi self-sufficient, for our mess tins could be used as small frying pans, and were held on the side of the horse in a canvas sling. These mess tins were more compact than the infantryman's, being no more than an inch deep, round and with a folding handle. Only once a regiment had camped for the night was it possible for the cooks to set about lighting a fire, racing to get a dixie of tea going and the food cooking. Each Troop carried two dixies; the lids were used to fry food on, while the dixies themselves each held about three gallons of stew. The stew stood astride whatever fire the cook had managed to rig up, be it on top of some bricks, if they were available, or above a small slit trench cut in the ground. The food was known as Bully Stew, and was the same day after day, day after day; boiled vegetables mixed with the contents of several one pound tins of bully beef. Our cook, a small stocky man, did his best with the limited resources, but Bully Stew only ever varied in two respects: the first depended on which vegetables were available, the second was the size of the portion.

The amount of stew we got would be slightly more or less dependent on whether the Regiment had recently suffered many casualties or not. In theory, the Regiment was supplied according to the number of men at any one time. If news of losses arrived too late to affect the food coming up on the ASC limbers, then we ate more although not necessarily better. For when we lost our cooks through injury or illness, it would be up to the rest of us to muck in and take over and take a turn as cook.

It was little wonder that with Bully being the only option, chicken stealing from local farms became rife and, being a born scrounger, I proved quite a dab hand at it. Chickens were popular targets for hungry soldiers. Not only did they remain fairly quiet, making it easy to sneak up and screw a neck, but the rest moved up to fill the gap, covering up the misdemeanour. Chickens were skinned, never plucked, so that we could bury the evidence, with little fear of being caught. If we were lucky, the morning might bring a few amusing theatricals as an irate farmer protested to our officers about his missing livestock. But rarely would he get any sympathy. Our officers were not immune to poaching themselves at times, and impatiently they would wave the farmer and his problem away.

There was only one occasion when we were nearly caught. One night, three of us crept on to a farm and stole a small pig, before clubbing it to death with an axe handle. We stuffed the pig into a sack and tore off up the road to a nearby stream where we cut its throat, leaving no trace of our activities. Wishing to eat the pig on a later occasion, we hid it under a blanket and settled down for the night. First thing in the morning, the farmer turned up and began complaining bitterly to one of our officers, we presumed about his pig. Then, to our great surprise, the officer suddenly ordered an immediate inspection. We looked at each other, 'Hell's teeth!' Quick thinking was required and the pig was grabbed, quickly wrapped in sacking, and shoved among the officer's valises on the Maltese cart – as it turned out, the only place not searched.

Along with the cooking, there was the job of providing latrines. Each Troop had one man, a pioneer – usually a lance corporal – who was detailed as toilet attendant but known to all as the rear admiral. On the move, he led a pack horse on which, among other things, were two shovels and two picks. When the regiment or squadron halted for the night, it was his job to dig three little trenches each around a foot deep and eight inches wide in the corner of a field. There was no screen, or any sort of cover at all, the earth was simply piled to one side of the holes and each trooper kicked a bit of the earth back in on top of whatever he had left behind. Finally, before the Troop moved out, it was, in theory, the pioneer's job to see that the holes were filled back in again.

Frequent contact with local civilians ensured memorable moments of humour. On one occasion I watched as some tommies, to the bewilderment of a farmer, tried to obtain eggs by strutting around a farmyard, squawking and dropping lumps of chalk from their behinds. As each man tried to trump the others with a yet better impression, so the others fell about laughing. The impressions were as much about having a good joke as about buying eggs.

Through miming, most soldiers made it clear what they were after, although that did not guarantee that local people were willing to understand. We were once at a crossroads and an officer had decided that, to site a machine-gun, a trench and breastworks would have to be dug. There was already a ditch to work from, but the two shovels and pick-axe on the Troop packhorse were not enough, so a group of us went to a nearby house. Perhaps the farmer had recently lost some chickens to soldiers, perhaps he did not want a trench dug so close to his house, whatever the reason, he seemed incapable of understanding what we wanted. 'Shovel, shovel, shuuvelll,' we explained to accompanying actions. Finally the farmer left us to return a few minutes later with his white cart horse, his *'cheval'*.

Fighting abated towards the end of November and the Regiment went into winter billets. My memory is hazy of this time, although two very youthful and upbeat letters which I sent to my parents from France found their way to the *Sussex Gazette*, and were published.

The first was dated November 3rd and confirmed that:

'I'm still going strong, we are capturing Germans every day and our artillery is playing hell with them. All our cavalry are armed with bayonets now and we are doing infantry work as well as cavalry. I have seen plenty of black chaps from India, they are in the trenches next to us. There are some good fighters, as mad as March hares. Now the Winter is coming on it is a bit nippy lodging at "Mrs Greenfields". Our Regiment has lost a lot of men. We lost most of them when we charged some German guns among some coal mines. We got covered with coal dust. I was one that came through safely. We were all as black as miners. We hear that Russia is doing well, as well as us.'

Shortly afterwards, a second letter dated November 16th noted that:

'I'm still alright. You say you were not allowed bonfires on the 5th. We had some awful fires, whole villages on fire and big farm buildings. They were too big to cook the breakfast on. I don't know what Kaiser Bill thinks General French's Contemptible Little Army is made of, but it is better than his big army. You would never believe how cheerful the British lads are going about their work whistling or smoking all the time and ever true to the old country.'

Christmas 1914 has become famous for the fraternisation which took place all the way along the line. This may have been the case, but I had no involvement in it, nor did I hear anything about it, although news of an impromptu Anglo/German truce is supposed to have caused a sensation back at home.

No matter where a soldier was that Christmas, he received a little festive cheer in the form of a Christmas tin, the personal gift, we were told, of Queen Mary. The tin contained a picture of the Queen, a packet of tobacco and twenty cigarettes. I wasn't a big smoker so I kept the contents for a souvenir. The cigarettes were stolen later in the war, but the picture and the tobacco I still own to this day.

Just before Christmas, Colonel Howell left for England, and I did not see him again until January. This left me at something of a loose end, for on Christmas Day all officers' servants were ordered to rejoin their respective squadrons for a festive dinner. Normally orderlies had their meals at the Regimental HQ, but it had closed down for that one day, and not having a squadron to go to, I was rather left to my own devices. There was one other man in the same position, so together we made our own makeshift Christmas dinner consisting of a Maconochie (an all-in-one dinner made up of things like beef, butter beans and carrots) and a tin of fruit we had managed to scrounge. It wasn't quite how my mother had made Christmas dinner, but it was the best, under the circumstances.

NOTES

1. Ben heard this story when he was taken as Major Bridges' horse orderly to the 4th Hussars later that month. The Pursuing Practice entailed a trooper, while riding, running his sword through a man from behind. As he rode past, the trooper retrieved his weapon by twisting his body round in the saddle and withdrawing the blade as the man fell. It was the Pursuing Practice that Harrison had apparently acted out while drunk, 'galloping' towards the Hussars' mess door, and impaling the polished oak with his sword.

   Lieutenant Archibald Harrison's name appears in the Army List for May 1914 but disappears from June 1914 onwards, perhaps giving some credence to the incident Ben described with the mess room door. His name does appear in the Army Medal Role as a member of the Intelligence Corps, but, rather adding to the mystery, it states that he embarked for France two days after he is supposed to have taken patrols out with the 4th Dragoon Guards on the night of August 21st. Harrison briefly took command of C Squadron after Captain Hornby was wounded in October. He left the Regiment on sick leave on December 14th 1914 and did not return, being transferred to the infantry in 1915.

2. Captain Fitzgerald was born and raised at Wexford in Ireland. The son of a wealthy family, he attended Eton College, and joined the 4th Dragoons straight from military college in 1907. At the outbreak of war he had been given a dispensation to marry, and a special ceremony had been held before the Regiment left for France. He had already ridden his luck when, during the battle of Mons, he was slightly wounded by a machine gun bullet which slit his cheek open. He was the first officer in the Regiment to lose his life.

3. The owner, Madame Loetitia Supply, then thirty six years old, was to face a sad future. Of the three civilians killed in Moulins during the war, two were members of her family, Blanche and Lucien, killed almost certainly by a shell which hit their home. Today their names appear on the village war memorial. The village itself underwent sporadic attack for much of the war, during which both her estaminet, the Café de la Gaîté, and barn were destroyed. The street, the Rue de la Fontaine, was, like most of the village, rebuilt after the war but, perhaps for obvious reasons, Madame Supply's home was not. Madame Supply continued to live in the village until her death in September 1950 when she was aged nearly seventy three. She now rests in the village cemetery.

4. During the confusion of the Retreat, both Regiments had been split up into isolated companies, the men following those officers left to lead them. These exhausted soldiers had collapsed in the streets of St Quentin, and slept where they lay, propped against walls or lying on pavements.

   The Dragoons had been acting as rearguard to the Division, covering the infantry's retreat, but had not expected to find any troops in the town. Arriving, Bridges posted two troops with machine guns to defend the town's approaches, and sent Lieutenant Harrison to assess the situation in St Quentin. He returned with the news that some 400 to 450 infantrymen were slumped on the cobblestones of the town's historic square, and all the way down the road to the

A very young
Benjamin (left)
in 1900.

Riding 'General'
in Danny Park,
April 1913.

Little Dene, Beddingham, near Lewes in Sussex, c. 1912. In the centre is Sidney Clouting, Ben's cousin, who was killed in a disastrous attack by the 1/5th Sussex on Aubers Ridge, May 9th 1915.

A raw recruit at Seaforth, Ben poses for a picture in his full dress uniform.

Captain Charles Beck Hornby (1883–1949), second in command of C Squadron, led the first attack by British troops on continental Europe for 99 years.

Church Parade, June 1914. Ben is third from the left.

Stables, May 1914. Left to right
Rear Row: Perkins, Bell, Unknown, Unknown
Front Row: Clouting, Sharp, Unknown

Stables, c. 1914.

The 4th R.I.D. Co
Ready for the German War 1914

A last picture before leaving Tidworth.

The consummate soldier, Adrian Carton de Wiart VC (1880–1963), wounded numerous times during the war.

Lieutenant Pat Fitzgerald (1886–1914). Married as war broke out, he became the first officer of the Regiment to be killed in action, September 13th 1914.

Trumpeter Patterson sounded the bugle for 'Troops Right Wheel' at Audregnies, but was captured after the attack.

(*Left*) Hitherto unidentified picture of a regiment disembarking at Boulogne, featured in 'The War Illustrated', but now known to be men of A Squadron, 4th Dragoon Guards, leaving HMT Winifredian.

The sugar factory, mid-way between Audregnies and Quiévrain.

Standing right, Pte Thomas Cumber, rescued under fire by Ben during the charge at Audregnies, August 24th 1914, was nevertheless taken prisoner. Photographed at Muncheberg POW camp, 40 miles east of Berlin.

Madame Supply, right, holding the baby, stands in front of her estaminet and barn. For two days she was to hide Ben and Lt Harrison, the 4th Dragoons' Intelligence Officer, under the noses of the Germans.

A farmhouse at Mont Notre Dame, south of the Aisne. Ben and Lt Harrison stayed overnight here in the company of some French Dragoons in September 1914.

Left to right, C Squadron's Tilney, Frost and Jervis.

4th Dragoon officers in the trenches at Vlamertinge 1915.

(*Right*) 4th Dragoon officers in Querrieu Wood, 1916.

(*Bottom Right*) Captain Hornby at Cerseuil, September 1914.

Left to right, Lt Aylmer, Lt Gallaher, Major Sewell, and Capt McGillycuddy, November 1914.

In billets at Sailly la Bourse.

Part of a letter written by Capt Hornby to Capt Carton de Wiart in which Ben's strength of character was mentioned at length.

The château at Potijze where Ben brought the injured de Wiart, and where he was to return the same night with the body of his friend Frank (Mickey) Lowe.

(*Below Left*) The Commonwealth War Graves signpost to Château Lawn Cemetery, where Lowe still rests.

(*Below Right*) Frank Lowe's grave, eighty years after he was killed by a stray bullet while walking on the Zonnebeke Road.

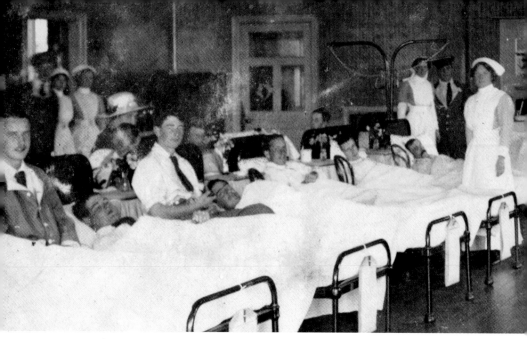

Queen's Ward, Graylingwell Hospital, circa July 1915. Ben is on the left, wearing a white shirt and tie.

Ben, top right, with a group of wounded soldiers, poses for a picture in the landscaped grounds of Graylingwell Hospital, August 1915.

MISSING TERRITORIAL.

———:o:———

PRIVATE S. CLOUTING.

Private Ben Clouting, 4th Dragoon Guards, son of Mr. and Mrs. Clouting, Littledene, near Lewes, who was wounded on Whit Monday, is still in Graylingwell Hospital, Chichester. His photograph appeared in a recent issue of the " Sussex Express."

His cousin, Private S. Clouting, No. 2462, 5th Batt. Royal Sussex Regiment, whose portrait appears above, has been missing since May 9th. Will any reader of the " Sussex Express " who has information of him kindly send same to 8, Cornfield-road, Reigate?

A newspaper cutting appealing for news on Ben's cousin, Sidney Clouting, missing since May 9th 1915. No trace of Sid was ever found.

The newspaper cutting dated July 1916 which blew across a field to Ben while he was waiting for rations at a brigade dump. Incredibly, it featured his father (far left) and his mother (4th right).

nich does so much to help the Actors' Orphanage Fund, | costers, drove from Daly's Theatre in a donkey cart. Th
rday. Mr. Lauri de Frece and Miss Alban, attired as | (*Daily Mirror* and L.N.A.)

SHEETS AS SUBSTITUTES FOR CARTS: A WAR-TIME EXPEDIENT.

our was scarce and horses unprocurable, so these women "carted" the hay from six acres in sheets. The photograph was taken at Croxley Green, Herts.

Home leave in 1917 at Croxley Green. The Clouting family moved here in 1916 after the riding accident to Ben's father.

Paris Plage, 1917. The two Bens, Ben Clouting (right) with Ben Spooner.

Were these the soldiers whom Lieutenant Stanley and the men of Ben's troop met on the Hohenzollern bridge on December 6th 1918?

The fighting over, A Squadron rides on to the Platz in front of Cologne Cathedral. The 4th (Royal Irish) Dragoon Guards had been the first troops to enter Germany, six days before.

May 1919, The 50th (Northumbrian) CCS, Huy. Ben, critically ill after an appendix operation, is being taken to a ward to die. He is carried by four German prisoners of war.

The same place today, off the Rue Grégoire Bodart, Huy. In 1919 the buildings were part of a teacher training college before being taken over as a hospital.

The opening of the memorial to the first action of the war, August 21st 1939 at Casteau. From left to right, L/Cpl JW Stevens, Unknown, Pte Mawson, Cpl Regan, Pte Rootes, Trumpeter Patterson, Corporal Tilney, Captain Hornby, Pte Clouting. All the men in this picture were either wounded or taken prisoner during the 1914-18 war.

The lady in the chauffeur-driven car, Louise Donnay de Casteau, (front right). Moments after the BEF's first encounter with the Germans, she asked Captain Hornby if she might go on duty at Mons.

The memorial shortly before its unveiling by Major-General Mullens, who commanded the Regiment when it went to France in August 1914.

Ben during a visit in May 1990.

Ben looks down the road to the village of Casteau where 1st Troop, C Squadron, engaged the enemy on August 22nd 1914.

The Menin Gate, Ypres. Ben stands under the names of a few of his Regiment who have no known graves.

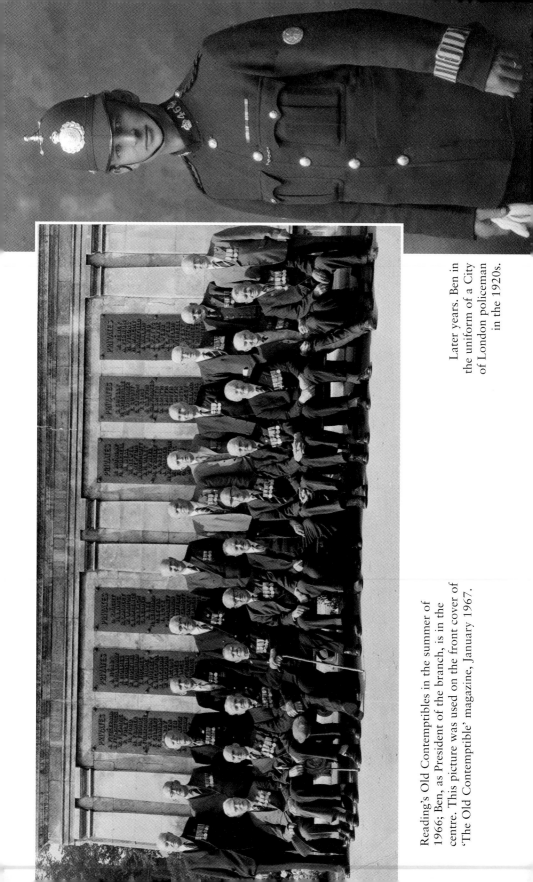

Later years. Ben in the uniform of a City of London policeman in the 1920s.

Reading's Old Contemptibles in the summer of 1966; Ben, as President of the branch, is in the centre. This picture was used on the front cover of 'The Old Contemptible' magazine, January 1967.

The Old Contemptibles' final pilgrimage, May 1990: Ben lays a wreath in memory of fallen comrades.

Enjoying lunch in Ypres with fellow Old Contemptible Archie Stanley (left).

Where it all started - Ben is filmed next to the house where the first shot was fired.

31st May 1990: a final parade before boarding the coach home. Standing L to R: William Thompson, Benjamin Clouting, Fred Dixon, Frank Sumpter, Tom Sharpe, Johnny Morris, Joe Armstrong, Victor Holden and Basil Farrer. Sitting L to R, G B Jameson, Bill Humphrey, Archie Stanley. Rear centre is Brigadier GMS Sprake, the then Honorary Secretary of the Old Contemptibles Association and to the right is Laura Parke, widow of Old Contemptible Charlie Parke.

Gatekeeper's lodge

Germans

La Roquette Château wall

Dragoons dismount here and fan out

LOOKING NORTH FROM CASTEAU

The location of the first shots between British and Germans troops, 22nd August 1914.

As the action began, Ben led his and three other horses behind this wall.

Château wall

Gatekeeper's lodge

Dragoons dismount here and the horses are taken under cover

Gateway

Horses taken behind the Château wall

Dragoons

The Dragoons fanned out on both sides of the road. Corporal Edward Thomas is credited with firing the first shot of the British Expeditionary Force from this spot.

LOOKING SOUTH FROM THE DIRECTION OF SOIGNIES

The Germans' point of view: looking south towards British positions. It was here that the retiring German cavalry halted and opened fire.

Dragoons dismount here

Germans halt here and open fire

LOOKING WEST

The charge of the 4th (Royal Irish) Dragoon Guards was driven to the right by heavy German fire (right).

LOOKING SOUTH

Under very heavy fire, and in increasing disarray, the Dragoons crossed the old Roman road.

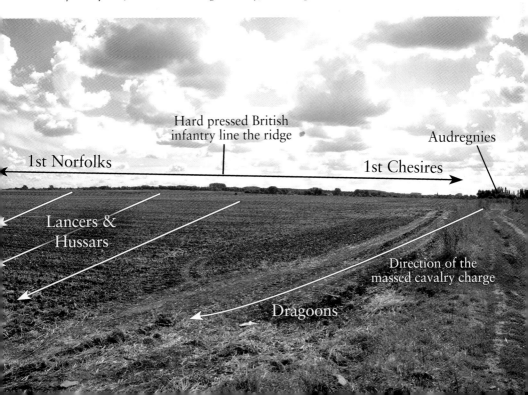

German Infantry and Artillery Batteries

Grounds of the
sugar factory

Remains of an old slag heap
used as cover to return fire

Old
Roman
road

LOOKING NORTH

In these fields, Ben Clouting's horse was shot from under him. He managed to stop a loose horse belonging to the 9th Lancers and, remounted, he rode out of the action.

LOOKING NORTH EAST

Ben headed towards the railway line in the middle distance, where he found Thomas Cumber badly wounded. Both men escaped the action although Cumber was taken prisoner soon afterwards.

German Infantry

German Batteries

Trees denote the line of the railway cutting

The cavalry is forced east towards the railway line and the village of Elouges

Sugar factory

train station from where the staff of the BEF's GHQ had left for Noyon on the last train that morning. Many of the men had had no food for two days or more, and had cast away their equipment. Some had been given white wine by friendly locals, and were now drunk; a few had been taken in, two sleeping the sleep of the dead under a couch in a chemist's back parlour.

Other than those of the Warwicks and Dublin Fusiliers, there were stragglers from several regiments, and at first few were in a mood to be moved on. 'Our old man has surrendered to the Germans, and we'll stick with him. We don't want any bloody cavalry interfering,' shouted one. Scarcely one soldier saluted any of the Dragoons' officers, and one is even recorded as pointing a rifle in Bridges' direction. Undeterred, Bridges spoke to the Mayor, asking him to requisition all available transport in the town in which to evacuate the troops. Ignoring the Mayor's protests that the men had already surrendered, Bridges took a copy of the incriminating note signed by Elkington and Mainwaring.

It was at this point that Bridges had had the idea of a toy band. Striking up with 'The British Grenadiers' and 'Tipperary', Bridges and his trumpeter walked around the square's fountain. 'I stopped playing and made them a short exhortation and told them I was going to take them back to their regiments,' recalled Bridges.

Eventually, wrote Osburn, 'We persuaded one of the colonels to march in front of his men. My recollection is that he looked very pale, entirely dazed, had no Sam Browne belt and leant heavily on his stick.'

It was after midnight when the long trail of troops finally left the town in thickening fog, Bridges leading the way. As they left, Osburn realised that his map-case was missing and returned 'to look for it in the now deserted Grande Place. As I sat on my horse alone there, taking a last look round, I heard an ominous sound – the metallic rattle on the cobbles of cavalry entering the town through one of the darkened side streets that led into the Grande Place.'

The following day, both Lieutenant-Colonels were relieved of their commands and subsequently court martialled on September 11th and 12th, at Chouy. Both were charged with 'Scandalous Conduct', the decision of the court being that both were guilty and would be cashiered.

Losing his battalion, Elkington joined the French Foreign Legion in which he served with distinction, being badly wounded in the leg. He was awarded the Croix de Guerre and the Médaille Militaire by the French and, as a result of his bravery, he was reinstated to his former rank by King George V in August 1916 and awarded a DSO.

John Ford Elkington was forty eight years old at the outbreak of war. Born in 1866 in Jamaica, he was educated in Guernsey before passing out of military college in 1885. He joined the Royal Warwickshire Regiment in 1886, serving as a Major in South Africa in 1900 and 1901, where he was awarded the Queen's South Africa Medal with four clasps. In 1904 he was made Lieutenant-Colonel, a rank he held when he took command of the first battalion in February 1914. He married relatively late in life, in 1908, and had a son the following year. After the war he chose never to wear his medals and walked with a pronounced limp for the rest of his life.

Mainwaring was two years older than Elkington, and had joined the Dublin Fusiliers in 1885. Like his counterpart, he served with his regiment for the next thirty years, going to South Africa in 1900, and taking command of the 2nd Dublin Fusiliers in March 1912. Unlike Elkington, Mainwaring was reinstated neither during nor after the war. Little is known of the rest of his life except that he retired to Derbyshire and died aged sixty six in 1930.

The events at St Quentin achieved great notoriety, with a four-verse poem, 'The Toy Band' being written by Sir Henry Newbolt, to which music was added by Sir Richard Paget. In 1994 an excellent book, *Dishonoured*, by Peter T. Scott, was published, giving the most detailed account yet of the events of that day.

CHAPTER SIX

Knee Deep in Mud

Ben
The Regiment remained in winter billets until January 1915 when Squadron and Troop training was begun again in earnest. The following month, training was stepped up as a move into the trenches in front of Ypres was expected at any time. As an officer's orderly, I avoided much of this training. However, in early February I was detailed to attend a course in the use of trench mortars, to be given by the 1st Field Squadron, Royal Engineers.

Long before the advent of Stokes mortars, we were shown a primitive contraption, made of what appeared to be a four-inch drain pipe welded to a base. At the bottom of the pipe there was a touch hole like that of the old muzzle-loading rifle, and to the side a primitive ratchet system to lever the mortar tube up and down. As we crowded round this object, we wondered at its construction while a sergeant began to talk us through its use. Several canvas gunpowder bags were to be dropped to the bottom of the tube, one of the mortar team piercing a bag so that a little gunpowder appeared at the touch hole. A plug of putee-like stuff called lutin was pressed around the touch hole and a fuse added, cut to a length so as to allow the team time to take cover. The bomb itself was ten inches long and had a wooden nose cone and a screw eye into which we hooked a piece of wire, enabling us to lower the bomb into the tube. Another fuse was cut and attached to the underneath of the bomb, the length of which varied according to the time required before detonation. Only then was the bomb carefully lowered into the barrel, making sure the fuse wasn't dislodged. The outside fuse which ran to the touch hole was lit by thick fusee matches, half-covered in phosphorous and developed to stay alight even in the windiest conditions. Once the fuse was lit, we were meant to clear off; the gunpowder both launching the missile and simultaneously lighting the fuse on the end of the bomb. The number of gun powder bags determined the distance the bomb was hurled, the maximum range being, I believe, no more than 200 yards.

The weather was quite good, and the ground dry, helping us to hone our skills for about a week before the Regiment took the trench mortar into the line, near Zillebeke. In the end I wasn't part of the team that fired the weapon in action, although I was to see a couple of rounds fired, watching them turn over and over as they flew, the fuse clearly fizzing on the outside.

During our training, we had not sought much cover as dummy bombs had been used. With live firing the team was more cautious, nipping round the corner into the next trench traverse. This was a wise move, for after the first half-a-dozen rounds a bomb detonated in the mortar, and blew the whole thing up on the spot. It was a sudden and violent end to our week's training, although thankfully no one was injured.

We remained in the line for a few days, when the principal danger was posed by snipers who killed at least one man while we were there and injured several others. After we were relieved, we were briefly employed digging trenches before a move to rest billets. A month before the German offensive at Ypres, Howell left the 4th Hussars,[1] and, one week later, I was allowed to rejoin the 4th Dragoons who were billeted on a prominent hill, known as the Mont des Cats. I had no sooner returned than Carton de Wiart rejoined the Regiment, taking command of A squadron, and asking me to look after his horses. I had not seen him since his visits to the Brands' stables, over two years before. In the meantime he had been sent to Somaliland at the outbreak of war, and in action had lost an eye, in place of which he now wore a patch.

Editor

After a period of recuperation, Captain de Wiart had left England for the Cavalry Base Depot at Rouen on March 31st 1915. However, eager to get to the front, he had travelled the same day to find the Regiment which was living, as de Wiart wrote, 'a comparatively dull life within sound of the guns of Ypres'. The War Diary merely states that the troopers were primarily engaged in rifle practice at a newly-installed rifle range at a Trappist monastery.

Ben

As soon as I took over de Wiart's horses, I joined up with the other orderlies billeted in a barn, close to the officers' quarters. These were towards the bottom of the hill in a small farmhouse, while the rest of the Regiment lived nearer a Trappist monastery, on top of the Mont des Cats.

This area was almost unmarked by war, having been the scene of just one brief fight late the previous year, when the 4th Hussars had been one of the regiments used in its capture. As a result the local farmers had stayed on the land, and a fairly normal life had resumed. Every Thursday, the farmer we lived with built a terrific fire in a big oven to bake bread. One or two of us would muck in to help knead the dough before it was placed in large bread troughs to bake. The bread was rather different from ours: flat rather than wide, with a cross made on top of the loaf so that when it was ready, a chunk could be easily hacked out of it. Helping the farmer bake the bread was his saucy fifteen-year-old daughter. She'd been taught all manner of rude words by the soldiers living in the area, and was not embarrassed to use them. *'Qu'est-ce que c'est*, cock?' she once took me aback with.

The farmers lived a traditional and to our minds, a primitive life. Like the urinals I had seen at Damousies, six months before, sanitation was basic. The farm on which we stayed had an open-air toilet cut into a rising footpath that led up to the farm barn, barely hidden for privacy by a canvas screen. This pathway was quite wide, into which a circular hole (about fifteen inches in diameter) had been dug to act as the toilet. In front were two foot marks, to guide the occupant to the perfect 'gun site' with droppings going straight into a pit underneath. Below the pathway, shuttered wooden doors had been built alongside the pit. These were opened once a year to allow the contents to flow or be shovelled into the midden. From there, the excrement would be carried away in carts and used as manure on the fields ploughed by the farmer's four large bullocks.

All manner of things were put in the pit. I saw some kittens dropped into the midden, while on another occasion I watched an old woman carry a couple of young puppies up the pathway, before throwing them in. The dogs' mother had followed the puppies up the path, but was shooed away by the old lady, who flapped her arms around aggressively, as she swore at the dog.

In France, the dog was an integral part of village and farm life and was not a luxury. Animals earned their keep, those that did not, or were surplus to requirements, had harsh and usually short lives. On the Mont des Cats, as with many villages we came to during the war, it was common to see the local milkman going round not with a pony but with a large dog as his main mode of transport. This dog would plod along, harnessed into a cart, on the back of which stood the village's milk churn. When not pulling the milk, the dog worked the butter churn. To the encouragement of *'Vite, Vite!'* the dog ran on a wheel like a treadmill, the motion of which turned the churn over and over, forming the butter.

While billeted in these towns and villages, we were paid in French or Belgian francs, lining up once a week to receive a five franc note, exchangeable anywhere and worth the equivalent of

Paper money printed and distributed by the various Belgian and French Chambers of Commerce, such as existed at Lille and Amiens. Soldiers could spend the notes only in the area in which they were issued, ensuring that many troops carried unspent notes with them in the hope of returning later.

five shillings. Once this money was broken into, however, we received smaller 'local' currency, or tokens with face values as little as ten centimes. This currency was manufactured by the various Chambers of Commerce such as existed in Amiens or Lille, and would be valid for a stated number of towns or communes and therefore of no value elsewhere. This meant we were forced either to spend our money before leaving the district or to keep it tucked into our haversacks in the hope that we would return a month or two later.

Editor
Like the Hussars, the Dragoons had had a fairly quiet time since the battles for Messines the previous October and November. They had spent a lot of time in the Bailleul area, refitting and training, during which time the winter monotony was broken up by inter-squadron and inter-troop sports. While the ranks had played football, some of the officers had hunted with the 2nd Cavalry Brigade Beagles, or had gone shooting with the Regiment's Machine Gun Officer, Lieutenant Aizlewood. He had had the forethought to bring out his own sporting rifles to France at the back end of 1914, but then to his, and the Regiment's, considerable frustration, the French banned hunting for the duration of the war, so the rifles and the beagles were reluctantly sent home. Beagling was exchanged for partridge chasing, and shooting for poaching, which provided the officers' mess on several occasions with welcome food.

Ben
To local people, soldiers were an undoubted mixed blessing. Behind the lines, British soldiers brought much money into local economies, with estaminets in particular making healthy profit from the coffee and omelettes served up by the thousand. Yet there was an undoubted downside too, for British and Empire soldiers were trying to liberate French and Belgian soil and many therefore had few qualms about poaching or stealing food to supplement otherwise poor diets. Some men became experts at procuring food, not least a corporal in C Squadron, 'Nasty' Carter of 1st Troop. He became known as the best scrounger in the Corps of Cavalry, and stories abounded within the Regiment of his antics.

The best known concerned an occasion when he had led a group of troopers to a local river in search of fish. The water being too low, 'Nasty' suggested shutting off the sluices, before fishing could begin in earnest. His clever idea, however, resulted in localised flooding, the guard reporting during the night that the horse lines were under water, with several dozen fish flapping about everywhere. Local villagers were known to have made any number of informal complaints to the Regiment about over-active scrounging in the area, but as officers too were often involved, they received little sympathy. Shortly before I returned to the Regiment, a funny incident had occurred when local peasants armed with various agricultural implements were seen chasing the new Medical Officer, Ingram, and Lieutenant Gallaher across muddy fields, both officers handicapped by struggling salmon, stuffed down the front of their breeches.

This incident raised Gallaher's stock even higher with the men. Gallaher was tremendously popular but particularly among those of his Troop, for he was a member of the famous tobacco family and his men never went short of a smoke. He was a brave man who was badly wounded on several occasions during the war. My abiding memory of him is of a scratch rugby game he organised, days after my return to the Regiment.

The game included both officers and men, something unthinkable before the war, and naturally included Gallaher, who by all accounts was a very good player. He produced a rugby ball and brought together two teams of anyone willing to have a go, although barely anyone knew the rules. Coming from the Sussex countryside, I could not recall having ever seen a game before, so I watched from the improvised touchline. Troopers went hurtling in all directions and tactics went west. In the midst of it all was Gallaher trying valiantly to bring about some sort of order. In one almighty scramble for the ball, however, he was heard to bellow, 'For God's sake, man, let go of my bloody ear!' underlining how hopeless his task was, and sending all who had heard it into fits of laughter.

To stiffen the resolve of the men behind the lines, they attended church services, given by a padre, in our case the Reverend Gibb, a padre who had been attached to the Regiment from the earliest days of the war. Services were often impromptu affairs, held in some field where we sang hymns such as 'Onward Christian Soldiers', and 'Fight The Good Fight', before listening to a morale-boosting sermon given by Gibb or perhaps a visiting padre. One particular padre, I recall, began his sermon with the words, 'Put your minds at rest. To start with, I'm 6 foot 5 inches, now that will stop you wondering how tall I am and you'll listen to what I've got to say.'

Padres to the cavalry were amiable men, but few were horsemen. Being in the cavalry, we could tell a horseman from the very moment he got on a horse, even in the way he got hold of the reins, or put his foot in the stirrup. One padre, I remember, was given the most docile horse the Regiment could find, and even then he had to be taught how to get on and off the old sheep. Later, I overheard this padre saying to Welch, our veterinary officer, that he'd seen his horse scratch his ear with his hind leg. Welch answered with apparent sincerity that this was a sure sign his horse had appendicitis. 'Are you sure that's what you saw?' Welch asked again, giving me a quick wink. The padre became quite concerned, 'Yes, yes, I'm sure.' I wasn't around for the conclusion of this enlightening discussion.

Throughout the war I tried to keep in touch with my family as regularly as possible, sending a note of how I was whenever we were out of the line. One of the quickest ways was on a printed Field Postcard, on which the soldier was only allowed to scrub out the official words, 'I am well/not well', 'I have/have not heard from you lately', that sort of thing. The soldier was only meant to date and sign it at the bottom, though some added the odd caustic word or two if they had not heard much for a while, one Irishman, I recall, writing 'never' when he came to 'I have received your parcel dated . . .' These cards were issued to us, one each, at regular intervals and were posted with the quartermaster. He passed them on to the duty officer for checking, destroying any which broke the strict rules on adding anything other than permitted. Letters were also censored by our troop officers, who must have become bored rigid, reading personal letter after personal letter before initialling envelopes and sending them on. To help matters all round, we were issued once a month with a green envelope, in which we could seal a letter knowing that it wouldn't be read by anyone in the Regiment. We were put on our honour not to reveal anything secret, signing the envelope to that effect. Most reached their destination sealed, although a sample was opened at the base to check soldiers were not abusing the trust. These envelopes were primarily aimed at married men, who felt they could not write anything personal to their wives when it would be read by others in the Regiment.

Receiving letters was more sporadic, mail being the last thing looked after when the Regiment was in the line. Letters arrived, but rumours abounded, both in France and back home, that parcels were robbed for chocolate and other foodstuffs. For this reason many troopers received disguised parcels. While we were in Nissen huts at Vlamertinge, a parcel arrived from my mother, on the outside of which was written 'comics'. 'Blimey,' I thought, 'who wants comics to read?' only to discover that my mother had used the comics as wrapping for a blackberry and apple tart. As there were several men who never received anything while in France, men who came from orphanages and the like, it was only fair that those who received parcels from home shared out the contents, particularly food.

Vlamertinge was one of the villages regularly used for billeting when the Regiment was out of the line. The cavalry often stayed farther behind the line than the infantry, as we had the luxury of riding as close as possible to the line before dismounting and entering the communication trenches, which twisted their way towards the front line. Similarly, as the Regiment left the line, it was met by the horses ridden up from the back areas, a job I undertook on several occasions. It was not necessarily an easy task. One frosty, moonlit evening we set out from Vlamertinge, each man riding one horse and leading three others. But no sooner had we hit the icy road than it became clear the horses were unable to keep their grip, so we were pulled up and told to put two frost cogs in the front two shoes of every horse.

Every horse shoe had nine holes for nails and four for variously-sized frost cogs, two cogs (size four) at the toe and two (size five) at the heel. As a matter of course, these holes had been filled with tow (strands of old rope, available from the farrier's tool kit) and were packed in place by dirt once the horse had replaced its foot on the ground. Every hole was threaded so that each frost cog could easily be screwed in like a little bolt, giving horses a better footing on icy ground, in the same way studs give footballers grip on a bad pitch.

The frost cogs were arrow-shaped, and sharp when new. Each was an inch long, including the thread, and was carried in a separate compartment in the sword frog. The frog also held the frost cog spanner, the tool designed to fix the cogs in place. The spanner was pointed at one end, so as to clean the tow out of the screw holes, while at the other end, the tool was stubbed with a square-shaped hole used to tighten the cogs.

Despite the moonlight, the relative darkness and intense cold made fitting cogs no easy job. The chill began to affect my fingers, gradually making them numb. I managed to misthread one cog and as I strained to tighten it my hand slipped, slicing it open across my palm. There was nothing more I could do but pass my spanner to someone else and try and stem the blood with my red and white spotted handkerchief. The handkerchief was filthy, but I had no choice but to keep it wrapped around my hand while we remounted and rode on. I was lucky, for it bled badly enough that I didn't catch an infection, before I had it seen to by the Medical Officer.

The trenches the Regiment occupied at this time were little more than shallow ditches joined together, and looked nothing like trenches ought to have done. There were no neat traverses, by which we could stop enfilade fire down the line, or localise the serious effects of a shell explosion in the trench. There were no parapets or paradoses to speak of, nor fire steps on which men could stand to peer out into No Man's Land. Instead, there was a quagmire of shallow holes in the ground, filled with oozing mud, for so shallow was the water table in the Ypres area that it was impossible to dig down more than a couple of feet without hitting water. Trenches, such as they were, had to be built partially above the land, but as often as not they were still waterlogged, with liquid mud coming up to our knees.

On entering the line we spread ourselves out. I always tried to team up with Spider Stevens. He was around six feet two inches tall, and when together we always tried to build up what passed for a parapet with sandbags. This we did as a precaution, for taller men tended to fall prey to a sniper's bullet more often than the smaller men, who did not have to crouch as far down. It was an incredible existence; it is impossible to describe just what it felt like to wear the same clothes day after day, all of us hopelessly lousy, without a bath in two months. At times we lived almost like animals. No one ever took any notice if a man was having a crap in the trench. Everyone was in the same situation; there was no privacy. In some trenches there might be a little recess for a latrine, or in quieter sectors we might even crawl over the parados to go in a shell hole behind the trench, but more often than not we simply went on a shovel and chucked it over the top.

All the time we were in the line, our bodies festered underneath our clothes. We were never allowed to remove our boots until out of the line, when we found half the sock came with the foot, half stopped where it was, stinking and rotten. As a result, trench foot was a major problem. The constant cold and wet affected the blood's circulation to the toes in particular, causing men's feet to swell disgustingly, turning them blue, then black. Bad cases had to be evacuated out of the line, and in the worst cases doctors were forced to amputate. Many techniques were adopted to avoid getting bad feet. Behind the line, where foot care was easier, I deliberately took size eleven boots, instead of my usual nine. This way I could pack my boots with lengths of straw, to keep my feet warm, just as I had seen French peasants do with their clogs, or 'sabots' as they were known. If straw wasn't available, newspaper would do just as well. When the weather was very bad, it was common to see a man with sandbags wrapped around his feet or tied around his puttees to protect his legs.

In an attempt to protect our feet, Wellington boots, or Trench

Waders, were issued to us. These came in just two sizes, nine and eleven, sufficient, the authorities obviously assumed, for all sizes of soldier. Attached to the top of these boots were two pieces of string which we held on to if we walked anywhere, for the suction power of the mud was so great that without them our feet would simply have left the boots.

When it rained, we wore our groundsheets. Before the war these had been rectangular, six foot by three foot, 'hearth rug' affairs; now they had been re-designed to form a cape around the shoulders. These groundsheets still had a rubber coating, but whereas at one time we had lain them on the ground to keep out the condensation or early morning dew, they now protected us from the worst of the rain that pattered against them or fell in rivulets from our caps. Worn as a macintosh, the groundsheet was a treasured possession and kept spirits up in the never-ending struggle to hold off the worst of the weather.

We lived in these extraordinary conditions for several days and nights, wet, cold and hungry, without even the comfort of a proper drink of tea. The food was never properly cooked and always filthy, while sometimes the hard biscuits we received as food supplements turned out to be the only food we got. These biscuits were so tough they required soaking in our tea before they softened enough to be eaten. Even then I pitied the poor devils with false teeth, for the two biscuits they received as a day's ration often proved beyond their capacity to break down. Some other biscuits we occasionally received were easier to eat but looked identical to the dog food, Spiller's Shapes, and became a standing joke with the troops.

In the front line, it could be lethal to give away the faintest trace of smoke or, at night, even a flicker of light. Making even lukewarm cups of tea was therefore a real art. One technique was to use four candle stumps stuck together with jam. Over this a billy can of water was held, which warmed slowly. It was important to ensure the flame was clean to avoid any smoke, though now and again when we could get hold of them, we used naphtha pellets, a white waxy substance that we could burn as an alternative to a naked flame. It was possible to have a smoke, but as a sniper could fix on a naked flame from anything up to a mile and a half away, at night we had to be very careful. As a solution, many used a simple style of lighter with a long wick half an inch thick. The wick wasn't lit by the flint but smouldered enough to light a cigarette or pipe, a small metal cap at the end of the lighter snuffing out any lingering burning. In the support lines there were fewer immediate dangers, for although still close to the German lines, we were far enough behind to risk brewing up warmer tea in a dixie. On these occasions a sandbag full of charcoal would be brought up, the dixie standing in amongst the smouldering charcoal which burnt slowly with a few wood chippings.

Clean water for tea or anything else was one of the most precious commodities in or out of the line, the general lack of it ensuring that we remained both thirsty and grimy. It was not unusual to go a couple of weeks without a good wash or shave, with annoying results should the hook at the top of our greatcoats catch in the whiskers on our neck or chin. When water was obtained for shaving, it was held, preciously, in a small tin and passed round for all to use. Now and again small tins of Ideal Milk appeared at the front, the lids of which were turned back as improvised handles. Filled with water, the tin stood in the ashes of the cook's fire or was held over candles in support lines to warm just sufficiently for us to shave. Having shared the tin round, we used the rest of the water in tiny amounts to wash with.

Before the advent of metal screw pickets and concertina wire, wooden posts were hammered into the ground with barbed wire wrapped around and tacked to the post. Barbed wire was used in great amounts by both sides to protect the front line but, like everything else that was needed for the trenches, this wire had to be carried up the line. A coil weighed fifty or sixty pounds, and through its centre a stake was put, allowing a man to carry it on his back. Parties of men would be sent down the line to bring more supplies up, and almost always included one particular man, a farmer before the war, who was immensely strong. He was a one-man-mule, for although everyone joked about his slow steady pace, no matter how strenuous the work, he could be relied upon to keep going at the same speed all day long.

At night, the wire and wooden posts were taken in front of the trenches and banged into place with heavy two-handed mallets, one trooper holding the post, the other knocking it into position. Even without the occasional stifled yowl of pain as a mallet gave a glancing blow to a hand, it was impossible to work without making some noise. A tap, tap, tap sound was inevitable, but as the Germans were often busy doing similar work a couple of hundred yards away, both sides adopted a policy of live and let live and there was rarely any shooting.

It was a good sign when the Germans were clearly in front of their trenches, for it meant we could get on with our work and relax a little more. Similarly, when no tapping was to be heard across No Man's Land, everyone became more agitated, terse voices whispering to those making excessive noise to 'shut that bloody sound up!' Every now and again the Germans sent up a flare to check what was going on. These flares gave off a terrific light and only gradually faded, with those on miniature parachutes lasting anything up to three minutes, which actually felt even longer. As a general rule we tried to fall to the ground before the flare burst, otherwise we stood stock still, turning our faces away from the German lines. Illumination of any sort was bad news. There was a cartoon drawn by the artist Bruce Bairnsfather printed at the time and it captured the feeling exactly. It featured a girl looking up at the moon, 'And to think that it's the same dear old moon that's looking down on him!' she dreams, and there's her sweetheart putting up the barbed wire and saying, 'This blinkin' moon will be the death of us'.

Only on one occasion did I fully venture out into No Man's Land, when I was selected to crawl out to a listening post. Where the opposing lines were closest, there was an on-going risk of a massive explosion when a portion of the front line and everyone in it would be obliterated by the detonation of gun cotton laid in a chamber under the trench floor. It was my job to go out with one other man to listen for sounds of German mining or counter-mining. There was no blacking up, we just went with a cord to pull if we wished to signal back, the sergeant warning the rest of the Troop who was out there. Squirming over the parapet, we went under our wire crawling forward some fifty yards into No Man's Land. It was a lousy job. The trenches were about two hundred yards apart there, and our job was simply to lie for two to three hours with just an ear to the ground listening for noises. It was tiring and frightening being out there and I was more than happy when a relief tapped my foot to say I could crawl back.

Just before dawn we 'stood to', when every man was put on alert in case the Germans wished to launch a sudden attack. After we were 'stood down', we would eat whatever breakfast was available and begin the day. When all was quiet we might become quite bored, one or two of us peering out through loopholes into No Man's Land or indulging in a little sniping. At one part of the line, I spotted a gap in a hedge past which a German could be seen to walk every now and again. We had a lake in front of us, then a ploughed field, so the hedge was anything up to a thousand yards away, making sniping, at best, rather hit and miss. Not being deterred, I and another man set up a sniping post. There wasn't enough time for either of us to spot the German, then aim and fire, so we took it in turns to aim at the gap, firing instantly the other gave the command. It was impossible to tell if we hit anyone, but it was one way of whiling away some time.

When it was quiet most officers stuck to their dugouts, word being passed down that such and such officer wanted to see so and so, just the duty officer making periodic patrols to see if everything was all right. There was an officer whom no one liked very much. One morning when everything was still, a single pistol shot came from the small dugout in which he had been sleeping. Immediately people began whispering to each other, 'Thank God he's shot himself,' when, blissfully unaware of the talk up top, the officer emerged with a broad smile and the tail of a mutilated mouse held high between his thumb and forefinger. 'I've got the little blighter,' he said triumphantly, tossing the mouse over the top before disappearing back into the dugout.

Shortly after this episode, the Germans launched the battle of 2nd Ypres, beginning with the first gas attack in warfare. The date was April 22nd 1915. The Germans had attacked north of Ypres, around Langemarck, and in no time at all had broken through, sweeping up and over Pilkem Ridge, to within a couple of miles of Ypres. We saw the French soldiers straggling back, coughing and wheezing. They gesticulated to us and said, 'Gaz, Gaz, Gaz', but we didn't know what was going on.

The fighting for Ypres intensified over the following days, but the Regiment was not directly involved. For a couple of days in early May we became engaged in digging a new line, as well as improving existing reserve trenches on the canal north of Ypres. Leaving our horses, we moved up towards the front, picking up some tools on the way. The Germans were shelling the area intermittently with shrapnel, but during the course of both nights we were largely left alone. All obstacles were moved to ensure the new trenches had a clear line of fire. We worked extremely hard, encouraged by the news that the quicker we finished the work, the sooner we could be on our way back to billets. We were not to be out of the action for long.

Editor

Owing to the weakened state of the 28th Division, the 1st Cavalry Division was sent into the line in support. Both the 1st and 2nd Cavalry Brigades were to man part of the GHQ line which ran from behind Zillebeke to near Wieltje. On May 9th, the 4th Dragoons marched up to the GHQ line at Potijze, arriving at 1pm, where they were instructed to continue to the front line trenches, to relieve infantry of the 85th Brigade.

The exact position of the trenches was unknown and as the Dragoons were being subjected to desultory shelling, Sewell, Gallaher and de Wiart halted the Regiment on the Zonnebeke road, before going ahead to rendezvous with a Captain from the Brigade, who would lead them into the line.

Then, as de Wiart recalled, 'an ominous feeling began to creep over me that we were going too far, as I knew the Germans had not broken our line. Suddenly the silence was split by a cry of *"Halt"* in obvious German, and we were fired on at the same moment . . . the next second I found myself sprawling on the ground with a damaged hand. I caught hold of it but it seemed to be a gory mess.'

De Wiart was able to stagger back along the road. 'By this time,' wrote de Wiart, 'I was beginning to feel very weak, called out, and luckily my voice was recognised. Some men came out to pick me up, and took me to the dressing station.'

Ben

I was one of those who ran forward to carry de Wiart back out of the exposed position. A bullet had smashed through his wrist and hand, destroying his wrist watch, bits of which were mixed up among the remnants of flesh. I heard later that the doctors tried hard to save his hand, and at one time he still had a stump with two fingers, but in the end those too had to be taken off. Four of us carried him out along the Zonnebeke road. He had lost a lot of blood, though he didn't appear to be in much pain. We took him back to a white château, Potijze Château, an impressive house that was being used as a dressing station. It was built in extensive grounds and surrounded by trees which were gradually being ripped apart by shell fragments. The house itself was pitted but intact, despite being less than a mile from the front lines. We carried him through a doorway and into a large candlelit room, full of wounded men. There was a terrible stench and we were glad to leave, but as we did so, de Wiart, weak as he was, turned to me, saying, 'Goodbye, Clouting, I hope it isn't long before you are home'.

Editor

Soon after the incident, one young and very tired staff officer appeared and led the Dragoons into their positions. The Dragoons' War Diary notes that the road was unprotected on each side to a total width of 175 yards, with everything being at sixes and sevens. The Dragoons took over the line at 2am, and were forced rapidly to rebuild and extend the trenches with German machine gunners at work just 200 yards away in their front line. At dawn B Squadron attempted to bring up rations, led by Lieutenant Gibb who was sniped and blinded in the process. Gibb was later taken to Potijze Château where both he and de Wiart were evacuated by the 85th Field Ambulance.

For the next four days, the Dragoons remained either in or just behind the line, while farther south, across the Menin Road, the Germans focused their attention this time on the 27th Division, subjecting it to intense artillery bombardment and ferocious infantry attacks. In their efforts to force a breach in the British line, the bombardment on other sectors of the salient was only marginally reduced, with the 4th Division, in neighbouring trenches to those of the Dragoons, repelling several attacks, while the Dragoons suffered, on the 10th, a day of shelling and sniping which killed seven and wounded as many. The 4th Dragoons' War Diary records on May 10th 1915, 'A good deal of artillery and rifle fire during the night. 8am our trenches were again shelled for two and a half hours. From 1pm to 3pm there was a tremendous bombardment of the fire trenches to our right front. 2nd Cav Bde now under orders of the 27th Div.'

Ben

Any number of shells were landing near the trenches we occupied, causing casualties. To keep me busy I volunteered to be a stretcher bearer, a temporary job but one which kept my mind off what was happening around me. By this time the trench system was well established, but even so the front line and communication trenches were not always linked, and a hair-raising sprint could be required to reach another part of the trench system. Sniping was at a premium, and each night I had my work cut out carrying those who had been wounded earlier in the day back to the dressing station at Potijze Château.

Because of continual heavy shelling and the presence of snipers, all work took place at night. The wounded were kept in close proximity for fast evacuation during darkness, though in a landscape pitted by shells, two onerous trips a night were all that was possible for any one team of stretcher bearers. If at all possible, soldiers avoided carrying a stretcher in twos. Over a short distance two was all right; over a long way in the dark, over rough terrain, it was very difficult. Volunteers would scout round and try to build a team of four men of similar weight and size, for three big men and one small one, even if he was strong, made the stretcher uneven. A balanced team cut down the need for rests, enabling us to change positions and hands on a stretcher with as little upset as possible.

The Reverend Gibb was wounded at more or less the same time as de Wiart. He had been shot through the temple, I would guess by a sniper, and four of us, including Mickey Lowe from my Troop, were given our first job of the night, carrying him out. He was a brave man, and always willing to share the dangers that we faced in the front line. We carried him out reasonably conscious, but though he survived the war he never regained his sight.

On our return, we were given the task of carrying one of our Sergeants out of the line. Like Reverend Gibb, Sergeant Bob Arnold had been badly wounded by a sniper's bullet. I hadn't been with him when he was wounded, but by all accounts he had been careless for a split second and suffered the consequences. A German, darting between trenches, had been shot and bowled over like a rabbit. Someone had made a quip about it along the lines of 'That got the so and so', and with that Arnold burst out laughing, raising himself momentarily above the height of the trench, a bullet whisking through both cheeks. The bullet had miraculously missed his teeth but despite our best efforts to stem the flow, he had bled profusely all day, so that by nightfall he was in serious danger of bleeding to death. There seemed no way of treating in effect four wounds. We tried to stop the bleeding by bandaging the outside of his face only to find he nearly choked; the more blood he lost, the weaker he became, so that by nightfall he had slipped into unconsciousness.

Arnold was a solidly built man, and weighed fifteen stones, making him extremely heavy to carry. Despite the seriousness of his injury, we could only make our way back slowly and we were forced to take several brief rests in the process. The journey was completed successfully (for I later heard Arnold was alive and well) and our small party began the trudge back. We were all physically strong but were exhausted, so that after the briefest of walks we halted on the road for a rest and a cigarette.

We hadn't halted long, indeed we had only just lit up, when Mickey Lowe muttered to us, 'Anyone who gets through this war will be a lucky blighter'. Lowe was several years older than myself and wore a good conduct stripe on his sleeve, but his patience and nerves had worn under the pressure of the last few weeks.

Almost as soon as he had spoken, Mickey grunted, half spun round and fell backwards. I caught him underneath his arms and slid him down to the ground, blood literally pumping out onto my riding breeches. He had been hit in the middle of the back by a stray bullet. And that was it. He never mentioned another word, the bullet seemed to knock him straight out and within three or four minutes he was gone. This was a terrific shock for me, for although I saw others killed in that war, although I saw many men dead, I, like everyone, just thanked the Lord it wasn't me. But this was different. He was one of us, one from our Squadron, a nice likeable man.

We carried him back to the Château, where we borrowed a

shovel and dug a hole in the lawn about eighteen inches deep. We emptied his pockets and took his two identification discs. Then we removed his jacket and laid him in the grave. It sounds strange but despite all the obscenity of war, it's still difficult to shovel earth onto a dead man's face, so we used his jacket to cover him up, before filling the grave back in. As was normal, we used a stick or bayonet to mark his place and tied one of the identification disks around a makeshift cross. Usually the other tag was handed to the Regimental padre, but as Gibb was himself wounded, we passed on Mickey's last effects to one of our officers.[2] That night an exhausted Regiment was relieved by a battalion of the East Surrey Regiment, and made its way back to Ypres.

Editor
On May 12th, the 2nd and 3rd Cavalry Brigades were amalgamated into what was briefly known as de Lisle's Cavalry Force. That evening, the Cavalry Force's first role was to be sent back into the line, taking over the line held by the 28th Division, which had by this time lost some 15,000 men in the three weeks since 2nd Ypres had officially begun. This time it was the Dragoons' turn to remain in the close support trenches, while the 18th Hussars and 9th Lancers went into the front line, just south of Wieltje.

During the hours of darkness, improvements were made in the line, but most of this work came to nothing, as just before dawn it began to pour with rain; this was joined at 3.30am by a thunderous German bombardment which lasted until after midday. The combination of incessant rain and shells caused havoc in the front line, where trenches gave way and quickly became a quagmire of filth and water.

On May 14th the Cavalry Force was dissolved, rejoining the Cavalry Corps. The Dragoons returned to the forward line of trenches, replacing troops from the 27th Division, and exchanging time as Duty Regiment in the front line with the 18th Hussars and 9th Lancers. A lull in the fighting meant casualties were noticeably lower, although the living conditions remained dreadful.

Ben
There were times when we fired at nothing just to let the Germans know that we were still there, alive in our collapsed trenches, if not always well. It seems strange now, the thought of shooting someone, but at that time I was a trained soldier and that was my life: killing someone who was trying to kill me. It was a natural state of affairs and I never had any hesitation whatever in having a pot, whether at nothing in particular or when I was sniping.

Sniping wasn't cost-free. The constant irritation our activities caused could bring swift retaliation from the other side, from a machine gun, mortar, even a battery. We were in the front line one afternoon, and I was having a pot across No Man's Land at a point where a few moments earlier I thought I'd seen some movement. I had loosed off two or three shots when, from behind me, Corporal Muggeridge suddenly appeared and ordered me off what existed of the firestep, saying he was in charge and that I was to stop firing.

Muggeridge and I had never got on. Although he belonged to my Troop, he'd lived in an adjoining barrack room before the war, and I had come under another Corporal, Cushy Harrison. For some reason I seemed to have rubbed up Muggeridge the wrong way, for he never flinched from trying to make my life harder. I had had as little to do with him as possible, but he too had come out with the original Regiment and was now also in A Squadron, so our paths inevitably crossed.

In France, Muggeridge had got a reputation for being windy. He was patently scared stiff of being killed, and my firing had made him fearful that we might receive retaliatory shelling from the German lines. His order to step down should have been the end of the matter, but he couldn't resist adding, 'Remember, Clouting, Carton de Wiart is no longer here to protect you now.' This I took as an awful snub. On one occasion before the war, I had been referred to as 'Carton de Wiart's grandchild,' and this had hurt my pride. Now, out in France, where we all lived under similar dangers, I lost my temper. Raising my rifle above my shoulder, I went to strike Muggeridge with the butt end. I had intended to jab him in the face, but a private behind me grabbed hold of my rifle's stock and said, 'Don't do it, Ben'. It gave me time to think. I'd got witnesses to what he'd said so the matter was never reported, although if I had I struck him I would have been in terrible trouble.

Undoubtedly Muggeridge, like many men, was fed up to the teeth, but what he had said was different. Men swore and cursed as it was often the only way to give vent to their feelings, either that or get up on the firestep and give Jerry three or four rounds, in which case they might stop a bullet. You'd hear chaps saying they'd put a bullet through their foot, to give themselves a blighty one, but that was just talk. A self-inflicted wound was a very serious crime and while accidents did happen – my future brother-in-law was shot in the groin by someone cleaning his rifle – an SIW was a very risky course of action to take, as likely to end up in a Court Martial as a trip home.

There were many times when I was fed up, and there were times when I was very frightened too, especially when shells fell too close, but I was lucky. For much of the war I was an orderly and had breaks from the trenches to look after an officer's horses, and it made a difference, as I realise now. There were those men who simply could not take the strain any longer and cracked up. It was awful to see a man with shell shock. It often happened when a shell had dropped nearby, and there had been an awful explosion, but not always. I remember one man simply breaking down and crying like a baby during a relatively quiet lull in the fighting. His name was Galtress, a regular soldier, and a good one, affectionately nicknamed Golly because of his thick mop of black hair. He'd come out with the Regiment and had been through the Mons retreat and all its hardships. Now, during 1915, he had been in and out of the line several times and there had been no signs of his increasing fatigue. We were in trenches near Bellewaarde Lake, when suddenly he just cracked up. He didn't run away or anything like that, he just sat on the floor of the trench sobbing his heart out and trembling like a leaf. Occasionally, when he began to lose control, we would have to gently hold him down, while his Corporal tried to get him to pull himself together, but to little avail. Galtress had had enough. Later he was sent down the line and that was the last I ever saw of him.[3]

For most men, cigarettes were one of the best ways to calm taut nerves. Many chain-smoked Woodbines to keep them going, and they were the first thing a man turned to when injured or in fear. Whenever a man was short of a cigarette or in need of one to keep the spirits up, one could always be cadged from a friend. Padres who came into the front line were never short of smokes; one padre, Woodbine Willie, became famous for his tobacco handouts, while within the Regiment, Lieutenant Gallaher had cigarettes sent out direct from the factory. I was one of the few who disliked fags, preferring a cherrywood pipe instead. Like everyone else, I found it a good antidote to frayed tempers, and continued to smoke throughout the rest of the war. We were issued with Capstan tobacco, but although it smelled lovely it was a bit too strong, and tended to burn my tongue. French tobacco, on the other hand, was finely chopped, very mild and burned freely. Most farmers grew their own tobacco, shredding it themselves, and because it burned so easily, always overloaded their pipes with the stuff. We could buy it almost anywhere behind the lines for just a few coppers, and I usually had some loose in my jacket pockets.

Our spell in the line was up and we were to be relieved by an infantry battalion. The change-over had already begun and we were making our way down a narrow communication trench as we bypassed the incoming battalion. Communication trenches were narrow at the best of times, but with heavily-laden troops coming into the line, the trench became very congested. Struggling past, I became aware of a log jam ahead. One of our Troop cooks, a strapping man, was causing all sorts of confusion as he squeezed by each incoming soldier. There was grumbling, swearing, heaving, and pushing, when amongst all of this I heard a voice say, 'The next time I meet that fat-gutted bugger I'll lay down and let him walk over me!' It was never going to be an easy proposition, but patently he considered lying down in the mud less painful than ever squeezing past our cook again.

Editor

After the attacks on May 13th, the ferocity of enemy shellfire decreased within the Salient. Only minor attacks were made by the Germans, and shellfire by both sides had become little more than desultory. This state of affairs continued until May 24th, by which time it was generally accepted that the 'Second Battle of Ypres,' was over.

The Official History records that the night of May 23rd/24th was quiet, the most distinct sound being that of German transport apparently heading south. '. . . it would be light about 2.30am and the troops on duty stood to arms, as usual, some fifteen minutes earlier. At 2.45am the enemy sent up four red lights, followed by two others, whereupon heavy fire was opened by guns, machine guns and rifles.'

The barrage of fire was followed by a dense cloud of chlorine gas, forty foot high. It was the largest gas attack of the war so far, covering four and a half miles, or most of the Vth Corps' front, from Hooge in the south to Turco Farm in the north. So close were the opposing trenches that the hissing of gas as it was released from cylinders could be clearly heard. The History records: 'The wind was light and the gas cloud in consequence moved very slowly, and from the air seemed almost stationary over the trenches.'

The Dragoons had been in the line around St Jean when they were relieved, arriving back at Ypres at 1am.

Ben

We had come out of the front line during the night of the 23rd of May, utterly worn out, unshaven and filthy. Others in our Brigade had taken over our stretch of line, while we wearily trudged back under the cover of darkness to Ypres. We collected our rations and ate them ravenously, before we got our heads down for some well-deserved sleep beneath the arches of an old brewery cellar, close to the town's ramparts.

A little before 4am, urgent calls to 'Stand to, stand to' woke me to the sound of thunderous fire which had broken out all along

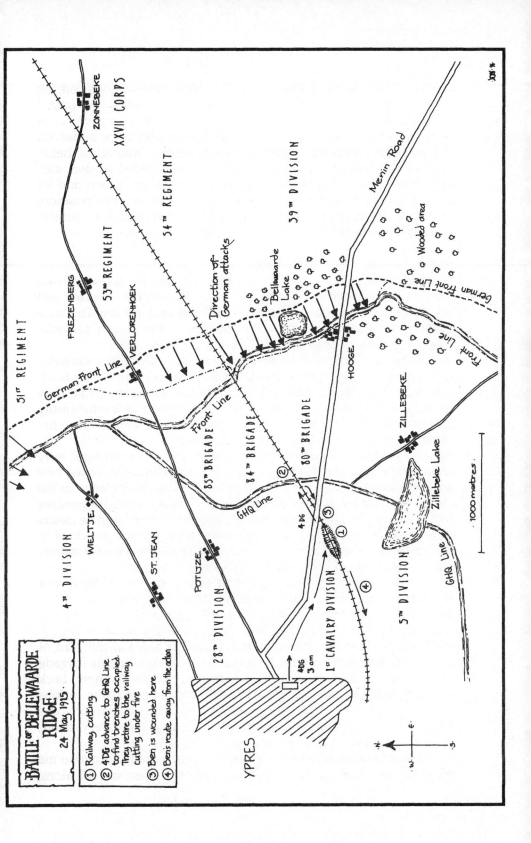

BATTLE of BELLEWAARDE RIDGE.
24 May 1915.

① Railway cutting
② 4DG advance to GHQ Line
to find trenches occupied.
They retire to the railway
cutting under fire
③ Ben is wounded here
④ Ben's route away from the action

YPRES

4 DIVISION

WELTJE

ST. JEAN

POTIZE

28TH DIVISION

406
3 am

1ST CAVALRY DIVISION

4 DG

② ① ③

④

5TH DIVISION

GHQ Line

Zillebeke Lake

ZILLEBEKE

GHQ Line

HOOGE

Front Line

Front Line

German Front Line

Bellewaarde Lake

Wooded area

German Front Line

80TH BRIGADE

84TH BRIGADE

85TH BRIGADE

Direction of
German attacks

39 DIVISION

Merin Road

54TH REGIMENT

53RD REGIMENT

VERLORENHOEK

FREZENBERG

51ST REGIMENT

XXVII CORPS

ZONNEBEKE

. 1000 metres .

N
W — E
S

the line. I was so tired I barely registered what was going on, but I somehow managed to haul myself to my feet, fumbling for my equipment.

It was light outside as we fell in under the ramparts, only to be dished out with extra equipment to carry up the line. I was detailed to draw the Troop rum in my waterbottle, and to carry 250 rounds of Vickers' machine gun ammunition packed in a wooden box, the strap of which I hooked on to the butt of my rifle and suspended over my shoulder. Others slung extra ammunition bandoliers around their necks, or trekked off with bags of bombs and cans of water.

The Germans had launched another gas attack and we had to go straight back to the front to close any gap in the line. There was a distinct whiff of gas in the air and our eyes were already smarting, so the order came round to don our gas masks. These masks were about the size of the palm of a hand, made of cotton wool and gauze. They had a little elastic band to keep them on our heads, and had been handed out just a couple of weeks earlier as the military's response to the first German gas attacks. To be activated, the masks had to be dampened and placed over the mouth and nostrils, and as water was forever in short supply, there was often no alternative but to urinate on them.

With everyone ready, we set off through the Lille Gate and up the Menin Road. It became evident that a great scrap was going on at the front, for the noise was indescribable. We were only lightly shelled on our way up, but we gritted our teeth nevertheless at the thought of what we were headed into. Several men, who had been caught by shrapnel bursts, lay dead along the road, while more men streamed past us, some wounded, others choking and exhausted by their exertions. The gas cloud, a yellowy fog, had been blown across the front by the prevailing winds. Like a thin mist, it had got everywhere and had obviously given the men at the front a real basin-full. Turning off at Hell Fire Corner, we crossed fields of mud, making our way towards the main support trenches, known as the GHQ line, but now under threat of becoming the front line. As we made our way forward, shrapnel began to rain on the support lines. Jerry gunners had spotted our arrival, just as news reached us that a battalion of the Durham Light Infantry had got into the line before us, taking our cover.

Editor
The Dragoons had in fact been ordered to a railway cutting south of the Menin Road at 4.30am, where they halted. News was then received that the GHQ Line north of the Menin Road had been captured and that the

Dragoons were to attack and help retake it. The CO went on ahead as the troops made their way across Hell Fire Corner and on towards the GHQ line. As they did so, the CO had just discovered that the part of the line supposedly in German hands was in fact crammed with over 400 men of the Divisional Reserve, the 15th and 19th Hussars, the 4th Green Howards and 5th Durham Light Infantry.

Ben

The order came to retire, but in effect it was every man for himself as we tore back towards the Menin Road. Troopers ran along the railway track or spread out into the fields either side, as whizz-bangs, fired by the Germans' 77mm field guns, dropped everywhere around us. The noise didn't quite muffle the shrieks and shouts as men tumbled like nine-pins, and the ground shuddered with the explosions. I managed to re-cross the Menin Road, but as I did so a shell fell directly behind me, sending my body sailing through the air. In an instant I found myself flat on my face, the stuffing completely knocked out of me. I stood up instinctively, and yelled as a searing pain shot through my ankle. Taking a few steps back to grasp my rifle, I saw the ammunition box, the one I had been carrying, cleft by a large shrapnel shard. Half hopping, half scrambling, I made off towards the railway cutting just yards ahead, and dived into the first available hole cut into the bank, to be joined almost immediately by another wounded man with shrapnel in his leg.

We sat there catching our breath, exchanging glances. His wound was light, a shrapnel ball plainly sticking out of his right thigh, just like a marble. My attention was drawn to my right ankle for the first time, but while it was clear that I had stopped a lump of shrapnel, rendering the ankle useless, I was loath to investigate further. Inside everyone's jackets there was a little pocket in which there was an absorbent pad and a khaki field dressing, so we could apply basic medical attention to wounds. However, it wasn't always easy to confront injury when it was your own. Clearly a lump of metal had ripped through the back of my boot, but fear over-rode any wish to look further.

Overall, I had been more lucky than I hardly dared admit. The ammunition box, balanced, as it was, behind my shoulder, had undoubtedly saved my life. Now I noticed that the inside of my riding breeches had been badly ripped by shrapnel. Luckier still, my ankle was probably bad enough to ensure a fast ticket back to Blighty. To steady our nerves, I took out the rum issue and drank some before passing it over to the other man. We were sitting in a small hollow in the left side of the cutting, over which had been put an old door, width-ways, on top of which dirt had been piled. Similar cubby holes lined the bank, with a couple of chaps in each, offering cover from the weather, but scant protection from shrapnel, and certainly not from a direct hit. For the time being, it was still the safest place to be while we sat things out. It was a beautiful day, and was clearly going to be a scorcher, as I was already sweating, and had begun to drink the rum in sips, to stave off thirst.

After two or three hours there was a relative pause in the firing, and as the heavy gas clouds too had thinned, the man opposite, who was not from my Regiment, made his move. 'Well, I think I'll get down to the field dressing station now. Good luck, mate,' and with that he took off, limping badly. After a few minutes I tried to follow him, but although I hadn't had a bad dose of gas, I was beginning to feel decidedly unwell, coughing and breathing heavily. There was no point in relying on stretcher bearers, but then again, my foot was useless. I needed a crutch or walking stick and the only thing to hand was my rifle. It would have to do.

Slithering out of the hole, I stood up, and there to my astonishment lay a worn-out farmhouse broom. It seemed incredible that in amongst all the wreckage there should be something so totally out of place, so utterly mundane as a broom. How it came to be there I'll never know, but it had a reasonably long shaft and an intact brush that fitted snugly under my arm. I put it on each railway sleeper so I didn't slip, and it let me get along fairly well, just hobbling and hobbling, as I carried my rifle in my left hand.

I followed the railway track until I saw a Red Cross flag, when I turned off and began to struggle across a field towards an Advanced Dressing Station. A doctor and an orderly came out and got each side of me, putting their arms under my shoulders, in order to cradle me the last few yards to the station where they put me directly into a waiting ambulance. 'Do your best to keep your eye on these,' said the doctor, then, 'All right, driver', and away we went. No one stopped to examine or bandage my foot.

There were two chaps gassed in the ambulance, one, poor devil, a Scotsman, was in a shocking state, fighting for his breath, and delirious. His breathing was short, gasping, and as he lay there he cried for his mother, 'Oh mother, God, oh mother, help me'. I watched him lie in agony for there was nothing I could do. There were two others in the van, one man, less seriously wounded, next to me, and underneath the young Jock, another man, also gassed, though not as badly.

We were driving steadily through Ypres, we hadn't been in it long, when suddenly the ambulance stopped dead, jolting everyone in the back. I shouted with surprise and the poor Jock groaned in pain, seconds before there was a resounding crash. Peering around the side of the ambulance I saw a cloud of dust drifting away from a veritable heap of bricks. The ambulance driver had seen a wall tottering, and had stopped just as the wall fell across the road. Had he driven on, we would undoubtedly have been crushed. There was no time to clear the rubble, so the driver was forced to take another route out of Ypres, to another town which I believe was Poperinge.

Editor

The Germans continued their attacks all morning before the initiative passed to the British, and counter-attacks were launched in the afternoon and early evening to regain much of the ground lost. Pressure on the 2nd Cavalry Brigade during the morning had been intense, the 18th Hussars and 9th Lancers in particular suffering severe casualties. Later, a squadron of the 4th Dragoons was pushed forward to support the 1st Cavalry Brigade between Zillebeke and Hooge, while the rest remained in the railway cutting until relieved at 9pm. The 4th Dragoons had suffered some seventy casualties, ten of them dead, while the Brigade had lost twenty three officers and 364 other ranks, around sixty per cent of its already depleted strength.

Ben was probably picked up by one of five Cavalry Field Ambulances which operated collection points and Advanced Dressing Stations just behind the line. If he was, then he was first taken to Vlamertinghe where the more severe gas cases were being treated with $ChCLl_3$, methylated spirits and ammonia stimulants, while the less serious cases were being quickly despatched to Casualty Clearing Stations. Among those being evacuated was Ben. He was driven to number 3 Casualty Clearing Station on the outskirts of Bailleul, ten miles south west of Ypres.[4] The CCS had only recently relocated from Poperinge, taking over one block of what had been an old lunatic asylum situated on the Bailleul to Ypres road. Doctors had estimated its capacity at no more than 350 men, yet during the month of May it admitted over 7,000 casualties. The influx of new patients naturally depended on the ferocity of the fighting. On May 9th they had received 808 patients; exactly a week later they had received none. May 24th, however, proved to be the most hectic day that month, for on top of the 111 wounded and sick patients still awaiting evacuation, the CCS admitted no fewer than 961 officers and men, of whom more than 600 were suffering from the effects of gas. It was, therefore, into organised pandemonium that Ben arrived.

No. 23454.
(If replying, please quote above No.)

Army Form B. 104—80.

Cavalry Record Office,

Canterbury Station.

8. 6. , 191 5.

SIR,

I regret to have to inform you that a report has this day been received from the War Office to the effect that (No.) 8292 (Rank) Pte (Name) Clouting B G. (Regiment) 4th Drag Gds is dangerously ill at Graylingwell War Hosp Chichester 24.5. suffering from Shell Wound R Ankle Severe

I am at the same time to express the sympathy and regret of the Army Council.

Any further information received in this office as to his condition or progress will be at once notified to you.

I am,

SIR,

Your obedient Servant,

To Mr W. Clouting
Lewes

Officer in charge of Records.

(K11219) Wt W 537—200,000—8/14. W & Co., Ltd.

Forms
B. 104-80
2

The dreaded letter: official notification of Ben's injury arrived at the Clouting home nearly three weeks after the event. However, the family already knew of this injury and had visited Ben in hospital.

Ben

By the time the ambulance arrived at the Casualty Clearing Station, I was panting badly and had a job to breathe from the effects of the gas. After being helped from the ambulance, I was left to wait for attention which, given the lightness of my wound, took a long time to arrive. When a nurse did come to see me, she asked where I was hit, and I motioned towards my foot. 'But what about all that there?' she asked, pointing to my tunic. It was still caked in the blood of 'Mickey' Lowe. 'It isn't mine,' was all I could bring myself to say, for all in all, I was feeling decidedly sick from the combined effects of chlorine gas and a large amount of the Troop's rum. The nurse returned, bringing with her a drink which made me violently and copiously sick almost as soon as I had touched it, but this eliminated much of the gas's worst effects and I suffered relatively little from that time onwards, although my sense of smell was permanently impaired.

Many of the more urgent cases were sent down the line late that afternoon, while the less serious, including myself, stayed the night there, near the railway station, in amongst the comforting signs of the Red Cross, which flew or were painted everywhere to underline to enemy aircraft the role of the place.

Next morning was another lovely, fine day and my spirits rose as I waited with others to be put on the ambulance train. Before embarkation, we were individually checked by a doctor to see if we were lying or sitting cases, sitting cases being those, like myself, who could walk or hop, for which we were designated 'walking wounded'. Four of us were put into a compartment, and as I sat by the window, a team of Belgian ladies got on and put very pretty hand-knitted stockings, with mauve bows, on those of us with wounded legs. When the train pulled out of the station, a small number of civilians cheered us off, in appreciation for which a number of us hoisted our stockinged legs out of the windows and gingerly waved them goodbye.

The train took us to Boulogne where, for the first time in months, I was to sleep in a proper bed. But I found I simply wasn't used to it and couldn't sleep, so I got out onto the floor. I was discovered by the night sister who made me get back into bed, but still I couldn't sleep, so I returned to the floor where I was allowed to stay, despite one more attempt by the sister to get me back into bed.

Editor

Ben had received little more than perfunctory treatment to his right ankle at Bailleul before he was evacuated with 257 other cases early the following afternoon, on Number 6 Ambulance Train, by way of St Omer to

Boulogne, arriving at 7.20pm. After one night in hospital, he sailed, on May 26th, in one of two Hospital Ships, the *St David*, or the *Dieppe*, arriving at Graylingwell War Hospital late that evening.

May 24th had turned out to be the final day in the battle that was to become known as Second Ypres. The Dragoons left the trenches sadly depleted, but were never again used as makeshift infantry as they had been during March, April and May 1915. The 2nd Cavalry Brigade had been thrown into the defence of Ypres and had helped save the day by their fighting tenacity, earning special praise from their commander in chief, Sir John French, when he inspected their ranks three weeks later.[5]

Ben

Two Red Cross orderlies carried me on a stretcher on board ship and placed me in the hold, where dozens of us lay in long rows. I discovered that a stretcher was a horrible thing to lie on because it was so narrow. The only way I could lie comfortably was on my back, because if I lay on my side, my knees hit the wooden poles. We sailed across at night and, though the trip was uncomfortable, we were going home to Blighty and that was all that mattered. I knew how lucky I was. I was going home with a much sought-after Blighty wound, while others were going home with limbs missing, or faces irreparably damaged.

We landed at Southampton early in the morning and were placed under cover on the quayside. Several ladies were milling around, offering soldiers sympathy, cigarettes, mugs of tea and cake, which were most welcome. One nurse came over to speak to me. 'What country do you come from?' she asked. I was covered in grime and filth, and my face was almost black from the bag of charcoal I had carried up the line a week or so before. A mixture of dust and sweat had helped to even out the 'tan' so that she had actually mistaken me for a colonial soldier. She was genuinely amazed, as she wiped away a little dirt, to find this boy underneath.

Those lightly wounded, like myself, waited patiently on our stretchers until orderlies came to help us to the hospital trains. If at all possible, the authorities tried to place soldiers in hospitals close to home. Even so, it was welcome news when I learnt I was on a train headed for Chichester, a town just 45 miles from home.

Officially my parents had still to be informed of my injury, but a sixth sense had already told them I was in trouble. Within two hours of my being wounded, my mother had collapsed, so I was later told. She had woken early and had become increasingly agitated, until all my father could get from her was 'my boy, my boy.' The local doctor was called, and after examining her confirmed she was suffering from severe shock, but for no apparent reason. 'How is the boy?' he asked. My father replied that I was well, for the family had only just received a card from me a couple of days before.

I had already arrived at Graylingwell War Hospital, Chichester, when my parents heard where I was. 'There's only one remedy for her shock and that is to take her to see Ben,' the doctor told my father, and with that he brought my mother, and one of my sisters, all the way over to see me, while he went off to see a friend in Chichester. It was ironic, but his name was Dr Steinhauser, a German who had been naturalised English and had been our doctor for many many years. His diagnosis was correct, and my mother was all right, but years later when I asked her about the incident, she said simply, 'I just knew you were in trouble'.

When my mother came to see me, she did not look in shock. On the contrary, she looked very well. It was the first time I had seen any of my family since January 1914, since when so many things had occurred. My mother sat by my bed for two hours and we talked and talked, during which she broke the bad news that my cousin Sidney had been missing in action since the 9th of May. He had only been in France a couple of months, she told me, and this had been the Regiment's first real action. There was some hope he might be a prisoner of war, but the family feared the worst.

Sid Clouting had enlisted at Hastings in the 5th Royal Sussex Regiment and had trained with the Battalion before embarking for France in February 1915. I found out in later years that after a spell acclimatising to the front line, the Battalion was selected to take part in an early morning attack on the German trenches near Aubers Ridge, but that the attack had utterly failed. The Regiment lost nearly 250 men; nearly 100 were killed, of whom Sidney Clouting was one. His body was never found.

At Graylingwell Hospital, preliminary examinations showed that the shrapnel had hit me just above the ankle joint and had come out through the tongue of my boot. I had no operation, rather my ankle was daily dressed and re-dressed when fragments of bone, puttee and boot, which gradually worked their way to the surface, were picked out. Nor did I received any physiotherapy, my ankle was simply bandaged and it was just a question of waiting until I felt I could try walking again.

The hospital was an ex-mental institution taken over for war work. It was large, with near enough 1,000 beds, and divided into many wards, including ours, Queen's Ward. It was staffed by full-time nurses, orderlies, and any number of volunteer helpers who gave many hours of their time, not just in providing nursing support, but in running an on-site library, canteen and even a Post Office. The local community did all they could to help our recovery. Soldiers did not draw pay while in hospital, so relief was provided by a Gift Fund, financed by local people, for the purchase of anything from fruit to musical instruments, games to stationery. On the wards we played endless card games, or, as the weather was so warm, we would go outside and sit on the lawns. For the more mobile, there was the opportunity to play bowls, indeed there was even a tennis court. We would sit, and talk, and reminisce and leg-pull. The trenches might have been a million miles away, for everyone wanted to forget what had happened in France, almost as if it had never occurred.

At night, the war returned for many on the ward. Chaps constantly shouted out in their sleep as though back in France, sometimes kicking out with their feet, or jerking their arms wildly. The most disturbed were those who were coming round after an operation, for there were no recovery wards, and men were brought back into the ward direct from the operating table. Usually a nurse would sit with them until they regained consciousness, or, when this wasn't possible, a soldier sat close by, ready to shout for help. Being only lightly wounded, I helped out on several occasions, mucking in to hold bandages as nurses dressed wounds on their rounds.

There was one man, a quiet fellow, who had both feet amputated during a particularly difficult operation and was taking a long time to come round from the anaesthetic. On finally waking, he launched, most unexpectedly, into a tirade of language that was just so awful the men on the ward held a handkerchief over his mouth, to protect the nurses. He had difficulty accepting what had happened and had become delirious, blaming everyone around him for his loss. He had been in hospital some time and had borne the pain without ever complaining as the doctors fought a losing battle to save his feet. When this man finally recovered, we told him what he had said, and he was very embarrassed.

By this time, soldiers were only being allowed out of the hospital if they were accompanied by an escort, who guaranteed to pick us up and bring us back by a pre-arranged time. The problem had been alcohol. Many soldiers had been returning drunk, as local people treated the wounded heroes to drink after drink in nearby pubs. The rule was now needed more than ever, for Australians and Canadians had begun arriving at Graylingwell since April and May, and these men seemed to have plenty of money – far more, it appeared, than the Tommy. Not only could these men rely on being bought drinks, but they could afford their own. The hospital was forced to introduce its own curfew, set at 10pm.

Garden parties, hosted by local families, were a well-appreciated source of outside entertainment. By July, I was hobbling around on crutches and the ward sister asked me if I would like to go to one such party. I readily agreed, and made sure I was at the front door at the appropriate time. I was pointed towards a carriage driven by an elderly coachman, but before climbing aboard, I stopped to stroke the horse. 'You fond of horses, Tommy?' he asked. I told him that not only was I from a cavalry regiment, but that I had grown up with horses on an estate near Lewes. 'You don't happen to know Bill Clouting?' he asked, to my astonishment. He and my father had worked together as stable lads at the home of Phillip Sassoon, before my dad married and moved away.

This coachman now worked for the lady to whose home several patients had been invited for tea. At the time, she was with the matron, but presently she reappeared to join us on the short trip to her home. 'You're never going to believe this, Miss, but I used to work with this soldier's father,' the coachman said. 'Good heavens, well then he must ride up on the box with you,' she answered.

There were plenty of invitations for wounded soldiers to attend various functions laid on for their benefit. On two occasions, I went to a garden party at Sir James Horlix's house, near Goodwood. Some twenty of us were picked up in a charabanc and taken over to his home for the afternoon, where we were met at the door by the butler and shown into the garden. We sat on garden seats to chat, while Sir James walked round to talk to each group of soldiers. Lemonade was served, and a tea of bread, butter and jam, as we sat around a large wooden table taken outside for the occasion.

Walking round the garden at one of Sir James's parties, I found a grass snake. This discovery put my mind into action, and asking for a jam jar, I managed to bottle the snake up, with the idea of taking it back to the hospital. It was only about a foot long, so there was little difficulty getting it onto the ward or concealing my activities, as I tied a bit of bandage round its neck and roped it to the rear leg of my bed. All the soldiers loved to play tricks on the nurses and I was no exception. I knew that last thing at night a nurse, would came round to tuck us into bed; it was as good a chance as any for a joke. Keeping a straight face was the hardest part, as I asked the nurse earnestly, 'Do please be careful and try not to step on my watchdog'. This particular nurse was well known for her nervousness and timidity and I eagerly followed the path of her eyes as she looked down. Then she saw the snake, gave a little yelp, and promptly fainted on top of me.

I had not quite expected this reaction, and while another nurse slapped her face to bring her round, the sister was called. Deep down, I would like to think this sister saw the funny side of the incident, but that, for the sake of ward discipline, she felt obliged to put on a good act to the contrary. Ward sisters had the ability to put the fear of God into junior nurses, VADs and even soldiers alike. Sitting in a hospital bed made me something of a captive audience, and I was left in no doubt as to what would happen if I ever tried a trick like that again. The dressing down finished with her telling me to get up, get dressed, and take the wretched creature up the garden, an orderly being to sent with me to ensure I left it there.

I left hospital in early September and was given a week's leave. I was still lame, although I no longer needed crutches and spent much of the week relaxing and exercising my foot. My brother William was still at school, but my two sisters had entered domestic service at a house near enough for them to still be living at home. Since the death of Charles Brand, the estate had been run down. Most of the animals had long been sold off, leaving my father to look after no more than a couple of mares and a couple of Shetland ponies, a far throw from the days when some eighteen horses stabled at Little Dene.

From Little Dene, I returned to the Regiment's depot at Newport, where I stayed for two or three weeks before I was moved back to the reserve Regiment at Tidworth. At Tidworth, I found Lieutenant Swallow working in a cushy job. Mullens would never have had him back, medically fit or not, so he was now seeing out the war as a Transport Officer, or some similar title. He came up to me and said, 'Oh hello, Clouting, how are you getting on?' A little harshly, I pointed out that I was about to leave for France again, yet to give Swallow his due he did not try and avoid me, quite the opposite. But deep in my heart I had the feeling he wasn't a man; he'd failed in action as a soldier.[6]

I need not have gone back so soon, but the Colonel wrote a letter to the depot asking for as many of the original Regiment to be sent back as soon as possible, and I wanted to go. Before I left, I had to go in front of a Medical Board consisting of an RAMC officer whose job it was to check the fitness of all those who were going back on a draft. 'Let me see you walk,' he asked. I tried very hard to hide my limp, but he spotted it and said. 'You're still lame. You needn't go back on this draft.' The role of the cavalry had been undermined since trench warfare began and many cavalrymen were going to be pushed into the Labour Corps, the infantry, or the newly formed Machine Gun Corps. This draft, however, was definitely going back to the 4th DG, and I wasn't going to miss that chance.

There were between fifty and sixty of us going back to France from Southampton to Boulogne, on another overnight journey. I can remember playing cards all through the darkness as we made our way across, and for once I did extremely well. From the port, we went by train straight back to the Regiment. I was quite happy going back; we were all regular soldiers and it was our life, our job.

It was late October, and I had only been back a matter of days when I found myself back in hospital once again, this time with impetigo. It had broken out around all my joints and on my hands, and on going sick I was immediately sent to a small isolation hospital. There were no wounded there, just sickness cases, impetigo, eczema, that sort of thing. The hospital was situated in a field. It was simply two marquees joined together, with a boarded floor, in the middle of which was a slow combustion stove, with a tall chimney which both took the fumes out of the tent and acted as a heater as well. This was the only heating in the marquee, and, it being the middle of winter, we all kept ourselves well snuggled down under the extra issue of blankets. The hospital was staffed by just male orderlies who were noticeably less sympathetic than the female nurses at Graylingwell, perfunctorily carrying out their duties. During the five weeks I was there my arms were kept plastered in ointment and wrapped in bandages; all I had to do was rest, my arms in slings so that I wasn't tempted to use them. Christmas came and went without much memorable cheer before I was released from hospital on the last day of 1915.

NOTES

1. Howell later served in Gallipoli and then with II Corps in France, where he was killed in October 1916 while making a reconnaissance of the front line near Poziers on the Somme.
2. Every year until his death in 1990, Ben would wear his Regimental tie on Armistice Day, and drink a single glass of sherry as a salute to the Regiment, but in particular to the memory of Mickey Lowe.
3. 7218 Private George Eric Galtress was born at Stantonbury in Buckinghamshire, and joined up at nearby Bletchley. He went out with the Dragoons in August 1914, but what happened after he broke down in the trenches is not clear. He is recorded as serving in the later battles of Loos and the Somme and it is known that he briefly served with the North Somerset Yeomanry before transferring to the 15th Warwickshires (2nd City of Birmingham Battalion) on September 23rd 1917. A brother, serving in the 12th Royal Fusiliers

had already been killed in June 1916, and George too was not to survive the war. He was killed in action on October 25th 1917, his name now being commemorated on the Tyne Cot Memorial, in the Ypres Salient.

4. His name appears in the Admission and Discharge Book for Field Service No 3 CCS at Bailleul, May 24th 1915-June 3rd 1915. It is interesting to note that Ben was the only 4th Dragoon Guardsman admitted to this CCS on May 24th.

5. The diary shows that in merely holding the line, the Dragoons lost thirty four men killed and 141 wounded in May. Comparative figures for the rest of the Brigade show that the 9th Lancers lost fifty five men killed, including the hero at Audregnies, Captain Francis Grenfell VC. The 18th Hussars lost seventy six men killed.

6. Lieutenant Swallow, then twenty three years old, remained with the 6th Reserve Regiment of Cavalry for the rest of the war, resigning his commission in July 1919. After the war, he returned to the rich lifestyle he had always known. He married, but had no children, dying of tuberculosis, a family illness, in 1940, aged forty nine.

CHAPTER SEVEN
A Different Life

Editor

Ben's release from hospital coincided with de Wiart's return to France, Ben quickly resuming his job as horse orderly. In March 1916 de Wiart left the Dragoons to be appointed second in command of the 7th Loyal North Lancs, and Ben went with him. It was the start of a string of commands as de Wiart quickly rose in seniority, taking command of the 8th Gloucesters, the 8th North Staffordshires, and, within a year, the 12th Infantry Brigade. Throughout this time Ben remained with de Wiart. However, owing to the restricted nature of Ben's job, looking after de Wiart's two horses, his memories leant more towards a series of cameos, than to a chronological recounting of events.

Ben

De Wiart rejoined the Regiment in January 1916 after a prolonged stay in England recovering from the injury he had received on the Zonnebeke road. The doctors had made several valiant attempts to save what was left of his hand but, as I read years later, de Wiart had finally given up, pulling the remaining two fingers off himself, forcing the doctors to reduce the hand to a stump. It was while he was in hospital that Bridges, then in command of the 19th Division, came into his hospital room and asked if he wished to return to France as second in command of the 7th Loyal North Lancashire Regiment, a battalion in Bridges' Division. De Wiart was more than happy to accept, and I resumed work as his horse orderly.

It was early on in the year when de Wiart took me to join the Loyal North Lancs, where, almost as soon as we arrived, I received a letter from my mother telling me dad had had a serious accident and was in hospital. My mother had been hankering after a change of lifestyle, and now that the estate had been run down in the years since Charlie Brand's death, my father had decided to leave Little Dene to take a post in Derby. My parents had been there for over twenty years and it was a wrench to leave, but my father had found a job teaching the daughter of a wealthy businessman to ride, and it seemed a good opportunity. One morning, he had been out alone exercising the horses when he passed a steamroller just as its safety valve blew. My father's horse jumped forward in

119

surprise, while the other, a pony he was leading, backed up. As it did so, the pony's lead rein became caught round my dad's leg, pulling him over the flank of his horse, which kicked out with both feet. My father was hit in the chest, and was taken to hospital on a two-wheeled butcher's cart with several broken ribs and coughing blood. Keen to get a three-day special leave to visit him, I went to see de Wiart to explain what had happened. 'Oh, that's bad news,' said de Wiart, sympathetically. But much as I hoped de Wiart would let me go, sympathy was all I got.

When we arrived, there had been some disorder in the Battalion; up to twenty men were in clink for minor things such as insubordination or dumb insolence. The first thing de Wiart did was to have them lined up before he walked up and down looking closely into each man's face. He said nothing until he had finished his inspection, then said, 'I now know all your faces. Return to your companies and do not come up before me again'.

He took the attitude that he should stamp his authority quickly on the Battalion, and although he could be tough, he was fair to both officers and men, and was respected for it. He could never suffer fools and expected an order to be carried out to the full. 'All out for physical training tomorrow morning,' meant 'all out' and not just the duty officer and men. When, the morning after this order was given, the Battalion's officers failed to appear, he gave all of them a real dressing down. This would never have occurred in front of any of the men, but we knew it had happened because, by God, they were all present the following morning.

De Wiart was a stickler for physical fitness, though not in the conventional sense of routine route marches. Rather, he would organise football matches, one platoon against another, the men playing in gas masks, with cigarettes for the winners. There were also cross-country runs, about seven miles long, some in full kit – haversack, waterbottle, 120 rounds of ammunition. As always, the whole Battalion ran, for he fervently believed that officers could not expect to lead their men if they weren't fit themselves. With his one eye, de Wiart could not run; instead he led the way on one of his mares, riding with just a blanket on the horse's back. Only occasionally would the Battalion go on route marches for fitness, in which case de Wiart got the men to sing. 'I don't care what they sing, so long as they sing!' I once heard him say.

Editor
Adrian Carton de Wiart was a remarkable man. The son of a Belgian lawyer, he was educated in England, going on to Oxford University to study law. He was there only a short time before he impulsively joined

up to see some action in the Boer War, but was shot almost on arrival in South Africa and returned to England, college and a hero's welcome. It was during the First World War that he showed apparent fearlessness in action. By the time Ben became his horse orderly, de Wiart had already lost an eye with the Camel Corps in Somaliland, and soon lost his hand at Ypres. Later, on the Somme, he survived a bullet wound to the back of the head, returning to suffer a serious wound in the leg, in 1918.

In total, he was wounded eleven times in action. Among his many honours (including a DSO with bar and the Croix de Guerre) he won the Victoria Cross at La Boisselle on July 3rd 1916, the only man to win the honour having neither British nor Commonwealth citizenship. The fact that he was Belgian had been overlooked when he was awarded the medal for 'conspicuous bravery, coolness and determination, during severe operations of a prolonged nature'.

As a person, de Wiart appears to have won the admiration, respect, even awe, of those around him. He was disciplined, dependable and supremely determined, and, perhaps unreasonably, expected those around him to behave likewise. In many ways he lived a 'Boy's Own Paper' lifestyle. His autobiography *Happy Odyssey* gives the impression of a consummate professional soldier. How many people could have written, 'To me war and politics seem bad mixers, like port and champagne. But if it wasn't for the politicians we wouldn't have wars, and I, for one, should have been done out of what is for me a very agreeable life'.

On June 15th, Major Carton de Wiart became acting Commanding Officer of the 8th Gloucesters, formally taking command one week later when he was promoted to Lieutenant-Colonel. It was with this battalion that de Wiart picked up a new servant, Holmes, with whom he formed a close bond.

Ben

Holmes looked after de Wiart's personal requirements and was absolutely devoted to him, never failing to turn him out marvellously. De Wiart had a parcel specially sent out from England every week with various goodies which kept him at the peak of physical condition. Nevertheless, missing a hand and an eye, he relied heavily on his personal servant, particularly when getting dressed in the morning and having his boots laced up. It inevitably brought the two in close contact.

Very few officers in an infantry regiment had horses, and consequently there were few other grooms around. The first and second in command, with perhaps one or two others such as the adjutant, would have a horse, but that was about all. De Wiart's horses were a light and a dark mare, the dark mare being my favourite by far. She was a pre-war horse, branded 4DG on her shoulder, and was given to me to look after when de Wiart first went to the North Lancs. She was remarkably tame and of all the horses I had during the war, probably ten in all, she was the most intelligent. I called her Nancy after a girlfriend I had met at Newport the previous autumn, and with whom I regularly corresponded. De Wiart referred to the horse simply as 'the brown mare' although she had a white muzzle in the centre of which was a pink diamond-shaped mark, about the size of a postage stamp, and so perfect it was almost as though it had been tattooed. She was the horse de Wiart rode with just a blanket for a saddle, yet, because I looked after her, she responded best of all to me.

Each morning, Holmes would come and tell me what de Wiart required that day. Most of the time I stayed amongst the men who drove the General Service wagons, looking after de Wiart's horses in the lines, where I fed and watered them three times a day. It was an easy life, for these horses were my sole concern, although de Wiart expected both to look absolutely spick and span and the saddlery to be in first class order. Occasionally I would get the farrier to look at the shoes, replacing those nails that had worn, but I was my own boss, you might say, because de Wiart was my boss and when he was not there I could do almost as I pleased. Occasionally I rode with him to Brigade or Divisional Head-quarters, often going through Albert, the town through which most men passed on the way to the front. The town was famous for a figure of the Madonna holding her Baby aloft at the top of a Basilica. Since 1915, this golden statue had hung at right angles, seemingly ready to fall at any time. It began a rumour that if she did, we would lose the war.

By this time, preparations for the battle of the Somme were in over-drive. The ASC were working day and night to bring supplies of every description closer to the front line, while huge numbers of troops were moving up to be billeted in villages close by. Our new Battalion, the 8th Gloucesters, had been undergoing intensive preparation for their part in the battle, practising their attack over the rolling chalk countryside, with fields taped out with known trench lines, so the soldiers could get an idea of the positions they were to take.

Every impression that this would be the decisive attack was maintained by the opening of the Somme bombardment. How long it lasted, I do not know, but it went on and on, day and night, with devastating ferocity, just as if half a dozen thunderstorms had been unleashed together. It was simply awesome. Even well behind the lines it seemed inconceivable that any Germans could survive such a pounding, although in the event most of them did.

Editor

The 'Big Push', as the Somme offensive became known, was meant decisively to break open the German defences, allowing the cavalry through to seize the town of Bapaume, some ten miles north east of Albert. However, in the wider, strategic sense, the attack was intended to open up the whole front, creating a mobile war. The cavalry would exploit the resulting 'gap', roll up the German flanks and drive them all the way back to Berlin. Among those who were to take part in the 'Push' were the 4th Dragoon Guards. Days before the attack, the Dragoons had been stationed at Querrier, some seventeen miles behind the lines, and it was here that they were given their plan of attack. On June 29th, de Wiart, possibly accompanied by Ben, rode to Querrier, where he joined Solly Flood, by then in charge of an infantry brigade, and other 4th Dragoon officers for dinner, and a 'good luck' for the days to come. As the great day approached, the Dragoons moved up with the rest of the Cavalry Brigade to Brisle, three miles from the trenches, but in the event July 1st was a disaster. In his personal diary, Lieutenant Wright of the 4th Dragoon Guards wrote, 'Twenty of our balloons are well up over the front line watching the progress of our infantry, and sending back information by wireless. We got news of our progress at 8.25am . . .There is nothing doing for the cavalry today and we are sent back to Querrier. We hear that our casualties are 15,000'. In the event, some 60,000 men had been killed or wounded on that day.

Ben

Throughout the initial stages, I remained with the transport, and consequently saw little of the battle. The Gloucesters were not used in the first attacks, but were held back in support, waiting for the order to move forward. The noise of the battle was tremendous and I felt for the men in the Battalion, who knew they would soon be headed into it.

On July 3rd, the 57th Brigade, of which the 8th Gloucesters were part, made an attack on La Boisselle, one of a number of heavily defended villages which had been a first day objective, but remained in German hands. The Brigade had gone in early that morning and fought all day, suffering a great number of casualties, de Wiart becoming the only senior officer left. He took charge, and typically displayed great courage, fighting off several German counter-attacks. It was for this action that he was awarded the Victoria Cross.

The 8th Gloucesters were withdrawn from the line shortly afterwards, hollow-eyed and utterly worn out. They looked shattered. However, within two or three weeks they were back, this time attacking High Wood, small, densely packed with trees, and strongly defended by the Germans who had constructed a trench line through one corner.

Just before this attack, de Wiart was wounded again, this time shot through the back of his head, ensuring he was soon on his way back to England again, and myself back to virtual self-employment. As a rule, de Wiart much preferred to wear his soft cap, and would only wear a steel helmet when extreme danger forced him to. Going into action he had, for some reason, left his cap on his horse and, because he was subsequently injured, it came into my possession. On his return to the Battalion a couple of months later, he had a new cap and never sought out his old one. Although I later jettisoned the cap, I kept the cap badge as a souvenir, which I still own.

During the summer of 1916, virtually everyone living around the transport lines came down with flu, one victim after another retiring to hastily-erected bivouacs for two or three days. The bivouacs had been made from our groundsheets, roped together through the eye holes and made into a sort of tent, with stacks of corn used to fill the area where tent flaps normally are.

Inside, the men lay in twos fully dressed under a pile of coats to sweat it out. The strain of flu was particularly virulent, and when I caught it, it knocked me out, leaving my head going round and round. We had a Transport Sergeant named Dredge, and throughout, he was like an old mother, crawling into the bivouacs to ply his patients with gruel – bread and milk – heavily laced with rum. It was his job to get his men back on the map and he took personal charge of 'medication', coming round with a friendly 'Get that down you, boy,' spoon-feeding us his concoctions from a little old saucepan.

Around this time, a couple of curious coincidences occurred, in which newspapers featured large. On the first occasion, I had been sent with a ration party to draw some rations for the Battalion, typically frozen beef, tins of bully beef, and hay for the horses. We had taken a GS wagon, and headed for an undamaged field well behind the lines where the ASC had set up a divisional dump. On arrival, we were told that our supply had not yet been made up and that we would have to wait. There were anything up to a hundred other men hanging around for rations, so we sat down on some bales of hay to chat. We were a mixed bunch. One was a popular, friendly man, an armourer, whose principal job was to mend jammed or broken guns. As we sat, he leaned across and offered me a drink from a flask he always carried with him. Without inquiring, I put my head back and drank, rocking forward as I choked and spluttered. 'My God, it's methylated spirits,' I

croaked, the meths burning my throat. He grinned, quite unconcerned. As an armourer, he received meths as part and parcel of
his work to remove grease, or clean a gun up. How he could drink
that stuff I could not begin to understand.

As we waited, I lazily began to watch a piece of newspaper
fluttering one way and then the other across the field. I could not
be bothered to go and pick it up, but it came closer and closer,
until I was able to shoot a foot out to trap it. It was the outside
cover of the continental issue of *The Daily Mirror*, printed primarily
for the benefit of the soldiers, although we rarely came across it,
and then usually a couple of weeks out of date. Still, there was
nothing else to do, so I picked it up for a quick look.

My eyes scanned the page and settled on a picture at the bottom.
'Well, I'll be jiggered!' I said excitedly, unable to believe my eyes.
'That is my mother. And that's my father!' The rest craned their
necks to see, equally astonished. The picture featured a group of
labourers carrying hay in large white sheets, two of whom were
clearly my parents. My mother had written to say that dad was
slowly on the mend, and here was the physical proof, in a field
on the Somme, during a war!

The picture had been printed to bolster the troops' morale, proving that loved ones at home were doing their bit for the war
effort. With all the horses and wagons commandeered for war
work, it showed that people were working hard to gather in the
harvest. Why the piece of paper blew to me, heaven only knows.
I folded the sheet carefully and put it in a pocket for safe keeping.

The second incident brought back memories of two years before,
when I had been picked, along with eleven other men, to shoot
the Colonels, Elkington and Mainwaring. Their court martial had
only cashiered them for attempting to surrender their commands,
and both officers appeared to vanish without trace.

One, Elkington, had joined the French Foreign Legion and
served with great distinction. As a result, the King decided to
reinstate him to his former rank in his Regiment and award him
the DSO. This story appeared in a newspaper, at the same time as
an officer, just out from England, arrived at the Battalion. His name
was Elkington (Acting Captain Christopher Garrett Elkington) and
I wondered if he just might be a relative. At the first opportunity
I asked him if he knew the Warwicks' Colonel. Not only did he
know him, but he said that he was his nephew. He only knew the
bare bones of the story of St Quentin, and was not aware of his
uncle's reinstatement, nor how close he came to being shot.

Editor
De Wiart returned in September to re-take command of the Battalion. Out of curiosity he went to the spot where he had been shot, and discovered the walking stick he had been carrying at the time of his injury. But, as he himself said, 'I felt I was becoming an individual target for the Hun,' and it was no surprise to anyone when six weeks later he was injured again by a shell fragment in his ankle. It was during his convalescence in England that he was presented with his VC by the King at Buckingham Palace on November 29th. Back out in France, de Wiart assumed temporary command of the 8th North Staffordshires, but soon left to take command of the 12th Infantry Brigade, in January 1917. Ben continued to serve de Wiart at Brigade Headquarters, where he remained for much of 1917.

Ben
That winter was the coldest of the whole war, with anything up to sixteen weeks of frost. Extra blankets were issued to all the men, coming up in bundles of ten on the wagons. Many of us wore leather or sheepskin jerkins to keep warm, while everyone was issued with a woollen hat which could be rolled up or down over the face.

The cold was such that any wounds or cuts suffered by the horses had to be cleaned with petrol, as water froze on the hair. Injuries were usually leg sores, or wounds to the horse's heel. These injuries were common when the rope which held the horses in the lines became entangled in the animals' fetlocks. The friction of the rope created a gall which was very difficult to heal. Only petrol could be used because it dried quickly and kept the dirt and mud out, although later that winter the veterinary officer gave us petroleum jelly to use instead.

We tried as hard as possible to give the horses shelter, often behind the walls of partially-destroyed houses, but they suffered very badly. Mules, however, proved far more successful in dealing with the exceptional weather conditions. These hardy creatures proved their importance when I saw a GS wagon stuck fast in the winter mud, despite the best efforts of two shire horses to move it. In the end the shires were unhitched and a team of four mules took over and walked away with it, their tiny feet coping much better with the suction of the mud.

During that winter, we took over some French dugouts built into the side of a steep bank, perhaps thirty feet high. Into this bank the French Engineers had built any number of small but elaborate dugouts. Each dugout entrance was covered with a piece of old sacking to keep out the worst of the cold, behind which a flight of eight steps led down to underground chambers that spread out laterally, in effect like a large 'T'. Each dugout could comfortably sleep six or more men and was heated at the apex of the 'T' by an oil drum which worked as a fireplace. This drum was attached to a smoke box which was coupled to a length of drainpipe fed up through the earth to the surface above. In the fireplace we burnt everything and anything we could get hold of, and on the whole kept warm. The only drawback to this comfortable existence were the tall chimneys. These proved a great temptation to pranksters who regularly stuffed rags down the funnels to smoke the men out.

Many of us were in poor health from the extremes of living outside, coupled with a poor diet. I was young and relatively fit, but suffered from various afflictions that came and went including large and painful abscesses on my arms, and one on the side of my face. I also endure several attacks of boils on my knees and at one time over twenty on my backside. These boils, like the abscesses, were intermittent, but when they were at their most virulent I simply could not ride, having to pass the time with a piece of lint pinned to my shirt tail. 'Do you think you can get hold of some Epsom Salts?' a transport man asked. 'If you can take a good spoonful every other morning, it might help.' Funnily enough, the canteens used to sell Epsom Salts in little penny packets and I found his advice worked very well.

Toothache was another common complaint which could drive a man half crazy with pain before he could see the MO for basic treatment. Once, in 1915, I had gone sick with toothache only to find that the MO had gone on leave to Paris, leaving just his medical orderly. The pain was terrible and I bullied the orderly into pulling the tooth out, despite his protestations. 'Just get a tooth pull and once you start, it doesn't matter what I do, you get it out,' I said. He tried three different tooth pulls and in the end, to his surprise and delight, the tooth came out. I was left to sit on a bale of hay with my head between my legs, spitting out the blood until I felt better.

There was so little activity at Brigade Headquarters that winter that we were given physical training lessons every morning to liven us all up. With time to kill, several men such as our blacksmith would make objects for fun. He was very skilful and on one occasion made a pair of ice skates with two pieces of wood and two pieces of iron fencing, for the River Somme had frozen over, and in places the ice was thick enough to skate on. Several of us used to go down to the river for a walk, and it was there that we watched a Frenchman catch ducks, with snares made of horse hair.

These snares caught the ducks which walked along the embankment, but far more roamed closer to the river, and could easily be picked off with a rifle. There were so many that at times it was possible to despatch two or even three in a row, if we got down low enough to the ground.

At first we shot ducks close to the river's edge, picking them out of the water at arm's length. However, it was clear that richer pickings would be had if we could get out on to the river itself. By this time the ice was too thin to walk on at the edges, so we improvised a canoe out of three barrels scrounged from a farm. Cutting them in two, we placed three halves in a line and, with two planks along the side to keep everything sturdy, nailed the boat together. A lance corporal sat in the front, and I sat in the back, then with two spades to paddle the craft out into the river, we collected the ducks we had shot, dropping them into the middle compartment.

It was while we were out collecting the ducks that the Military Police turned up and called us in, arresting us as we landed. There had apparently been several casualties from bullets ricocheting off the ice and wounding soldiers. An order banning such actions had been posted, but no one had told us.

Firing had gone on all along the river, and these MPs' orders were to clamp down heavily on this activity, posting patrols at various intervals along the banks. Our rifles were collected, as were a sample number of ducks as evidence, and we were marched to a provost marshal's office, where our particulars were taken by a grumpy officer. Just before we were dismissed, the corporal I had been boating with asked earnestly, 'Does that mean we have lost our ducks, sir?' whereupon I laughed and we got a dressing down before we were allowed to leave. We had been bluntly told that we would hear more about the matter but nothing ever came of it, probably because we had donated several ducks to the officers' mess before we were caught.

Editor

Brigade Headquarters remained on the Somme throughout the winter of 1916–17, moving in February close to the village of Suzanne, three or four miles behind the line. Wherever Headquarters was, it was never far behind the lines, perhaps in an old farmhouse, as opposed to a Battalion HQ which was often just a bivouac in the corner of a field, but there was not a great deal of difference apart from, as Ben said, 'a little more brass and braid'.

Ben

When de Wiart was made Brigadier, the idea was that he would run the four battalions from Brigade Headquarters. This he found very difficult to do, as temperamentally he could never be far away from the action, and consequently he continued to be wounded. I believe he was requested to go back to Brigade HQ, but still remained much closer to the line, saying he could run it just as well from there.

Sometime in March, we moved to the town of Arras. This had once been a very attractive town, but it had been badly knocked about, although it still managed to maintain much of its character. Below the town, there was a labyrinth of inter-connected caves that ran for miles and miles, all the way up to the battle front at Vimy Ridge. These caves, widely used for storage by the inhabitants, were also ideal for billeting troops. During quiet periods, several of us used to go mooching around in these caves or walking above ground in the town's once beautiful shopping squares. In the rubble of one shop, I picked up a white enamelled chamber pot, with an attractive blue rim. The pot was brand new and might come in useful, so I took it back to Brigade Headquarters. Every now and again, one of the canteens in Arras would get a few barrels of beer, always pretty weak stuff but better than nothing. Soldiers used to line up with containers of all kinds to collect the beer, and I would go down and get the chamber pot filled up, to a chorus of comments all around. The pot could carry about four litres, which we would carefully take back to Headquarters where it was shared out. It became something of a standing joke, although it was surprising the number of men who wouldn't drink from it.

Despite the destruction of the town, there were any number of estaminets still open, which the soldiers visited for a bit of company and something to eat and drink. 'Encore, Madame, café avec Cognac,' was the stock phrase, although this was gradually shortened to either 'Café avec,' or 'Encore avec'. 'Café avec' was not real coffee but either burnt barley or roast acorns, a large pot of which always stood in the embers of a peat fire. After a drink was ordered, Madame would pour a little coffee into a smaller pot, returning it to the embers to heat more thoroughly. She then gave us some home-made sugar, which, on the first occasion I was there, I thought was a barley sugar sweet and promptly ate it. Only afterwards did I discover that it was supposed to be held in the mouth to sweeten the coffee.

I often went to this particular café, and as an entertainment sometimes went down with de Wiart's horse, Nancy. Once there, she would half follow me in, with just her head and front feet through the door, to the amusement of the customers. Nancy liked being made a fuss of, and it became a bit of a show. I would ask the owner for sugar, but withheld it until Nancy kissed me. '*brassez moi*' I would say in French, and as I raised my face, she would lean over and nuzzle her face in mine.

She was a horse that I never had to call. I would just clap my hands and she would race across the field, giving a sort of chuckle as she arrived. It was possible to ride her down the road without anything on her at all, not even a headcollar, steering her with the pressure of my knees. At night, if we were in a barn, she would lie down and place her head on my legs and I'd put my arm round her neck.

Nancy had a remarkable temperament and, like most cavalry horses, stood up well to the noise of gunfire. While out riding on one occasion, I was about to pass a 4.5 inch howitzer, when I was stopped by a member of the gun team, as the gun was about to fire. The 4.5 inch howitzer was a big gun. On the road, it was pulled by six draught horses, and would be manoeuvred into position by a caterpillar tractor, before being carefully hidden, usually in a hedgerow, surrounded by camouflage netting. Enemy balloonists always tried hard to pin-point a heavy gun in action, but while they might see a gun fire, any wind moved the after-smoke away quickly enough to disguise the exact location. The trick was to ensure that everyone near the gun stood stock still, as sudden movement after firing would keep the balloonists' eyes on the spot. Only after a couple of minutes had passed would a whistle blow to give the all clear.

I was no farther than twenty yards away from the howitzer when I was stopped, at which point one of the gun crew said, 'I think you had better get off your horse and hold her head'. 'She won't mind,' I replied. This surprised him. 'Put the lanyard in her mouth and she will fire it for you,' I assured him. I gave Nancy a stroke and talked to her as they fired. There was a flash and a thunderous bang, but Nancy didn't show the slightest bit of interest.

She was a most lovable mare, and when I was later sent down to an equitation school in 1917, I was genuinely sad to leave her. She was killed at the end of the war when a shell burst almost underneath her, but, though it seems hard, I was glad. So many of the Regiment's horses were handed over to local farmers at the end of the war, and there was no knowing what might have happened to her.

Before the Battle of Arras, I went with de Wiart to Paris Plage, a small town by the sea. We had gone for an officers' conference, one of the many they used to have before a major attack. Amongst the other orderlies milling around, I spotted Ben Spooner, a trooper from C Squadron. He had been a troop officer's servant before the war and, like myself, had come out with the Regiment in August 1914. I don't remember what we talked about particularly, but we had several hours to kill before we rejoined our officers, so we decided to have a walk round the town. In Paris Plage there was a photographic shop, and we dived in there to have our pictures taken together, picking them up just before we were due to be back.

The Battle of Arras began on April 9th and lasted until mid-May. The Brigade had been in intensive training for quite a while before-hand, as it was to be used early on in the assault. The weather was very cold and frosty, and after a preliminary bombardment the Brigade attacked, capturing most of their objectives, I believe. Early on in the battle, de Wiart suffered another, if minor, wound to his ear, and for the next few weeks was forced to ride around with a great pad bandaged on to the side of his head. This would have looked all right, had I not also suffered a minor head wound soon afterwards, which ensured that my head too was bandaged. We must have looked a funny pair riding around, officer and servant both swathed with khaki bandages, but otherwise in fine fettle.

I got my head wound while we were billeted in the village of St Nicolas, which was close to the front line and was almost totally destroyed. My accommodation was in a dug out, and I sat there listening to the sound of shells coming over. The shelling was fairly sporadic, but every now and again one dropped nearby. 'Cor, that was a near one!' I said, and stuck my head outside the dugout entrance to see where it had landed.

When I came round, I found myself at a field dressing station, propped up on a bale of hay with a veterinary sergeant busily cutting my hair off, with shears used to trim the hair from a horse's heels and ears. He did this prior to an inspection by the MO, who told me that I had been blessed with a very thick skull. Apparently a shrapnel ball had ricocheted off my bare head just as I poked it out of the dugout but, apart from a very sore head, there was thankfully no other damage. 'By God, you are a lucky man,' the MO said, 'if that had been me, I would have been dead.' He told me that he had a thin skull and certainly wouldn't have survived without a helmet on. My head was dressed and, as I was well enough to carry on, I went back to Brigade. On my return, de Wiart asked after my welfare. 'It didn't do me a lot of good, sir, but I'm not too bad,' I replied, wondering afterwards whether I had not sounded a little sarcastic. I wore the bandage for at least a month, although I had a headache for six.

One afternoon, Holmes came to see me. De Wiart was worried that the dark mare – Nancy – had come down with sunstroke, and he wanted me to pay special attention to her. It was important to get her out of the sun, and so for several days I looked after her in the remains of a house on the outskirts of Arras. The house had lost its roof, but had just enough of the ground floor ceiling left to afford cover. Discovering an old bath tub, I filled it with water from a shallow well nearby, and on the orders of a veterinary officer periodically bathed Nancy's head to get her temperature down. Pushing her head down between her front legs, I used a bit of old sacking to squeeze the water over her, just enough to keep her head cool.

There was an open-air swimming pool quite close to where I was. It still had water in it, and several men from Brigade Headquarters used to go down and have a swim, together with several goldfish which had somehow found their way into the pool. An unofficial sports day was organised on one occasion, with prizes being awarded for the different races. The high board was also still in position, and an impromptu diving contest was held, won by one of the officers.

When I wasn't at the pool, I was back at the house looking after Nancy. Standing in the doorway one morning, I noticed a cart coming up the road towards my house, driven, curiously enough, by a gendarme, with an elderly Frenchman sitting next to him. Stopping at my house, the gendarme climbed down and began speaking some incomprehensible French at me, pulling various papers from his pocket as he spoke. I didn't know what he wanted, but I guessed the papers had something to do with the house, for they clearly wished to go in. Pushing past, they went to move some loose floor boards in one corner of the house, which I had deliberately placed over a cellar trap-door in case it gave way under Nancy's weight.

Not knowing what they wanted, I became annoyed, telling them that the horse was 'très malade' and should not be disturbed. But both men ignored what I said, and carried on scurrying around until they had got into the cellar, from which they reappeared moments later clutching several bottles of wine. Had any soldiers known of this treasure trove, the cellar would have been stripped bare long ago, and I now felt doubly annoyed at missing out on such a hoard. Doubtless, the owner wanted to secure his wines before he lost everything to the war, and was clearly intent on filling his wagon with as much wine as his tired grey horse could be expected to pull. I watched as they made endless trips to the cellar, before the old man handed me the last four bottles and pushed off, leaving me to replace the floorboards!

At Brigade HQ, we could expect to receive rations roughly every three days, although quite what food might arrive was another matter. The strangest that a group of eight of us received, as a two-day ration, was a whole 56lb cheese, a tin of biscuits, and some tins of Tickler's Plum Jam. Quite what we were supposed to do with a whole cheese, none of us knew, until one of the corporals suggested we made toasted cheese. Putting a dixie over a fire, we began to chop the cheese into it, alternatively adding water to make it more runny and bran to thicken it. All we ended up with was an unpleasant, gooey mess which we spooned onto the biscuits, and ate with a dollop of the Tickler's jam.

Tickler's was the worst of the various jams available, because it tasted of paraffin. The best was Colonial Conserve, but most of that seemed to vanish into the officers' mess long before we saw it. Tins of corned beef were also very common. Like the jams, they varied greatly in quality; the worst of them, on a hot day, could literally be poured out of the can, being almost entirely liquid fat. Actually pleasant to eat were the circular loaves of white bread, cut across the top so that they broke more easily. Unfortunately, they were too often put into sacks straight after baking, and were consequently pretty flat when they came out again.

To supplement our diet, volunteers walked to the nearest YMCA marquee, although this might be ten miles away. If the sergeant in charge gave his permission, the lads pooled what money they had on them before one or more volunteers, a couple of horses' nose bags in hand, started the long but usually pleasant walk. The idea was to go and fetch whatever was available, tins of fruit, chocolate, cigarettes, tins of Capstan tobacco, and to share out the proceeds equally on return. As these trips made a change from the routine of life at Headquarters, I volunteered many times and on one of these trips actually met an old school friend, Will Sherlock.

It was an odd meeting, for we were both quite alone on a long straight road, in fact we had walked towards each other for a full ten minutes before a hand shot out and a voice shouted, 'Ben Clouting!' I looked closely. 'Will Sherlock! My goodness!' We had grown up together and been to the same school at Beddingham. His parents had been farm workers who lived within a mile of my family, so I had seen a lot of him. He had joined the Artillery and was out on an errand for the battery. We stopped and had a natter, and talked about the past and what had happened to friends, and then we parted and I never saw or heard of him again, not even to know if he survived the war.

Of all the creatures an outside life brought a soldier into contact with, lice were the most hated and rats the most loathed. Lice had been with us since the Mons Retreat, when the discovery that I was infested by them had a great effect on me. We'd never been warned about them before the war, indeed, I had never seen them but I knew what they were. Smaller than ants, they were white fat things like little grubs and laid their eggs wherever there was body hair, sticking on before spreading out into all one's clothes. Where they originally came from I never knew, some said from straw, but all I know is that for three or four days I had become frantic to get rid of them. I did not think I could tell anyone; I felt embarrassed and ashamed. I dumped my underpants in the hope that that would help, but of course it made no difference at all. Little did I know that everyone else was just as lousy. No one said anything at first, but then in talk the truth came out.

From that time onwards, we all suffered from interminable itching as these creatures roamed around our clothes, leaving blotchy red bite marks wherever they stopped to feast. To get rid of them, a burning candle was run up and down the seams, killing off most of the tiny white eggs as well as the live lice; alternatively, we cracked them between our thumb nails.

Every now and again, we were given baths in brewery vats, where a ladder was used to climb down into three or four feet of water, heated by a steam pipe. After little more than a couple of minutes, we would be ordered out to be rinsed off with a cold bucket of water before being reunited with our clothes. These had been taken away to be deloused using hot air, but this treatment provided only temporary relief and we were soon lousy again. In 1916, my parents had sent me a green shaving-type stick which boldly – and inaccurately – claimed to cure the problem. However, miracle cures aside, only boiling our clothes seemed to get rid of the lice.

By 1917, we had got hold of square biscuit tins in which to boil our underclothes, but we had to be careful on two counts. The first was, if the unit was forced to move unexpectedly. This happened only once, but it proved costly. For having hastily rolled up my wet clothes, I shoved them into my saddle bag, only to discover later than the leather of the saddle had stained and mottled my shirt. The second was, that we had to make sure there was a good supply of water, for otherwise the tin's soldered edges would melt on the open fire. However, if all was well we boiled our cotton underpants and flannelette shirts (known as grey-backs) before pegging them out to dry, finally, although not indefinitely, lice-free.

It was perhaps while our clothes were drying that we would join in one of the many organised ratting expeditions. Soldiers' attitudes to the rats differed greatly. Some hated them, and never got used to their loathsome presence. Others, especially those from the countryside, like myself, or those who had worked on farms, were not particularly bothered by them. During the period I had been in the trenches in 1915, there had been an enormous number of rats which ran along the top of the trenches, or swam, snout above the water, through the sodden front and support lines. These rats could be the size of small cats, for there were any number of dead bodies near the lines on which to feed.

That they ate the dead bodies was only natural, but it hardly endeared them to the men. This explained why ratting was such a popular pastime with officers' servants and transport men alike. Ratting took place either around deserted farmhouses, or among holes in a hedgerow. A whole afternoon could be taken up, packing cordite into the holes before the rats were smoked out in their dozens. Earlier in the war, ratting had been something of a laborious exercise, as cartridge cases were emptied from hundreds of .202 bullets to get enough cordite to prove effective. By 1917, when more shells were available, it was possible to get hold of a shell case, or better still, the cordite that was packed separately to fire the big guns.

Howitzer cordite gave off a nasty green gas and was packed into a hole from which a trail of cordite was drawn. Once the trail was lit, a clod of earth was quickly packed around the cordite in the hole, forcing the fumes down the tunnels and the rats out. There was a great deal of excitement as we laid into the rats with sticks and clubs, scattering them squealing in all directions, as we killed just as many as we possibly could.

Since the outbreak of war I had had just one leave, those seven days at my parents' home after my discharge from hospital. However, in August 1917 I was given a three-day pass to England. It was not a long leave by any standards, but I was delighted to get the chance to go home, and I was soon on my way down the line to catch a troop train to the channel ports. The train was packed with soldiers, most exhausted, all filthy, but to a man, glad to be going home and in good spirits. As the train trundled its way through the French countryside, a rumour filtered through to us that there was a nurse aboard and that she was being sent home because she was pregnant. Whether there was any truth in this, heaven only knows, but the men began musing as to whether she would get a wound stripe, and the baby, a blue chevron for being on active service.

It had taken a long time for my father to recover from his injury in 1916. For several months, my parents had lived with an aunt of mine in Twickenham, where dad had convalesced until well enough to take on light work at Croxley Green. He was looking after a pony, and in exchange, they were allowed to live in 'Elmcote' cottage, a house belonging to a soldier on duty in France. It was really an act of kindness, the house being rented on the understanding that, when the soldier returned, they would move out.

As a three-day pass began and ended with the Transport Officer at Dover, I was anxious to get home as soon as the brief formalities were over. Once past the officer, I had to make my way to London, where I took the Bakerloo Line to Watford. Armed with my parents' new address, I finally arrived at Croxley Green station a little after 2am, where a taxi driver patriotically gave me a free lift home.

My father was very disgruntled at being woken up by my knock, leaning out of the window to discover what on earth was going on. 'It's our Ben, it's our Ben!' I heard my sisters shouting, followed by a racing of feet as they arrived at the door, candle in hand. Nobody went to bed that night; the whole family was together and we sat and just talked and talked.

The next day, I outlined where I had been and what I'd seen, and showed them those souvenirs I had brought home, including the newspaper picture of my parents. They had bought the home issue of *The Daily Mirror* for several weeks in the expectation of seeing it, but it was never published in the UK.

In no time at all I was on my way again. Everybody put a brave face on it, and rather than a sad farewell at the station, I left my family at the front gate. To hide her fears, my mother became almost jolly, following me out of the house, while pretending to blow a trumpet and singing 'Come to the Zulu war, boys.' I had sung it as a lad, when I had played soldiers with my red-tipped sword. This was my send-off, and, after I had gone, my mother went inside, and cried as if her heart was absolutely broken. It was days before she got over it for, as I learnt later, she was not only distraught at my going but felt that by singing that song, she was in effect sending me off to be killed. I had already been wounded twice, and both my parents felt that sooner or later I would get hit again.

I headed back to Belgium, to Ypres, where the battle for Passchendaele was in full swing. The battle, 3rd Ypres as it was also known, was a fiasco. In the whole war, I never saw anything or anywhere worse than the wasteland through which the infantry had to fight. It was desolate but for the tree stumps where a wood once grew or the few bricks where a building had been, and sometimes the hulks of tanks, jammed deep in the mud, wrecked by enemy fire.

The first tank I had seen was soon after their first use during the Somme Battle the previous September. At that time, prior to their attack, the roads on which they were to drive had been taped off and put out of bounds. Only later did we hear fantastic stories about what they could do, and I wondered why they had not been more successful. To my mind, they looked unwieldy, with the wheels at the back to help steer and the little turrets on each side. I had always been grateful not to have served in them, and up at Ypres it was possible to get a good look inside. They were cramped death traps. The tanks I saw were generally burnt out and, on more than one occasion, I saw the grisly remains of their crews fried inside. These tanks had the smallest of trap doors to get in and out through, and it must have been a ghastly end when the tank was knocked out and the crew was unable to escape.

As far as the eye could see, everything was devastated, the only signs of human habitation being the endless miles of duckboards that traversed the battlefield. To step off the duckboards was to risk death, for most of the shell holes lay lip to lip, full of mud or contaminated water. As men had literally drowned in the quagmire, wire netting was spread over the duckboards, to help soldiers keep their footing. I used these duckboards during September and October 1917, as I crossed and re-crossed the battlefield, taking rations to any of the Brigade's beleaguered battalions in the front line. We used mules to make the journey, picking them up from the divisional dump where they had either been allocated to take up the usual rations of bully beef and biscuits, or to carry the most important cargo, water. Water was taken up in old petrol cans, into which we dropped a lighted match to burn off any excess fuel, before swilling them out and filling them up. The cans held two gallons of water, four cans being hung on each side of a mule. Every can weighed some twenty pounds, so that a fully-laden mule was expected to carry eight cans, or 160 pounds of water. We would go up the line in the afternoon, so that we would arrive near the front at twilight, this being anything up to two miles from the actual battle line. Mules were co-operative creatures and would go where horses couldn't but the ground was so pitted that we could only travel so far before passage became impossible. Normally we headed for a pre-determined spot, to be met by the

Regiment's Quartermaster with his ration party from the line. He would set up a post, perhaps with some camouflage netting hung up on tree stumps, so that when we arrived we could off-load the mules under cover, before picking up the empty cans and beginning our journey back. His ration party then lugged the Battalion's food and water the rest of the way.

Slogging our way up, we would pass other parties of one sort or another, coming down parallel tracks or squeezing past on our own. We rarely stopped, other than to pass on any useful tips, preferring to press on as quickly as possible so we could begin our way back correspondingly early.

Yet there is one image that has stuck in my mind, and if I could paint, I would paint it today. It would be of a soldier with his right arm blown off, a piece of dressing pinned across his wound, leading another man who had been blinded. The two were on a parallel line of duckboards to ours, the blinded man, bandages draped across his eyes, walking behind. He was holding onto his comrade's left shoulder as he was led back down the line, and it was unbelievably pathetic. As such, it was not an abnormal sight, indeed it didn't even begin to turn my stomach. Yet it was a moment somehow framed in time, and I have never forgotten it.

Most of us were quite callous by that time; the dead were simply the unlucky ones. Death was one of those things, and if it came to burying a man, the act of handling him meant nothing, it was just a thing you did out of humanity. There was no shortage of shell holes in which to bury the dead, making it quite easy to roll them down into a hole with little ceremony, and cover them up. They were not you, that was the important thing, and although that sounds callous, it did breed an unbelievable comradeship amongst the living. Throughout my army life, I never really had a bosom pal, and if anything, was something of a loner. Yet even I felt a comradeship then that I never experienced again, and it was the one thing I missed more than anything else after the war.

Those trips up the line never became any easier; they were always difficult and hazardous. Exposed and vulnerable on the duckboards, it was not hard to feel that life was very tenuous at times. Once, late in the afternoon, we felt sure the Germans had seen our small column, for although any sudden shelling felt quite personal, there seemed no other reason why they should send over two batches of shells, 'coal boxes', or 'Jack Johnsons' as they were also known. There were ten of us, each leading a mule in single file, when they began landing all around us, between sixty and eighty yards away. They didn't land all at once but in two salvoes of four, with the range near enough dead right. If they could see us, then it needed just a slight readjustment and we could be wiped out in one go. There was no cover in front, so I shouted that we should turn and chase back to a small mound we had passed. I had barely got the words out when the second salvo come over, throwing earth over twenty feet into the air. There was a terrific crash followed by a black cloud of smoke. I was frightened, bloody frightened. My self-control drained away and I found myself muttering, 'Oh God, help me, please God, help me'. I could visualise the next round landing in the middle of us, and there we were, trying to turn heavily-laden mules around. Time seemed to freeze, but in the end we all reached the comparative safety of the knoll and there we waited until the Germans laid off. We had been lucky. 'Coal boxes' could cause awful casualties, but the mud was so thick that the shells were ploughing deep into the ground, severely reducing their effectiveness.

CHAPTER EIGHT

1918: From Cayeux to Cologne

Ben

In November 1917, de Wiart was wounded again. This time he had been hit by a shell splinter in the hip, the wound subsequently turning septic. He had been sent back to England, and had therefore been forced to give up command of the Brigade. Whenever de Wiart had been absent before, I had remained with the transport of whichever unit I was with. This time he was likely to be away for a long time, so it was decided that I should return to the Regiment.

No sooner had I got back, than I was 'claimed' by Captain Jackie Aylmer. He was due to be sent as an instructor to the Cavalry School of Equitation at Cayeux-sur-Mer, a small, undistinguished town, where the mouth of the River Somme meets the sea. 'I want you to take over my two horses at the school,' he had ordered. He had been out with the Regiment since 1914 and even now was still absolutely mustard. Nicknamed Foxy because of his sharp features, Aylmer was a consummate soldier and an excellent horseman, which went a long way in a cavalry regiment. Very popular with the other officers, Aylmer came from a wealthy family where he only had to hold his finger up and everybody bowed. He had a sharp temper, and had always expected the impossible from us. He was, suffice to say, not very popular with the troops.

Aylmer was not a big strapping man, whereas men like Hornby and Bridges really stood out. When officers were in uniform, some of them really looked the part and others did not. The uniform did not make the man, nor was it necessarily even the way an officer commanded his men; there was something else, almost indefinable, a certain stature: Hornby and Bridges walked and looked like soldiers. In the cavalry, more than anywhere, skills such as horsemanship were important, and there were officers, we would say, who could not ride a hoof pick, an instrument used to clear dirt and stones from a horse's hoof. The pre-war gulf between officers and men still existed among surviving officers like Aylmer and Bridges, but the war had forced a change, in that those who came along afterwards, the new officers, the civilian businessmen, lawyers, those who would never have joined the army but for war, dealt with everyday practicalities differently from pre-war officers.

Many orderlies whose officers had been wounded were sent down to Cayeux, taking their horses with them to be used at the school. However, I would look after Aylmer's and therefore had to say a fond farewell to de Wiart's two mares, and especially Nancy, before I got on my way. At Cayeux I soon found that I was to be billeted, along with three other cavalrymen, at an estaminet belonging to a pleasant couple, Monsieur and Madame Daye. Monsieur Daye was in the artillery but lived at home while serving Cayeux's local shore battery. He had at one time been at the front but had been gassed, as a result of which he suffered from bronchial trouble and was now seeing out the war protecting the town's lighthouse. Each evening, he left the estaminet to join his battery of 75s down near the beach, although why it should have been necessary to guard a lighthouse which wasn't actually working, appeared to us a curious waste of resources. Quite what that battery was expected to do to repel a naval attack was, in any case, even more obscure.

Not that this was any of my concern. I was at Cayeux to groom Aylmer's horses, turning them out each day for officers to ride at the equitation school. The stalls in which the grooms worked were very modern by the standards of the day, and were situated in the grounds of a large private house. I was given two stalls in which to look after the horses before I took them over to the outdoor school for the morning's lessons. After the ride I collected the horses, fed, watered and groomed them, before turning them out again in the afternoon, if they were needed. I never taught the officers to ride, and only occasionally was I expected to do any guard duties; otherwise I was free to do what I liked.

At the school there was a very unruly horse that no one would ride. She was a large black horse, and frightened many of the inexperienced officers by rearing up and walking two or three paces forward in an attempt to throw her rider. As a result this horse was passed on to the grooms to be dealt with, and I quickly took it upon myself to straighten her out. There were one or two old tricks used in the army to 'cure' an unruly horse. One was to give the horse a thwack on the top of the head with a bottle of water. The idea was that as the bottle broke, the horse sensed blood running down its neck, and generally decided it was not worth giving the rider any more trouble.

In dealing with a rearing horse, my father had taught me that it was best to pull the animal right over as it stood up on its hind legs. The art was to slip one's feet out of the stirrups while giving the reins a sharp pull, helping the horse to fall on to its back. When

141

any horse falls to the ground, the first thing it must do in order to stand up is to raise its head. This is different, for example, from a cow, which always gets up back feet first, and means that if the rider is quick and sits on the horse's head, the animal is effectively immobilised. This is exactly what I did, handing out a hiding on her flank, before showing her the whip that I had used. It was a very effective solution and I subsequently had no further problems.

Life was quite easy. As far as possible I kept out of Aylmer's way, getting on extremely well with my co-billeters, a Jock from the Scots Greys, a Corporal from the 16th Lancers, and another man from the 3rd Dragoons, all, like myself, servants to instructors at the school. We all worked together and were quite competitive to see who could turn out the best horses. Occasionally we took the horses down to the sea for a swim, or, as the tide went out a long way and the sand was firm, exercised them along the beach.

We whiled away many hours at the estaminet which Madame Daye ran with her cousin, Jeanne, an elderly spinster who helped her out. Both were very kind and helpful, and, although they were under no obligation to feed us, took our rations, which they cooked and supplemented with extra food, very often horse meat. To many cavalrymen, the idea of eating horse meat was inconceivable. In the cavalry, horses were branded to show to which Regiment they belonged. In my Regiment, 4DG appeared on the right shoulder, while a number and a single letter A, B or C was burnt into a horse's hind hoof denoting the Squadron. These horses not only belonged to the Regiment but almost became an extension of the cavalryman himself. Eating horse meat was therefore almost a form of cannibalism.

Early in the war, we had had a horse which got five bullet wounds in the backside from a machine gun. These wounds were not fatal, and as trained horses were a valuable commodity, a twitch was used to steady the horse, as our veterinary officer attempted to dig the bullets out with large tweezers. In the end four were removed but the fifth could not be budged, so it was decided that, as French troops were in the same field as ourselves, the horse would be poleaxed and handed over to them to eat. The French were happy to have this unexpected gift and, as a friendly gesture, gave our cook the liver, which had gone down a treat until one trooper asked, 'By God, this liver's good, bobajig [Hindustani for cook], where did you get it?' 'It's C40's,' cook replied. This trooper immediately retched and brought the whole lot up. 'You dirty bastard, that was my horse!' Other troopers were also unhappy about what they had eaten, but it didn't bother me one little bit, in fact I quite enjoyed it.

At the estaminet Madame Daye, in particular, tried to get us to speak our pidgin French, while she replied in English. Her English was quite good, and in the end she even began writing to my mother to tell her how we were all getting on, and indeed my mother replied, thanking her for looking after us. Her husband, when we saw him, was a lively man who turned out to have been something of a local comedian before the war. When home, he ran the next best thing to a local cinema, a drill hall with wooden benches in which he would show silent French films to anyone who was interested. As the compère, he would dress up as a clown and tell a few jokes before the show, all of which were beyond our French. He knew that I could sing, and now and again got me to peal off a few impromptu songs to the accompaniment of a pianist who failed, with aplomb, ever to get in the right key. If there were no other would-be stars, the show began, and he would come and sit next to me and try to translate the captions which ran with the film.

Besides the 'cinema', the only other place of note was a brothel about two miles outside the town. This was a very large house which served as an exclusive all-round entertainment club for all other ranks, and had official sanction. It was properly run, with roulette tables, and Crown and Anchor games, while there were anything up to ten girls working there under the management of a madame. If not actually working, these girls would wander round the room and talk to the troops; there was no obligation for soldiers to jump into bed with them.

Troops from the riding school were free to do as they wished after work, and most made their way down to the brothel, although by no means were they the only ones there. Farther up the road was a large convalescent camp, but while the Military Police stopped the camp patients coming into the town, the same restriction didn't apply to the brothel, which consequently was always full. On pay days it would be packed, and at times it would be a job to get to the gambling tables to lay a bet. There was a great atmosphere on these nights, and with so much money flying about, it was very exciting.

The girls were examined every day by an elderly doctor who often popped into the café in which I was billeted for a Cognac coffee and a chat. We would pull his leg about his job, and as he spoke fairly good English, he joked with us and let us in on all the latest goings on. His talk to us about his work at the brothel was an absolute eye-opener for me as he relayed his daily anecdotes to us: 'I said to one of the young girls, "You look a bit sore, how many soldiers did you have last night?" She made a quick tally and told me "fifty-six". "You had better have three or four days off," and I put her on the sick list.'

In March, the Germans launched what turned out to be their final fling on the Western front, against Gough's Fifth Army. Despite the tremendous events that unfolded at this time, I remained with the other grooms at Cayeux, when many other non-combatant soldiers, such as cooks, transport men and labourers were being combed out of the back areas to bolster the crumbling front line.

The fighting at the front was ferocious, although we didn't know how close to a complete breakthrough the Germans came, as they regained all the land that they had lost over the previous twenty months. At Cayeux, my co-billeters were glad to be well out of it, but I was becoming restless. I considered myself a fighting soldier, and I was bored with being everybody's servant. Being at Cayeux felt like being in the peacetime army again, and I increasingly became tired of the school, and in the end asked if I could be returned to my Regiment. When I got back to the billet I told the others, and they all pronounced me mad for giving up such an easy job. They were all content to see out the war in luxury. The corporal in particular had had three days' leave to get married in England, and had no intention of going anywhere near the front again, if he had any say in the matter.

My decision was partly prompted by an incident which had hurt my pride. During the war, those soldiers who were orderlies, or those considered 'too familiar' with officers, were sometimes shunned, or made to feel they were having an easy time. I had nearly come to blows with one man, over a slight, while in the trenches in 1915; on another occasion, in 1917, I had again been upset by an underhand remark. I had been out exercising de Wiart's horses. Both were fine, thoroughbred horses and as such were a sure sign of 'familiarity' with officers. I was riding one and leading the other, when I happened to pass a stationary battery of artillery, and as I passed, one of the drivers turned to his mate and shouted, 'And what did you do in the war, Daddy?' We were all miles behind the line, but he, at least, would probably be heading towards it, and that was enough for him to feel I was having a cushy number. I rode on because it was my business to ride on, but it stung me. On my left sleeve I had two wound stripes, and on my right, a red and three blue chevrons, denoting how many years I had served in France. The red signified that I was an Old Contemptible and I would dearly have loved to have offered him my sleeve with a 'Wipe your nose on that!' Within the Regiment, I was considered close to de Wiart because he knew my father, but it was his personal servant, Holmes, whom de Wiart picked up in 1916, who was his great favourite. When I gave up being an orderly, the atmosphere changed, for I had returned to the fold; I was one of them again.

The only people I felt I would miss were Madame Daye and her husband. They had been so kind, that years after the war I attempted to get in touch with them. They had moved to Amiens to set up a cinema in the 1920s, but both had died quite young, the husband no doubt from the gas poisoning.

Just before I was due to return to the Regiment, I paid a final visit to the brothel. The place was humming as usual when, all of a sudden, the house was raided by five officers. All had been drinking and had come, we assumed, from the officers' convalescent home a little farther out of the town. Officers never came into the place, and as they arrived everyone fell silent. I'm not sure what they thought they were going to find, and I supposed that they had come out of curiosity or boredom, but as they began to push their rank around, a big Australian, who ran a Crown and Anchor game, took charge of the situation. Making his way to the biggest of the officers, he said, 'Sir, if you are a man you will take your jacket off and fight me. If you are a gentleman you will take the others and leave'. It was the perfect line to take, for the officers had no option but to go.

Leaving the school, I received a rail warrant and headed back towards the front. It was July and the German attacks had mostly petered out, and now there was a temporary lull while both sides caught their breath. Back with the Regiment, I discovered de Wiart had returned to France in April and had been given command of another brigade, in the Bantam Division. But with his uncanny ability to attract enemy fire, he had been badly wounded, this time in the left leg, and had returned to England. To all intents and purposes this finished his war, although he managed to scrape back to France just in time to see the Armistice.

The Regiment had just received a new draft of men and had gone into training, principally musketry. However, in case we were required to act as infantry, we practised advancing in a line with bayonets fixed. At this time it was late summer and we were bivouacked in a large field, the men taking cover under a thick hedge that ran all the way around the field. My own billet was in a small gap in a hedge, where I and another man had rigged up a little cover using a ground sheet.

One morning, the order came round that the following day we were due for a special parade, and that we were to turn out in pre-war kit. Many of us had collected various bits of excess baggage along the way; I, for example, had a French cook's knife,

145

while, carefully folded on the back of my saddle, I had a marvellous blanket that had once belonged to a German officer. Like everyone else, I had also picked up various pots and pans, and the odd souvenir. Before the parade began, all these personal belongings were to be left at the side of the field, and just to make sure, we were warned that our troop sergeants would be making a thorough inspection of our saddlery.

The following morning we stood by our horses in preparation for the special parade. Behind us the hedgerow appeared as if ready to host a giant jumble sale, only there were to be no buyers or sellers. For we were given the order to mount and the Regiment promptly moved out, riding to an identical field, perhaps ten miles from where we had been. The Regiment had pulled a fast one to shake each squadron out of all its excess baggage. Everyone was very annoyed, but our officers were eager to cut down all superfluous weight on the horses, as the Germans had begun to retreat and the cavalry might come into its own.

The casualty rate among officers during the war, especially junior ones, had ensured that even in the rarefied atmosphere of the regular cavalry, where breeding and money had meant so much, one or two ex-rankers had been made up to officers while I had been away. It was for this reason that, on my 21st birthday, I decided to put in for a commission. At the time, we were still billeted out in the open, and I went to find the orderly sergeant to fill in the appropriate form. When it came to which school I had gone to, I wrote 'National Church School' and in the end it was this that proved my undoing. My application was refused. When I asked one of the clerical orderlies why, he told me it was the village school I had gone to. 'The old school tie, boy,' he said. It was one of those things. I had had enough of being an orderly and this was a chance, or so it had seemed, to get on. By putting in for a commission, I was accepting that, if it was granted, I would eventually have been moved to another regiment, but I was willing to accept the change.

That I should have considered a commission showed how times had changed; that it was refused, proved that not every rule could be broken. I was somewhat peeved, but in time I realised I would not have been able to carry myself as an officer; I simply didn't have the language or the words. Sergeant Dusty Miller, perhaps in an attempt to lift my spirits, received permission to make me up to a lance-corporal. Throwing two lance-corporal stripes at me, he said, 'Put those on your sleeves and mount the guard tonight, and that's an order'.

Increasing numbers of German prisoners could be seen, trudging back to our makeshift prison cages. Many were ridiculously young and looked as if their world had fallen to pieces. They looked dishevelled, their equipment dilapidated, for their lines of supply were finally breaking down, and many soldiers were left to scrounge around for their food. Right at the end of the war, I stopped at a farmhouse to find the owners in tears: the Germans had passed through the previous night, and had eaten their old guard dog, cooking it at the farm before moving on. Passing one hastily-erected POW cage, holding sixty or seventy newly-captured Germans, our curiosity was sufficiently aroused that we went over and had a look. Most of the Germans appeared very hungry and tired, and only seemed interested in swapping what bits and pieces they still owned for food. Several Germans passed over various trinkets, but one in particular caught my eye. He looked exhausted and was offering a watch for a tin of corned beef. The exchange agreed, the watch was flipped over the fence as the three-quarter pound tin sailed in the opposite direction. The German was so worn out that he completely missed the tin, which thudded into his eye leaving him with a bad swelling to add to his general misery.

By no means all the Germans were giving up. The enemy's rearguard action was tenacious, and often caused grievous casualties, as well-placed machine guns caught infantrymen out in the open, or artillery raked battalions on the move.

On one night in early October, Jerry gunners caught a battalion of Jocks and a battery of artillery, in the same road at the same time. I rode past the carnage hours afterwards. It was clear that the Germans had been deadly accurate, for there were any number of dead Scotsmen in their kilts sprawled about between shattered guns and dead horses. The debris continued for several hundred yards all down the road, underlining the congestion of traffic that there must have been at the time. At least four guns had been knocked out, lying upside-down or on their sides, with dead gunners and drivers strewn around.

The shelling had happened on a road just outside a village, through which I had had to pass on my way to discover where the Regiment's rations were due to be dumped that night. The village had been badly knocked about, leaving everything in chaos. Evidently the place was a major thoroughfare, for troops and artillery were all moving up to keep pace with the German retreat, so I decided it would be easier to make my through the town's outskirts and found a passage safely through.

That evening, I returned to the village with the Regiment. The destruction had largely been cleared; only the village, now cloaked in darkness, was crowded with fresh battalions all making their way forward. By this time our Colonel was losing his temper. 'Can't anyone get us out of this bloody hole?' I rode forward to say that I had passed that way in the morning and knew a route around the village. I was told to lead on, and took the Regiment single file along the track and out the other side of the village.

During the last weeks of the war, I was used as a ground scout. I carried a lance with a pair of fish tail wire cutters, screwed on about a foot below the top of the shaft. The lance was held by a sling attached to the forearm, and was carried with the shaft held tightly under the arm. The tip of the lance could pick barbed or telephone wire and steer it into the cutters, the mere act of riding forward usually being enough to cut the wire. The ground scouts rode ahead, and to a certain extent picked the route the following squadrons would take. When crossing open country, they had to be very circumspect about which wires they broke. Telephone lines which the engineers might have run forward in the night might be carrying vital information, and naturally we feared cutting our own communications.

On the night of November 10th, we bivouacked in a field not far from Mons, and awaited further orders. The Germans were in full retreat, stopping only to fight the briefest rearguard actions, while their pioneers and engineers worked feverishly to delay our advance. At first light, we moved off a short distance to a road where we dismounted and stood at our horses' heads, facing the centre of the road. Each side of the road was lined with fully matured poplar trees into which German engineers had drilled, laying explosives. The intention had been to blow them across the road, but most had either failed to go off or had been defused by our engineers, the explosives being left to protrude from the tree trunks.

We had received information that some Germans were making a stand near a village called Ath, and that at 2pm the infantry was to make a frontal assault, supported by cavalry. Two regiments of cavalry, we and, I believe, the 18th Hussars, were to attack around Ath's flanks, cutting off the enemy's retreat, although our orders were not to worry about Ath itself, but to sweep past and harass any Germans we happened to come across. We were to be guided in the attack by what we found.

That morning, our Troop officer came round with a map to show us broadly the direction we were to take. At this time we were a few miles away from our target, for while rifle fire was quite distinct, it was nowhere near us. There would be further instructions before the attack went in, but meantime we checked our saddlery and all our equipment before the Regiment moved on again. It was fully light, and we were much nearer the firing line when we halted once again along a hedge-lined road that helped to conceal our presence. I had just begun to re-check my saddlery when I saw an old Douglas motorbike speeding towards us with a despatch rider frantically waving his helmet. As he came closer, I could hear him shouting, 'It's all over, boys, there's an Armistice. It's all over'. At first I didn't know what he meant. What was all over? I hadn't a clue. In fact, what was an Armistice? I'd never heard the word.

There wasn't any real excitement or jubilation at the news; naturally we were relieved, and I'm sure a weight lifted from our shoulders, but that was about all. The war everyone had hoped would end, had ended, but so too had a way of life. Now it had apparently dragged to a close, I, for one, felt almost ambivalent. I was unemotional by nature, and my jumbled thoughts, such as I had at 11 o'clock that November morning, went unspoken.

Immediately after the motorbike had sped away, the order came, 'All officers to the front!' (the front being wherever the Colonel was at the time). It was quickly followed by 'All senior NCOs to the front!', instructions being relayed through the NCOs to the troops that as of 11am we were to cease all offensive action. It was about 9am by this time, and there was still plenty of gunfire around Ath as it took time for the message to get round. Our sister Regiment, the 7th Dragoon Guards, launched, at the point of the sword, an attack in the last hour of the war. It seems funny that we didn't know anything about the eleventh hour of the eleventh day of the eleventh month, in fact many men didn't know what the date was; most were concerned only to live day to day.[1]

Editor
On November 11th 1918, the Regimental Diary records that the Brigade halted west of Beloeil, and the Dragoons billeted for the night at Quevan-camps. 'The men,' it says, 'were under cover but the horses were out.'

Ben
That evening we moved into a field and put the lines down. We were close to a small village, and during the evening some local people came out and brought us wine, which they had no doubt gone to great pains to hide during four years of occupation. I had a drink and joined in some of the light-hearted chat, but there were no particular celebrations, and the men remained quiet and subdued. While we had all lived under the threat of injury or death, there was a common purpose, but all of a sudden the threat

had been lifted. At the time I didn't know what to think, but years later I could recognise that there were some feelings of bitterness which didn't really go until I had left the army.

It was a bitterly cold Armistice night. Orders were issued that all our blankets were to be put on the horses and that we were to sleep under our coats. Later, a couple of officers came round. They had got wind that some troopers had pinched their blankets back, their walk-round pre-empting a flurry of activity as several men scrambled to reunite horses with covers. Meanwhile the rest of us kept warm, as we'd often done, by sleeping in groups of three, huddling together on ground sheets under our knee-length warm coats. A local farmer let us help ourselves to straw to pad the ground, and we used our saddles as wind breaks. We finally settled down with our cap comforters pressed down firmly on our heads and our coats pulled over our shoulders. It was an uncomfortable night, we ached with the cold, our legs were stiff, our extremities chilled to the bone. In the morning there was some half-hearted merriment as men stood their frozen coats upright, as testimony to the cold.

For the next three or four days a phoney war continued, with occasional gunfire, and now and again the explosion of a delayed mine. These mines had been laid before the Armistice and were wired to explode once Jerry had pulled back, destroying crossroads, or other important junctions. At one crossroads we saw how the Germans had placed an eight-inch shell into each of four holes, wiring them together to blow the place to smithereens. The Engineers had got there just in time and disconnected them, leaving the shells sitting idly in their pits, their nose cones peeping above the road.

Before the Regiment received orders to ride for Germany, we were told to polish and clean everything to pre-war standards, or as near as humanly possible. We had no polish, but by cracking up old bricks, of which there was an ample supply, we made brick dust, an abrasive which, when used with a dab of water, could clean steel and polish buttons up a treat. It was the authorities' plan to show the German people that we were a victorious army, by the high level of smartness.

It was somewhat ironic that while our equipment and uniforms looked the part, the men wearing them were anything but healthy. Flu, or the 'parasite of unknown origin', as it was known, had taken hold of Europe that winter, so that as we rode towards Cologne we began to lose men, all of whom were quickly whisked to hospital. Our farrier was one of the first to drop, leaving the Troop without anyone to tend the horses, should a shoe come loose and need replacing. As luck would have it, the first horse to have problems was mine, so, having no option, I got hold of the farrier's kit and shoed my own horse, using what knowledge I'd picked up watching others. Evidently my efforts were considered good enough, because within no time at all I was made temporary farrier, and was subsequently assigned to look after another Troop as well. Each evening, it was my job to take the farrier's kit and walk round checking the horses' hooves, putting a nail in here and there, so as to avoid disruption when the Squadron was on the move. I continued the job almost until we reached Cologne, when reinforcement shoeing smiths arrived to take over.

Editor

Although an occupation of Berlin was seriously considered, there would have been immense practical problems supplying Allied armies stationed hundreds of miles into enemy territory. Such a scheme would have required a massive increase in manpower to guard vital supply lines, so instead the Allies decided to occupy the Rhineland. This region was not only the jewel in the crown of Germany's industrial power but, with the natural barrier of the mighty river Rhine, was an area easily defendable should hostilities resume.

In December 1918, the occupying force was to be troops of the 2nd Army, under General Sir Hubert Plumer. At the forefront of the Army, the 4th Dragoons, part of the 1st Cavalry Division, were commanded, by a quirk of fate, by forty-seven-year-old Major-General Richard Mullens, who had led the 4th Dragoons to France in August 1914. The advance guard was to be the 2nd Cavalry Brigade under Brigadier-General A Lawson. He would go ahead of the Army, reaching the Franco-German frontier at the end of the month.

Ben

As our Regiment had been first into action back in 1914, we were given the privilege of being the first troops to cross into German territory. As far as I know, the whole British Army stood still on 1st December 1918 while the 4th Dragoon Guards crossed a frost-covered frontier early one morning. We passed through several villages where the inhabitants came out to watch us pass by, including one small town where the Bürgermeister turned out to take the salute.

Editor

On December 1st at 5am, the 2nd Cavalry Brigade moved off, crossing the frontier at 9am near Eicherscheid, a town near Malmédy. Orders were given that, as far as possible, men of 1914 should be put in the vanguard of the advance as it crossed into Germany, and according to one war correspondent and author, Ferdinand Tuohy, it was the 4th Dragoon Guards who were the first to cross. By 4th December, the 1st Cavalry Division had reached Düren, approximately twenty miles from Cologne, but pushed on in response to urgent calls from the city's Mayor, Konrad Adenauer, to arrive and fill the dangerous power vacuum left by the departure of retreating German forces.

Ben

On December 6th, we entered Cologne, where we were to stay for the next four months. On that first day, I was part of an advance guard which rode ahead of the main body of Dragoons into the town. One squadron, A I believe, formed up in the square outside the Cathedral, while two troops under the command of 2nd Lieutenant Stanley rode on past the Cathedral to check that the Germans had crossed to the other side of the Rhine – the preliminary dividing line between the two armies.

The Troop was meant to go to the middle of the magnificent Hohenzollern Bridge, a broad-spanned bridge guarded at both ends by huge stone towers, and wide enough to take both conventional traffic and two railway tracks. Instead, on reaching the middle, Stanley said, 'Come on, let's go over and have a look'. At the command of 'Carry swords', we rode right over to the far side, whereupon the German sentries turned out and presented arms, Stanley returning the salute before riding forward to speak to the one officer present. We were there some minutes before we about-wheeled and rode back to rejoin the Regiment.

Editor

2nd Lieutenant Stanley had been ordered to lead both the 3rd and 4th Troops of C Squadron, and one section from the 2nd Machine Gun Squadron, to take over the bridge. Posting sentries at the western end and positioning a sub-section of machine guns to cover the crossing, Stanley led the two troops over the bridge, only to find a ten-man German guard formed up across the roadway at the other end. Intimating through a mixture of hand signals and broken French that he expected them to leave, Stanley gave the German officer in charge half an hour to remove the detachment. Refusing to move without the authority of the General commanding the Rhine bridges, the officer did agree to inform his superiors of the Dragoons' presence. Some minutes later, a staff car drew up, and out stepped a much-decorated German General who, on meeting 2nd Lieutenant Stanley, asked if he was aware that the British were not due to cross the bridge until the 12th. At this point a compromise was reached, giving control of two-thirds of the bridge to the British, enabling them, as Stanley later recalled, to 'keep observation of the Germans while they could not ascertain our movements at the Western end'. A chalk line was drawn across the bridge to signify the divide, while a German officer was ordered to report each sunrise to the British, informing them of when the Germans would withdraw from the eastern third of the bridge.

Ben

Before we crossed the Rhine, the Regiment's horses were taken up to the city zoo, while the Regiment went into billets at the Artillery Depot in Nippes. The following day, December 7th, I was sent with a section of six men to take over a little fort half a dozen miles away. The fort consisted of six anti-aircraft guns, all out of action with their breech blocks taken away. Our orders were to stay there until relieved. We were shown on a map where to go and had little difficulty finding it, although the trooper sent on later with our rations got hopelessly lost. This forced us to improvise, so, taking a break from the monotony of guarding the fort, we nipped off into a neighbouring field of turnips, where we were able to close in on a stray hare. The hare was duly despatched, cooked and served up with a loaf of poor quality bread, obtained from a local shop. This was the main event of an otherwise uneventful stay, and we returned three days later as the Regiment was awaiting permission to cross the Rhine, where it was to move into the vacated cavalry barracks in Deutz, overlooking the river.

Editor

The 4th Dragoon Guards unofficially crossed into Deutz on December 11th, a day early, to relieve congestion on the west bank. B squadron subsequently stayed in Deutz while A and C Squadrons returned the following morning to take part in a parade across the river.

Ben

It was a dull, overcast day when we assembled on the square in front of the Cathedral to make final preparations for the official crossing of the Hohenzollern Bridge. Shortly before 10am, a bugle call brought us to attention, followed by the order to mount and draw swords. We were in immaculate condition and must have brought home to the crowds of people watching that we were not just a victorious army, but a disciplined one too. As we moved off, the bands struck up with 'Rule Britannia', then as the Regiment swung round the Cathedral, I saw General Plumer ready to take the salute standing before a huge Union Jack.

No sooner had the Regiment crossed the bridge than it rode into

Deutz and beyond, fanning out east of the Rhine into a twenty-five-mile-deep de-militarised zone, which the Germans had vacated the day before. The Regiment was billeted in neighbouring villages as units were sent out. For three days I went with ten men, criss-crossing the buffer zone to ensure that the Germans' withdrawal was complete. It was a leisurely trip and we did not encounter any problems, returning to stay at our billet, a little pub near Wermelskirchen, north-east of Cologne. After this initial phase was completed, the Regiment rode back to Deutz to take over the vacated cavalry barracks. From here, a troop of cavalry would leave each day to ride around Cologne to ensure all was well and to remind the local population just who was in charge.

From now until the following June, when the final peace treaty was signed, all army personnel continued to live under the dictates of the Armistice. On our arrival, we were encouraged to walk around in pairs for self-protection, and were told to carry side-arms when out of barracks. We were still at war, and the authorities were keen to keep contact between us and civilians to a minimum. Back in Deutz, the routine of barrack life returned. There was the usual work to be done, guard duty, some troop training and musketry, and inter-regimental and Brigade sports. There were lectures, too, on all sorts of topics, such as health care, horsemanship and post-war reconstruction, while every now and again we had morale-boosting visits from various dignitaries including, on at least two occasions, the Prince of Wales.

Throughout the war, the Prince had been seen all across the front, meeting troops and generally getting involved. I had seen him around Christmas 1914, when with the 4th Hussars, and in January 1919, I saw him again when he came and visited Deutz Barracks. I was instructed to mount a double guard of twelve men, so that at the appropriate moment the men could be turned out of the guard room and lined up with swords at the slope. As the Prince passed, I was to give the order 'Royal salute, carry swords!', followed, once the Prince and his escort had passed, with 'Slope swords, guard dismiss!' His visits were always impeccably organised, and there was always something being done to which his attention could be drawn. When, a couple of months later, the Prince passed through again, he was given a display of whisping, whereby we massaged our horses' flanks and backs with a twist of hay, looped into a figure eight and knotted. On cue, the Prince turned up to watch our work, stopping to stroke a horse before passing through the rest of the stables.

The last stables of the day was at 5pm, following which, time was our own. Like most, I would leave the barracks to make my way across the bridge into the city centre where, in the bustle of the early evening, we would pass among demobilised German soldiers, still in their army tunics, trousers and overcoats. Personally, I had no point of contact with these soldiers, although I felt no hostility towards them. We had entered a country in chaos, whose population was starving, and, bar the odd diehard, most Germans were just glad the war was all over. In all my time in Cologne there was, with the exception of the odd minor incident, no conflict between them and us, and on the whole the British troops were very well-behaved.

If anyone could be said to be resentful, it was some of the older civilians. One, a pub owner, a real 'Hun' with a short haircut on top of a bullet head, went out of his way to make it clear that he didn't want to serve us. We were 'Englishers' and whenever we entered his pub he became surly and eyed us with great suspicion. Unluckily for him, his pub was close to the barracks, and so he had to get used to us. We made a point of sitting at the bar and talking to his two daughters who were at school and were learning English. Quite why he never stopped them talking to us, I never fathomed, for he certainly didn't approve, and watched us all the time, clearly resenting our presence. But we were in charge and he had to muck in like everybody else. We were anxious to pick up some basic German and so spent several evenings trying to converse with these girls, drinking the mild beer served there and occasionally slipping the girls a couple of chocolate bars brought from the army canteen.

For the first time in my life, I had considerable freedom and I was intent on enjoying those evenings around the city. I watched English films at the Army Picture House, sat in the seats restricted to troops at the theatre, or retreated to the reserved circle at the opera. I acquired my first taste for opera in Cologne after I saw 'Madame Butterfly', performed by a sixteen-stone 'Madame'. Her considerable bulk as a butterfly tickled me no end, though this probably helped enhance her singing, which was wonderful, and encouraged me to go to other performances, including 'The Flying Dutchman' and 'The Mikado'.

Everything was cheap, for we were paid in German marks, and with their currency in a continual state of slow depreciation against the pound, we were able to buy luxuries we could never have afforded back home. On one of my regular shopping trips, I bought a fine pair of cut-throat razors in a case, which had been made in Solingen (the German equivalent to Sheffield), and which I used for many, many years afterwards.

There was a down-side to all this new-found wealth, for the mix of a hungry population and the huge influx of relatively wealthy soldiers created a prostitute, and subsequently a VD, problem that the authorities were at first unable to control. There were so many prostitutes among the street doorways that the main shopping street, the Hohe Strasse, became known as the Whore Strasse. We were warned about contact with prostitutes, and any soldier who became infected could have his wages docked, and certainly would have lost his extra sixpence good conduct pay. In Cologne we were regularly checked for early signs of VD, with the short-arm inspection, an afternoon indoor medical which all personnel were ordered to attend. We were formed up in two lines and told to drop our pants, pulling up our shirts as the medical officer walked by, so that he could have a peer at our private parts. These inspections had taken place pretty well every fortnight, but it was a 'catch early', not a preventative, treatment, and there was a period when we were losing a trooper a day through VD, far more than during the war.

The short arm parade was mildly embarrassing, but we got used to it, and common sense told us it was necessary. What I objected to was the introduction, in February, of the 'catch all' Early Treatment, or E.T. room. With VD rife, orders were given that any soldier returning to barracks after 6pm, irrespective of where he might have been, had to go for early treatment against any infection. This was easily enforced, as any soldier coming back had to pass through the guard room on his way to his barrack block. The sergeant of the guard's job would be to direct each trooper into the E.T. room where observation screens ensured that soldiers didn't cheat on the treatment. Whether or not anyone did watch I don't know, but the screens proved enough of a deterrent on their own.

The E.T. room was sparsely furnished, containing three cubicles, any one of which a trooper entered. There he'd find a bowl of warm water to which disinfectant was added, and he washed himself and threw away the water so the bowl could be refilled for the next man. Following this, each man picked up a tube with a nozzle on the end, and injected the end of his privates with an anti-bacterial ointment. If there were two or three men using the cubicles there was plenty of tomfoolery, with troopers telling each other where to put the tube. The treatment finished, each trooper left by another door, signing a book as he went confirming he'd followed the procedures.

Not surprisingly, no one liked the E.T. room, and it annoyed me in particular that, having been to the Opera or for a drink, I was expected to go through this rigmarole. I decided to find a way around the E.T. room and found a solution by way of the forage barn doors. They were huge doors on hinges that opened on to the street, enabling wagons to enter the barracks during the day to deliver hay. Though always padlocked when not in use, one of the doors had a diamond-shaped hole cut into it at chest height, through which the guards could confirm deliveries as they arrived. Once in the barn, anyone could exit through a small personnel hatch built into the doors at the rear, and, as this door was never locked, it allowed anyone using it direct access on to the barrack square.

Toying with the idea of trying to climb through the hole, I waited until the next occasion I was due to act as corporal of the guard. I knew that if I climbed through and couldn't get back, I could always walk round and come through the guardhouse again. No one would take any notice because I was on duty.

It was always going to be a tight squeeze, and I had to remove my bandolier and tunic to make it, putting my arms and head through first, then wriggling until I landed in a crumpled heap on the far side. There were no further problems returning and so I decided, 'Right, that's my way in when I'm back late at night, and to hell with the E.T. room'.

Flushed with my success, I told another corporal with whom I used to go around town. He was a lot smaller and had no trouble climbing through even with his bandolier on. As the guardroom never took a soldier's name when he left the barracks, only when he returned, no one would realise we were missing. For a month to six weeks we successfully used the forage door as our means of entry back into barracks, but, as with all good things, this route was eventually blocked off. I made the mistake of letting on to our squadron cook how we were avoiding the E.T. room, never dreaming he'd try it himself, for he was considerably larger than I was. He, like everyone else, hated the E.T. room, and returning late one evening decided to have a go. After much straining, he apparently got his head and shoulders through with his feet off the floor, but couldn't get any farther. It was then that he discovered that he couldn't get back, either; and jammed unceremoniously in the barn door, he was finally forced to call for the guard. I don't know which way they got him out, but I do know that next day the hole was criss-crossed with barbed wire, firmly held in place by big staples. Common sense might have told the cook he couldn't get through, but he tried and that was the end of our little trick.

In early March, as our time in Cologne was drawing to a close, I was sent for and interviewed by one of our Squadron leaders.

He told me the Life Guards were losing all their war volunteers and were looking around for men to help rebuild the Regiment, and would I like to transfer, being of the right stature. I declined the offer, saying with all respect that I'd had 'enough of wearing a tin hat, and didn't want a tin waistcoat as well'. Asked to explain, I replied that I had joined the 4th Dragoon Guards and that I'd finish in it. He dismissed me with a 'Fair enough' and nothing further was said.

The Regiment left Cologne at the end of March. Some hundred of us left on horseback, three days before the main body of Dragoons. Our destination was to be the port of Antwerp, where the Regiment would embark for Kingstown in Ireland, but first we were to make for the Belgian town of Verviers. At Verviers, we would rendezvous with the rest of the Regiment, due to make the trip down on the train.

Billeting officers went ahead of our party, so that on our arrival we were split up and put into pre-arranged accommodation. I and another corporal were billeted in a house owned by the local cobbler. We slept there, but collected our own rations which the lady of the house cooked for us. The shoemaker interested us, as he made shoes with wooden nails, since metal nails were unobtainable by the end of the war. He claimed the wooden nails lasted nearly as long as the metal.

We stayed in Verviers for the best part of a month, during which time the Regiment slimmed to a skeleton force of around 250 men. Those who had joined for the duration of the war were demobbed, leaving a rump of old regular soldiers to occupy themselves, while veterinary officers chose the best horses to return to Ireland, disposing of the remainder to Belgian farmers for farm work.

To keep ourselves occupied, leisurely four-mile route marches were undertaken, carrying just belts and bayonets. We marched to attention through villages but otherwise walked at ease and sang, timing our arrival back in Verviers for 12.30pm, where we broke up to have a beer in the estaminets, and a meal in the mess room. Afternoons were free for us to do as we liked, with the usual inter-troop football matches to pass the time.

Just before the Regiment was due to leave for Antwerp, we returned from a route march and dispersed as normal for our mid-day drink. On leaving the estaminet half-an-hour later, I trotted down some steps when, out of the blue, a stab of pain caused me to bend double.

NOTES

1. It was a Regiment very different from that which had boarded *HMT Winifredian* on August 16th 1914. Precise casualty figures for the 4th Dragoon Guards are unobtainable; however, the following statistics should be taken as the minimum casualty figures for the Regiment. Of the 551 officers and men who went to France on the *Winifredian*, eighty four had been killed in action or had died of wounds or illness. A further 199 had been wounded, twenty seven of them on two or more occasions, while seventy six men were taken prisoners of war. A minimum of 359 men, or sixty five per cent of the men on that ship, had become casualties. These figures exclude those who were transferred to other regiments during the war, of whom an unknown number were subsequently wounded, and at least four were killed.

CHAPTER NINE

They think it's all over . . .

Ben

At first I thought I had got bad wind, but as the day wore on I began to feel terrible and by night time I was in agony, hanging over the side of the bed in a desperate attempt to relieve the pain. The shoemaker and his wife finally called the doctor, who gave me a brief examination, promising he would see me again in the morning. This was of little comfort, but as there was nothing else to do, I stuck the night out until he reappeared to say that he had made arrangements for me to go to hospital as I had appendicitis. 'I can't go to hospital now! The Regiment's due to go home tomorrow,' I said. But the doctor replied, 'I'm sorry. I've made enquiries and there is neither a suitable hospital in Antwerp, nor a doctor on the ship. Your Regiment is going to Ireland and I dare not take the chance. You must go into hospital'.

It was pointless arguing, for I could no longer stand and had to be carried from the house on a stretcher. As I left, the shoemaker's wife who had been so charming, touchingly began to cry. However, I was the second soldier billeted at her house to be carried off in this way, so perhaps she thought she was cursed. The ambulance whisked me off to the town of Huy, to a former school, converted into a hospital for British troops.[1]

On the ward, I was left in the care of nurses who were instructed to do nothing but feed me periodically with warm milk. I continued to be in severe pain, yet saw no doctor and received no other treatment until an orderly came round the ward, checking medical details. The hospital was due to close and the orderly was looking to see who might be moved farther down the line. 'Oh, we've been looking for you,' he said cheerfully, 'you've been put in the wrong ward.'

A doctor was sent for and, with another doctor in attendance, he gently proceeded to feel and prod me before announcing that they'd operate in the morning. Yet within minutes orderlies returned to shave and put long stockings on me before I was stretchered to the operating theatre. A chloroform-laced mask was placed over my face and I was told to start counting.

I woke to find myself back in the ward, with most of the pain gone, and feeling altogether much better. My general chirpiness returned to the extent that I posed for a picture the following day, a nurse and an orderly perched on the end of my bed. All in all it seemed a matter of swift recuperation and a fast ticket back to the Regiment. My optimism was misplaced. Within days pleurisy set in with a vengeance, reducing me to a physical wreck; filling my lungs with putrid liquid and leaving me gasping for breath.

My condition worsened, and gave such cause for alarm that I was placed on the critically ill list, unable either to talk or perform the merest exertion. Only the shallowest breathing kept me going, so that as my condition deteriorated, so did the doctor's prognosis. I would become too weak to fight my condition and was therefore likely to die at any time. It was decided, therefore, to move me from the ward, so that my death would not have a detrimental effect on those remaining.

Four Germans, all POWs who worked at the hospital, came to the ward, picked up my bed and carried me off outside and across a courtyard to another building.[2] As we ventured into the fresh air I became aware of a doctor crossing the yard in front of me when suddenly he stopped, turned, and snapped a photograph of our group.

The new ward was a converted classroom containing a dozen beds, all occupied by dangerously ill patients. On the first night, orderlies came to remove two soldiers who died on either side of me, and came back again and again over the next few days as nine of our number went the same way. My survival was due almost entirely to the devoted attention of a Scottish nurse, who came each evening to put her arm round my neck and feed me Brandy Mixture, a concoction of egg, cinnamon water and brandy. As she held a cup to my mouth she encouraged me to take just that bit more. 'Come on, just a wee drop more for old Scottie,' she would insist, and although I didn't want it at the time, it gave me sufficient strength to pull through.

I suppose I had been there ten days when the doctor I had seen in the courtyard reappeared and ventured to my bed. 'Here's a little souvenir for you,' he whispered, and deposited something on the small locker that stood by my side. Although fully conscious, it was a while before I troubled to take a look, but was delighted to find he had left the photograph taken in the courtyard. I discovered that this doctor was due to go home and had been taking pictures of the hospital and the staff for mementoes. He was on his way to the X-ray dark room to develop the film, when he passed our party outside.[3]

With the hospital itself marked for closure, I had to be

transferred by ambulance some eight or nine miles to Namur, accompanied by a nurse and an orderly. I had various tubes sticking out of me, and as I was loaded aboard, I heard a doctor instructing the driver that on no account should he jar me on the journey.

The new hospital was a large renovated house providing pleasant surroundings for the two months I remained at Namur. It was here that I underwent a further operation to drain an abscess, during which the surgeons came across a date stone, the root, they thought, of all the trouble. As if not in enough distress, I was also undergoing intermittent treatment to have liquid pumped from my lungs. This entailed freezing my back before one end of a rubber tube was fed into my chest with the aid of a long needle, the other end of the tube being connected to a glass cylinder. The needle removed, the air was systematically pumped from the cylinder, the vacuum sucking, drip by drip, about one and a half test tubes of the fluid from my lung. It was an experience likened to being sucked inside out, and, unable to face any more while conscious, I was put under ether during further treatment.

My ward was run by a sister whom nobody liked. Her name was Sister Hoyle, and she was super-efficient, a nurse to her very fingertips, but with the habit of being very snappy and sharp with people. Everything had to be straight, the beds perfectly aligned, the sheets flawlessly tucked in, even the bed wheels turned so that they all faced the same way. Nothing was to be out of place, and the other nurses lived in fear of making a mistake.

These nurses came daily to re-dress my surgery scar, using a many-tailed bandage around my midriff; a bandage made of strips of overlapping cloth, loosely pinned over cotton wool. This allowed the liquids that bubbled up from around the operation scars to be mopped up. Meanwhile, should I require extra attention, a wooden spoon was brought and placed at the side of my bed, with which to bang on a chair.

Unsure whether I would ever get home, I one day asked a nurse to write to my mother, saying that although unable to write, I nevertheless wanted to thank her for everything she had done for me. My parents knew that I was in hospital, and had been told officially that I was poorly after a second operation. Yet it was important that I didn't say goodbye as such and, only after it had been very carefully worded, was the letter sent.[4]

In the neighbouring bed to mine there was a young Belgian seriously ill with severe constipation. The doctors had operated and had left a bucket underneath his body to collect a slow stream of effluent, but the stench was overpowering. It was then that

Sister Hoyle went out into the garden and returned with a huge bunch of lilac which she arranged in an earthenware pot and placed on the chair beside my bed. 'Bury your nose in that,' she whispered, and from that day she became an angel to me – she could do no wrong.[5]

My condition slowly began to improve and by the last week of June, I was considered fit enough to travel by ambulance train to the 14th Stationary Hospital at Boulogne. The hospital was made up of many uninspiring Nissen huts joined together, but the weather was fine and on warm days the orderlies would half-wheel, half-carry the patients' beds out on to the cliffs so we could enjoy fresh air and sunshine. Three or four of us were allowed to relax and even eat our dinners out there, our beds backing onto the sea. While I was dozing one day, a charabanc full of nurses momentarily stopped on the road directly opposite us and as I looked my eyes fixed on one face. I looked again, she looked at me, and then I thrust my hand in the air and waved. It was Sister Hoyle. She acknowledged my wave, and within twenty minutes was scooting back along the cliffs to see how I was. The hospital at Namur was now closing and she was finally on her way home. We chatted for a short time, before she had to go, promising as she did so to tell the doctors my full case history so I would receive the very best attention. That one visit did me the power of good, and I have always been sad that we never met again.

With the worst over, it was now just a case of slow recuperation. I was to be confined to bed for some four tiresome months in all, propped upright so that my muscles wouldn't tighten on the tubes that straggled from my stomach. To stop me sliding down the bed, a pillow called a Donkey was placed behind me, while strategically-positioned cotton wool cups under my heels and a water cushion under my backside helped avoid the worst that bedsores would bring. When finally allowed to sleep normally, I discovered that I could barely sleep on my side as it hurt so much.

The first few times that I was allowed out of bed were to sit still in a chair while my bed was remade. These few minutes were precious after six months lying on a matress and, although I struggled to get up, I had a taste for this renewed independence. I had a target in mind, for after months of bed pans, I wanted, more than anything, to go to a toilet on my own. As the toilets were at the far end of the hut, a few trial runs were needed before the day came when, labouring from bed rail to bed rail, I finally reached the objective. This one trip had, however, exhausted me and I had to call for an orderly to take me back to bed in a wheelchair.

Around the first anniversary of the Armistice, I finally got home to England and to the Royal Herbert Hospital in Woolwich. I had an aunt and uncle living locally, who came over and took me out, and as I got better I was able to go and see them. As a soldier, wearing the hospital blue uniform, I was entitled to free travel on Woolwich's electric trams and was usually invited to sit pride of place next to the driver.

It was at The Royal Herbert that I learnt to walk again. Having been invalided for so long, my weight had tumbled to seven stone, and everything was flabby. I was really just skin and bones. At the same time, I was on a strict diet of mince and milk, week in and week out, so it took time to build up both my stamina and leg muscles. Through perseverance, I gradually taught myself to walk slowly round the ward with the nurse and her trolley, helping to hold a bucket as she changed the dirty swabs and put new dressings on wounds.

Even into 1920, men were still dying from their wounds. Yet, although I saw some terrible sights and found myself holding many a chap's hand when the pain became unbearable, the sights themselves didn't turn my stomach in the least. It was fascinating to see what the doctors were able to achieve, one surgeon, Major Swan, working wonders with two particular cases.

The first had lost part of his upper lip, to which new skin had been grafted, grown after surgeons managed to join the man's arm to his stomach. The growth of skin in between was cut away from the stomach but not away from the arm, which for the following six weeks was strapped to the upper lip. The graft was successful, and by the time I was discharged, the man had at least a provisional lump of flesh which the surgeons could later shape.

The second had been hit by a large shard of shrapnel which shattered the femur in his thigh. So badly damaged was his leg that, after patching up, it was found to be three inches shorter than the other. An orderly told me that Major Swan was certain he could lengthen the leg to within half an inch of its original size, but that it would be a nasty operation. The patient was willing to go along with this, so during the operation Major Swan cut the bone at an angle, as two orderlies were instructed to pull the leg. Where the two bones still met, he screwed a metal plate into place to give it support while the bone knitted together, the man's leg being kept in traction all the while. It took months to succeed, during which time I helped to dress the wounds and saw this metal plate in action. The leg would always be stiff, but so pleased was Major Swan with the result that the metal plate was later inscribed with details of the operation, mounted on a piece of mahogany and presented to the delighted patient.

After four months at the Royal Herbert, I asked to be discharged. It was March 1920, and I'd been nearly a year in various hospitals. While I was grateful for all that had been done, I was thoroughly tired of the whole experience. The doctors were reluctant to let me return to the Regiment, back once again at Tidworth, and insisted that if discharged, I must have a letter from the Squadron Sergeant Major stating that I would be put on twelve months' light duty, and that under no circumstances would I go riding.

The letter arrived, and I was discharged from the Royal Herbert for a week at my parents' cottage at Croxley Green. While I was there, my girl friend, Betty Shepard – a class mate of my elder sister's – came to see me. I'd kept in contact with her since 1916, but though I had known her well beforehand, our relationship, which had been on paper until then, didn't work out once we met, and we quickly split up.

It felt strange to return to Tidworth. The Regiment had been back into the swing of peace time soldiering for a full year, since its return from Germany, and there were many new, as well as old, faces. I returned to barrack life with B Squadron, but was quickly moved to one of the cubicle rooms next to the stairway, as I had been made an Orderly Sergeant and drill instructor to the regiment of recruits. The drill instructor's job was unofficial. The RSM, 'Liz' Barrett, an old soldier and long-standing favourite in the Regiment, was meant to drill the three Squadrons, every Friday. However, he was suffering from bouts of laryngitis and needed someone to call out the commands as he gave them quietly behind. I didn't mind, I was on light duties and had plenty of time on my hands. To fill the day, a young doctor recommended that I took up the art of Indian club swinging to build up my stomach muscles. Standing on an upturned beer box, I would windmill two clubs around, building up the weight gradually, until I could swing two rifles around for up to an hour a day.

One of the perks of being a member of the Corporals' Mess was that the small swindles that went on within the Regiment usually filtered down to us first. One fiddle concerned a prized book of passes someone had pinched, enabling myself and two others almost unlimited possibilities to leave Tidworth Camp. The book contained anything up to a hundred passes, an assortment of white and pink slips, the former giving permission to leave the camp, the latter to use the trains for free. I had palled up with a girl, Clarice Plumb, who worked in a haberdashery store in Swindon, and so 'allowed' myself once weekly visits, setting off at 5pm to give myself plenty of time to cover the twenty-six-mile trip from Tidworth to town. Despite the train passes, I preferred to cycle to

Swindon, for I didn't want to court suspicion; by going across country, I knew I'd never meet a policeman, whereas on the train there would be one checking passes at Ludgershall station, one possibly at Andover, and another at Swindon. Each slip had to be signed by an officer and we practised forging signatures including Lieutenant Fetherstonhaugh's, which proved too flourishing to duplicate faithfully, and Captain Misa's, which was simple. Many years later, the back of a regimental reunion dinner menu gave me the opportunity to pen Misa's signature for his informal inspection. 'We got many passes on that one,' I told him with a grin. His reply was humorous and unprintable.

As an Orderly Sergeant, it was my duty to take the roll call at 6.15am, thereby ensuring our swindle went undetected. After I spent the evening with Clarice, I would sleep at the YMCA in Swindon, being woken at 4am, in time for a cup of tea and a bun before I cycled into barracks. Everything was timed to a tee, so I was surprised when, one morning, he woke me an hour early. 'Just wait until you look outside, there's two inches of snow.' This threw a great spanner in the works. Fearing I would give the game away, I dressed quickly and ran downstairs, and grabbing my bike set off as fast as I could. I was forced to remove the bike's mudguards as they clogged up in the snow, but my luck was in, and when I came across a stretch where a milk lorry with twin tyres had driven, I was able to ride in the tracks and make good time to Ludgershall. I had to half-cycle, half-run, but I got into barracks just as reveille sounded. I chucked my bike in the corner and immediately started shouting, 'Come on, show a leg'. I had a Corporal, nicknamed Bandy Nylon, who would take the roll call, but as I hadn't made any arrangements, I would have been in trouble.

Not long after returning to the Regiment I was very fortunate to have General Pitman pin the Mons medal on my chest after a Sunday Church parade. I and one other trooper had not received our medals, and following a special ceremony outside Mooltan Barracks, we were given the privilege of standing on a dais with the General and taking the salute of the Regiment as it marched past. I was very proud, as one might imagine, and was congratulated on my smartness.

Only three months after rejoining the Regiment I decided to put

Opposite:
Ben's final discharge from the army after serving seven years with the Colours and five on the Army Reserve. It is interesting to note the false date of birth. To be accepted into the army, Ben had to conceal his age: he was in fact born in 1897 not 1895.

Serial No. bay 13241

Army Form B. 2079D.

Certificate of discharge from (a) ....Section "B" Army Reserve....

No. 389251. Rank Trooper

Name CLOUTING Benjamin George
(Surname) (Christian names in full)

Corps from which } 4th Dragoon Guards
discharged }

N.B.—The following particulars refer only to the engagement from which the man is now being discharged :—

Enlisted at Lewes on 28.8. 1913

(b) 1914 Star
British War Medal
Victory Medal

Medals, Clasps, Decorations, Mentions in Despatches. Any special acts of gallantry or distinguished conduct brought to notice in brigade or superior orders.

Discharged in consequence of ...termination of first... ...period of engagement under... Para 484 (VII) Kings Regulations.

AFTER HAVING SERVED :—

(c) with the Colours (h) Six years.
Three hundred and sixty days.

(d) in Section "B" ARMY RESERVE (h) Five years.
Five days.

(e) in Section "D" ARMY RESERVE (h) } Nil years.
(f) in the SUPPLEMENTARY RESERVE (h) } Nil
(g) in the TERRITORIAL ARMY (h) Nil days.

Date of discharge 27.8. 25.

Description of the above-named man on Enlistment :—

Year of birth 1895 Marks or Scars Scar small of
Height 5 ft 8½ ins. back. Hairy birthmark
Complexion Fair inner side left knee
Eyes Blue Hair Dk Brown

Place Canterbury. Whitehead SSM { Signature and Rank.

Date 12.8.25. Officer i/c Cavalry Records.

Special attention is directed to the Notes on reverse.

(158AJ) (329885) Wt. W2038/P7270 (15) Gp.152 50000 4-25 W & S Ltd. Forms/B2079/28 P.T.O.

in my papers and leave. The Regiment was going to India and I didn't really want to go, and though I'd never regretted joining the army, five years of war had been a basin-full and I wanted the freedom I'd never had since a boy. Many things had changed within the Regiment, and now so many of the old faces had gone, I felt even more of a loner. I felt, too, that I'd learnt the drill to a high standard with pre-war men, superior to those who were now joining up, and that made me bitter against those who seemed slack or less able. This was how I felt and I wasn't well respected because of it. To those who had joined up after the war, I was a faceless, stern drill instructor; it quickly brought me to the conclusion that all in all I'd truthfully had enough.

Out in civilian life, my father was very poorly. Although he was bravely struggling on as a landscape gardener to make ends meet, he nevertheless desperately needed help. With leave owing, I was able to depart from the Regiment a month early, handing in my bandolier and sword, then the rest of my kit to stores, in exchange for which I received a new suit. I left Tidworth, and to all intents and purposes that appeared to be the end of my army service. I didn't then, nor have I ever, regretted going to the war. I was aware that as a cavalryman and as an orderly, I had had a cushier time than some others, but nevertheless I had served throughout the war, and had been wounded twice. I had also been slightly gassed, with the effect that I suffered serious nose bleeds during dry weather for the next fifty years, and I have never regained the ability to smell gas (a potentially serious drawback in the kitchen). I did not suffer from any psychological problems after the war, or even from nightmares. I did have the habit of ducking if there was a sudden loud noise, but that was only a distant reflex to diving for the ground when shrapnel burst overhead, and in time even this tendency to flinch diminished. I left the Regiment with many memories, with the opportunity to attend regimental reunions, and £29–6s war gratuity to set me up for life!

It was late June when I eventually teamed up with my father. But he was more ill than I had realised and within a month he was dead from a mixed infection of the lungs. In eight years, so much had changed: Charlie Brand's death, Sid's death, and a year later the death of my grandmother who had raised him. Old friends from childhood had gone: Harold Clark and Janie Weaver's brother, George. He had joined the Sussex Yeomanry and died of dysentery shortly after being evacuated from Gallipoli in January 1916, just one of several boys from Beddingham, Firle and Glynde killed in the war, with whom I had gone to school.

Now my father's death left me unexpectedly at a loose end, and with high unemployment, I wasn't hopeful of finding work. My brother, who was employed at The Sun Engraving Company in Watford, managed to get me temporary work at the printing works, stacking waste paper in 100-lb bundles, before bailing, then binding them up ready for sale. The nationwide recession was biting, and it wasn't long before the company began cutting staff, and I was told that being the last in, I could expect to be the first out. It was hardly an ideal job, and was something of a come-down from life in the army. I began to toy with the idea of emigrating, having heard that the Hudson's Bay Company in North America were taking on people, but mother begged me not to go: 'You've been away ever since you left school, I never see anything of you.' So instead, I began to look at the police force, and was told that if my papers were accepted, I would be kept on at the paper firm until I was called for training.

Industrial unrest was rife at this time, and in April 1921 two thirds of the very powerful Triple Alliance (of the miners, railwaymen and transport workers) had gone on strike. The miners had begun the industrial action and the railwaymen had followed in support. The mines were privately owned at this time, but so seriously did the Government take this action, that it mobilised Navy stokers to look after the pits and pumps to stop them flooding. These sailors complained that they were being intimidated by the strikers, so the Government mobilised a number of soldiers to look after the sailors. I happened to be one who received papers to rejoin the Regiment.

A travel warrant was sent, with orders to proceed to the Dragoons' new depot at Dunbar. But I was in need of a break and in no particular hurry, so I set about a sightseeing tour of Scotland. I'd never seen Scotland before and by 'mistakenly' getting on the wrong trains, visits to Perth, Inverness and overnight stays at hotels in the depths of the Scottish Highlands, were made possible. Declining attempts by train guards to charge excess fares on some of my more outrageous detours, I merely explained that if platform guards were unable to direct me to the right coaches, that was hardly my fault. I was three days late into Dunbar and my absence commented on, but nothing more.

Having just arrived, I took a look around the camp when suddenly I heard 'Cronkie, Cronkie!' I turned and to my surprise saw Cumber running down the road, before flinging his arms round me in an embrace. There was so much to talk about that we spent the rest of the afternoon and evening just reminiscing, and swapping stories. His face was still scarred from his fall on the railway, but otherwise he was fine. It was the first time I'd seen him since that day at Audregnies, and when I was moved on a few days later, it was sadly the last.

I was temporarily made an Orderly Sergeant again. However, I declined to revert to being a drill instructor as I was training to be a singer and, toying with turning professional, I didn't want to damage my voice. Most troopers were kicking their heels around, until some of us were sent down to Tidworth from where a draft had just been sent to the mines in South Wales. An attack of the flu hit the camp, and I came down with a bad attack of quinsy, which laid me up in hospital. Apart from that, the next couple of months were spent whiling away time at Tidworth with a number of sailors who, having also been called up, were found to be excess to requirements.

In June I was finally discharged from the army, joining the City of London Police Force in November 1921. Shortly afterwards, an indirect approach was made by Sir Tom Bridges as to whether I wished to go as his servant to Australia, where he had been made its new Governor. It was a great honour, but I now had a new career, and I declined.

I remained on the army reserve for a further six years, until I had completed the statutory twelve years in the forces, when I was released from all military obligations in August 1927. I had finally reached the end of the line.

NOTES

1. This was Number 50 Casualty Clearing Station and was stationed in Huy from December 22nd 1918 onwards in what was an *Ecole Normale*, a teacher training college. The hospital remained at Huy until it was closed down on June 7th 1919, the remaining patients being transferred to the 48 CCS at Namur. The buildings at Huy still exist, in almost identical condition to that of 1919, just off the Rue Grégoire Bodart, near the river.
2. The Allies compelled 193,000 German POWs to stay on and work as part of the Clearing Up Army in France and Belgium.
3. Four Royal Army Medical doctors were serving at Huy at this time, Captains W Simpson, RW Swayne, F Morres, and CH Hicks.
4. When Ben's mother died in 1947, he found an old sewing box in which she had stashed every letter and postcard he had ever sent during the war, including the letter written by the nurse.
5. Sister Annie Lord Hoyle of the Territorial Force Nursing Service had served in France since October 1914. After the war, she worked at Namur from May 24th 1919 until July 6th 1919, after which she proceeded to Boulogne to report to the Matron-in-Chief, prior to returning to England.

Epilogue

When Ben finally left the army in 1921, he left the war, although the war did not quite leave him, for the slight dose of chlorine gas he received in 1915 ensured that he had bad nose bleeds every May for the next fifty years. Fortunately, the wound to his ankle did not trouble him afterwards, and, like many soldiers with 'exemplary' service records, he was able to join the police force, first in the City of London, then later at Eastbourne. He might have made the police a long term career, but a business proposition put to him in 1934 led to his leaving the force and setting up a window-cleaning service in Reading, a business that was to last him literally a lifetime. Ben built the County Window Cleaning Service up from scratch, and was awarded a Royal Warrant in 1950 to wash the windows of Windsor Castle. As late as 1990, he continued arriving at work at 6.30am every weekday to ensure that the vans were full of petrol and had the right ladders for their respective jobs. Ben had given up window-cleaning, but when the need arose he still turned out, washing the window of Mothercare in Reading town centre on one occasion, to the surprise of the staff, when he was aged nearly 90.

He married Beatrice in 1923, and later had two children, Derek and Pearl, both of whom married and continued to live in Reading, Derek eventually taking over his father's company. Ben had over sixty one years of marriage before his wife died, curiously enough on the seventieth anniversary of that first shot, on August 22nd 1984. Ben continued to keep busy, and remained healthy almost until the end. He died on August 13th 1990. It was speculated at the time that he was aiming to die on the 22nd; whether he was or not, I do not know, but knowing Ben I could well believe it.

Select Bibliography

Unpublished Sources
The Public Record Office
  Unit War Diaries: WO 95, and Medical Records, MH 106.

The Imperial War Museum
  The Photocopied Diary of Lieutenant Chance, 4th Dragoon Guards
  The Diary of Corporal W A Hardy, 4th Dragoon Guards

The National Army Museum
  The Rikards Records

The Museum of the Royal Dragoon Guards, York
  The Diary of Lieutenant A Wright
  The Regimental Magazines of the 4th/7th Dragoon Guards, which
    contained the personal recollections of: Corporal Dyer, Second Lieu-
    tenant Stanley, Corporal Tilney, and other anonymous articles.

Published Books
Bridges, Sir Tom, *Alarms and Excursions*, Longmans Green & Co, 1938.
Carton de Wiart, Adrian, *Happy Odyssey*, Jonathan Cape, London, 1950.
De Lisle, General Sir Henry B, *Reminiscences of Sport and War*, London, 1939.
Edmonds, Sir James E, *Military Operations, France and Belgium, 1914*, Vols 1, 2 & 3, Macmillan, 1925.
Edmonds, Sir James E, *The Occupation of the Rhineland, 1918–1929*, The Imperial War Museum, HMSO, 1987.
Gibb, Rev Harold, *Record of the 4th Royal Irish Dragoon Guards in the Great War 1914–1918*, Canterbury, 1925.
Holmes, Richard, *Riding the Retreat, Mons To The Marne 1914 Revisited*, Jonathan Cape, London, 1995.
Macdonald, Lyn, *1914*, Michael Joseph, London, 1987.
Osburn, Arthur, *Unwilling Passenger*, Faber & Faber, London, 1926.
Scott, Peter T, *Dishonoured*, Tom Donovan Publishing, London, 1994.
Thwaites, Norman, *Velvet & Vinegar*, Grayson & Grayson, London, 1932.

Index